T0319597

The Venture Capital State

A volume in the series

Cornell Studies in Political Economy
edited by Peter J. Katzenstein

A list of titles in this series is available at cornellpress.cornell.edu.

The Venture Capital State

The Silicon Valley Model
in East Asia

Robyn Klingler-Vidra

Cornell University Press
Ithaca and London

Publication of this book has been made possible by a generous grant from the Chiang Ching-kuo Foundation for International Scholarly Exchange.

First published 2018 by Cornell University Press

Printed in the United States of America

Library of Congress Cataloging-in-Publication Data

Names: Klingler-Vidra, Robyn, author.
Title: The venture capital state : the Silicon Valley model in East Asia / Robyn Klingler-Vidra.
Description: Ithaca : Cornell University Press, 2018. | Series: Cornell studies in political economy | Includes bibliographical references and index.
Identifiers: LCCN 2017052058 | ISBN 9781501723377 (cloth : alk. paper) | ISBN 9781501723391 (epub/mobi) | ISBN 9781501723384 (pdf)
Subjects: LCSH: Venture capital—Government policy—East Asia—Case studies. | Capital market—Government policy—East Asia—Case studies. | Technological innovations—Finance—Government policy—East Asia—Case studies. | Diffusion of innovations—East Asia—Case studies. | East Asia—Economic policy—Case studies.
Classification: LCC HG4751. K573 2018 | DDC 332/.04154095—dc23
LC record available at https://lccn.loc.gov/2017052058

To Eze

Contents

Illustrations

Figures

Tables

Acknowledgments

I owe a debt of gratitude to all the policymakers, venture capitalists, industry association leaders, international organization staff, academics, and entrepreneurs who offered me their time, insights, and data. In each country I benefited from at least one particularly helpful contact who provided further introductions. In Hong Kong, Brandon Sedloff opened his Rolodex; in Taiwan, Emilie Tsai and James Hill were essential to obtaining interviews; and Meng Wong offered his considered analysis and access to policymaking in Singapore. I am also grateful for the financial support that made this book's East Asian fieldwork possible. Fieldwork conducted in Hong Kong and Taiwan in 2011 and 2012 was financed by a London School of Economics and Political Science (LSE) international relations department grant. The second major installment of East Asian fieldwork was carried out while based at the National University of Singapore Lee Kuan Yew School of Public Policy in 2012 on a research exchange. Interviews in Israel and Hong Kong between 2013 and 2015 were supported by a Senior Research Fellowship with Coller Institute of Venture at Tel Aviv University. Access to key sources in Israel was made swiftly available by Zvika Halfin.

Academic communities at the LSE and King's College London offered friendship, tough questions, and valuable recommendations. Feedback on conference presentations—at the New Approaches to Building Markets in Asia conference (October 2011, Singapore), International Studies Association annual conventions (2012–17), the *International Studies Review* presidential special issue on diffusion workshop (July 2013, Berlin) and the "What Is Patient Capital, and Where Does It Exist?" workshop for the *Socio-Economic Review* special issue on patient capital (February 2016, Berlin)—proved immensely helpful. Participation in the Warwick Manuscript Development workshop in October 2014, organized by Len Seabrooke, was especially valuable. T. J. Pempel, my discussant at the workshop, gave feedback and encouragement that had a remarkably positive impact on the book taking shape. Sylvia Maxfield and Magnus Ryner both offered crucial mentorship when my focus waned, and Valbona Muzaka, Iain Hardie, Lawrence Saez, Covadonga Meseguer, and Peter Kingstone were generous in giving feedback on key portions of the book. My research program has been shaped by collaborations with Dan Breznitz, Martin Kenney, Etel Solingen, Ramon Pacheco Pardo, Sylvia Maxfield, Elizabeth Thurbon, Ka Ho Mok, Lena Rethel, Poh Kam Wong, Richard Deeg, Toby James Carroll, Darryl Jarvis, and Philip Schleifer. My project with Robert Wade on "policy distraction" has helped focus this book's argumentation (this is, of course, in addition to the motivational role his seminal work *Governing the Market* played in undertaking this line of research in the first place). Robert Falkner guided the formulation of the project's aim and continues to serve as my model of the consummate professional and collegial academic.

I thank my nonacademic editing team, consisting of my brother, Robert Klingler, and my husband, Eze Vidra. They kept me focused on answering the all-important "so what?" question. Eze has motivated me, shared his expertise, and offered unwavering support over the years and across the rounds of edits. For all this, and so much more love, encouragement, and partnership, I dedicate this book to him. I would like to thank our children, Rafael and Maya, for bringing immense joy to my life and forcing me to slow down and see this book in the bigger picture. I thank my parents, Renee and Robert, for the opportunity to pursue this enchanting academic path, and for my loving family in the United States and Israel for their support along the way. Last but certainly not least, I thank the Cornell University Press team: Roger Haydon for his professionalism and humor; Peter Katzenstein for his tremendous ability to deliver constructive criticism that consistently struck at the core of the book's issues, both theoretical and empirical; and two external reviewers for their instructive suggestions.

Abbreviations

ARF	Applied Research Fund (Hong Kong)
AVCPEC	Asian Venture Capital and Private Equity Council
CEPD	Council for Economic Planning and Development (Taiwan)
CIER	Chung-Hua Institution for Economic Research
DPP	Democratic Progressive Party (Taiwan)
EC	Economic Committee (Singapore)
EDB	Economic Development Board (Singapore)
ERISA	Employee Retirement Income Security Act (United States)
ESVF	Early-Stage Venture Funding (Singapore)
ExCo	Executive Council (Hong Kong)
GIO	Government Information Office Executive Yuan, Republic of China
GIP	Global Investor Program (Singapore)
GIS	Government Information Services (Hong Kong)
HKVCA	Hong Kong Private Equity and Venture Capital Association
ICT	information and communications technology
IDB	Industrial Development Bureau (Taiwan)
III	Institute for Information Industry (Taiwan)
IPO	initial public offering
ITB	Innovation and Technology Bureau (Hong Kong)
ITC	Innovation and Technology Commission (Hong Kong)
ITRI	Industrial Technology Research Institute (Taiwan)
KMT	Kuomintang (Taiwan)
LegCo	Legislative Council (Hong Kong)
LP	limited partnership
MITI	Ministry of International Trade and Industry (Japan)

MNC	multinational corporation
MoEA	Ministry of Economic Affairs (Taiwan)
MoF	Ministry of Finance (Hong Kong, Taiwan, Singapore)
MTI	Ministry of Trade and Industry (Singapore)
NDC	National Development Council (Taiwan)
NDF	National Development Fund (Taiwan)
NDP	National Development Plan (Taiwan)
NRF	National Research Foundation (Singapore)
NSTB	National Science and Technology Board (Singapore)
NVCA	National Venture Capital Association (United States)
NZVIF	New Zealand Venture Investment Fund
OCS	Office of the Chief Scientist (Israel)
PAP	People's Action Party (Singapore)
PRC	People's Republic of China
R&D	research and development
ROC	Republic of China
SAR	Special Administrative Region
SME	small- and medium-sized enterprise
SVCA	Singapore Private Equity and Venture Capital Association
TIER	Taiwan Institute of Economic Research
TIF	Technopreneurship Investment Fund (Singapore)
TVCA	Taiwan Private Equity and Venture Capital Association
VC	venture capital
VoC	varieties of capitalism

The Venture Capital State

1

The Venture Capital State

> The road to the free market was opened and kept open by an enormous increase in continuous, centrally organized and controlled interventionism.
>
> —Karl Polanyi, *The Great Transformation*

Rumors abounded as twelve North Korean government officials spent two weeks in Silicon Valley during the spring of 2011. What we know of their northern California trip is that the delegates—surrounded by security officers in a visit enshrouded in secrecy—spent a hundred minutes at the Googleplex in Mountain View and joined a lunch seminar at Stanford University. Their itinerary was reportedly motivated by a desire to build up North Korea's "own internet expertise." The North Korean policymakers wanted to learn what the Silicon Valley cluster was all about, and what aided its ephemeral success. We could presume that they came to study Silicon Valley with an eye toward developing Pyongyang as a hub of innovation and entrepreneurship.

The North Korean delegates are perhaps the least likely in a long list of policymakers, acting on behalf of cities, provinces, and countries around the globe, to study the drivers of Silicon Valley's success. Policymakers visit the valley to learn how to create their own system of innovation (Nelson and Winter 1982; Lundvall 1992) and to build a bridge to Silicon Valley (Rapo and Seulamo-Vargas 2010; Saxenian 2008). As an expression of their aspirations, policymakers go on to craft Silicon monikers for their locale. The British government's promotion of the Silicon Roundabout in London, Taiwan's use of the Silicon Island, and Skolkovo being created as Russia's Silicon Valley are just a few examples.[1]

Many of these policymakers study one particular component of the Silicon Valley cluster: its venture capital (VC) industry. They learn about the cluster's VC element for two reasons. First, VC epitomizes the neoliberal essence of Silicon Valley: private investors allocating money to high-growth, but high-risk, start-ups—in exchange for an ownership stake—that strive to disrupt existing markets (Lerner 2002).[2] If a local Silicon Valley is to be created, then a VC market—akin to the one that financed and nurtured the meteoric rise of start-ups in Silicon Valley—is a necessary component of the free market fabric.

Second, venture capital is widely recognized as an engine of innovation and entrepreneurship (Gompers and Lerner 1999; OECD 1996; National Venture Capital Association 2012). In the post–global financial crisis world, as policymakers in advanced economies work to resuscitate economic activity, they hope that venture capital's "smart money" for start-ups fosters innovation and high-quality job creation. Policymakers in emerging markets see venture capital as a tool for advancing the knowledge-based economy capabilities essential to competing in the services and technology-centric segments of the global economy. Policymakers in emerging market countries hope that an escape from the "middle income trap" can be attained through competition in high value-added sectors, such as those that venture capitalists invest in (Paus 2014). Venture capital promotion is conceptualized as one of the tools capable of driving advanced and developing states' ability to compete on the innovation frontier. Such innovation capacity brings greater productivity—and, according to mainstream economic theory—sustainable growth and competitiveness (OECD 2007).

In light of its positive associations with innovation and entrepreneurship, venture capital holds a unique position in the minds of the public and policymakers. Unlike other investment classes, such as hedge funds and sovereign wealth funds, which are criticized for their dubious impact on firms and markets, venture capital is conceptualized as part of the financial sector that society cannot afford to live without. The *Wall Street Journal* went so far as to dub venture capital "Humanity's Last Great Hope" for its purported ability to identify and nurture transformative technologies (Mims 2014). National Venture Capital Association research corroborates this sentiment: 40 percent of all the companies that have gone public in the United States between 1974 and 2015 received VC funding in their ascent. Those 556 companies account for 85 percent of all research and development (R&D) spending, 63 percent of the public equities market capitalization, and employ more than 3 million people.

Concurrent to the rising exuberance for venture capital is the increased restraint on public R&D coffers. Downward pressure on spending since 2008 stems from the promulgation of austerity measures, leaving governments increasingly unable to fund basic research. Yet R&D spending is often viewed as central to national industrial strategy, particularly in the technology sector

(Spencer and Brander 1983). European Union member states have struggled to achieve the 3 percent R&D spending targets set in 2002, as they spend, on average, 2 percent (Eurostat 2015). This shortfall fuels claims that there is not enough investment in innovation. Venture capitalists are put forward as the answer, as they are private investors flush with money, networks, and expertise. It is in this context that policymakers' interest in deploying purposive action to build VC clusters along the lines of Silicon Valley's venture capital industry—now conceptualized to be singularly capable of advancing entrepreneurship and innovation, which is believed to be central to spurring economic growth—has never been greater.

Puzzle

At least forty-five countries have utilized public policies aimed at creating local Silicon Valley–like venture capital markets. These "venture capital states" span a remarkable range, from Russia and Canada, Finland and the United Kingdom, and China and Chile. The diffusion of VC policy transcends ideological lines, as neoliberal and socialist states, liberal market economies and coordinated market economies, and left- and right-wing governments alike pursue policy actions.[3] Efforts are not only attempted by advanced economies; policymakers in numerous emerging economies (including all of the BRICS) have also acted. Figure 1.1 below illustrates the breadth of venture capital policy diffusion, specifying the cumulative number of states initiating policies since the United States first catalyzed VC activity by providing loans to venture capital managers via the SBIC program in 1958.

North Korean policymakers' interest in Silicon Valley, along with the VC policy diffusion trend depicted in figure 1.1, paints a picture of states converging in their efforts to replicate the Silicon Valley model. More specifically, the diffusion of the VC policy model appears to be driving economically, spatially, and culturally different states to reach "universal convergence" on yet another component of the American capitalist model (Kuczynski and Williamson 2003, 325).

Diffusion scholars expect this type of result as the temporal clustering of economic policies and government regime types comes from states having increasingly less scope for distinctive policy choices due to globalization's advance (Elkins and Simmons 2005; Braun and Gilardi 2006; Busch and Jörgens 2005; Holzinger and Knill 2005; Haggard and Maxfield, 1996; Goodman and Pauly 1993). In 1979, Kenneth Waltz contended that policymakers are socialized into following similar paths through emulation, praise, and ridicule mechanisms. Organizational sociologists such as Paul DiMaggio and Woody Powell (1983) assert that the preponderance of a "world culture" explains the "non-rational" adoption of similar policies across states. Policymakers pursue similar, highly acclaimed policies like that of trying to

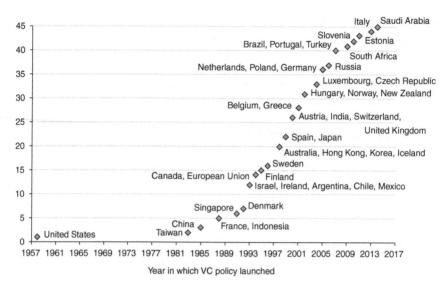

Figure 1.1 State launches of VC policy efforts (cumulative number) 1957–2017

Sources: European Venture Capital Association, Latin American Venture Capital Association, European Union, OECD, World Bank, and individual country sources. *Methodology*: Chart indicates each country's initial VC policy launch date, and the curve represents the cumulative number of VC policy launches. Sample is all OECD, G-20, BRICS, and Asian Tiger countries. All forty-five states launched VC policies by 2014. The forty-five states included in the sample are Argentina, Australia, Austria, Belgium, Brazil, Canada, Chile, China, Czech Republic, Denmark, Estonia, Finland, France, Germany, Greece, Hong Kong, Hungary, Iceland, India, Indonesia, Ireland, Israel, Italy, Japan, Korea, Luxembourg, Mexico, Netherlands, New Zealand, Norway, Poland, Portugal, Russia, Saudi Arabia, Singapore, Slovak Republic, Slovenia, South Africa, Spain, Sweden, Switzerland, Taiwan, Turkey, United Kingdom and the United States. The sample also includes the European Union as an entity.

create a Silicon Valley as "social proof" that they "belong" (Axelrod 1986). Particularly relevant to this study of the diffusion of a highly revered model, Florini (1996) argues that diffusion is likely when the model emanates from a "prominent" state that is viewed as successful. Canonizing the conceptualization of mechanisms that drive diffusion processes, Simmons et al. (2006) distill the mechanisms by which convergence occurs: coercive forces, competitive pressures, learning, or imitation processes. The overarching orientation of this scholarship is the assumption that, at some critical "tipping point," international influences "become more important than domestic politics" (Finnemore and Sikkink 1998, 902), trumping the potential for domestic context in repudiating—or reshaping—the internationally disseminated object.[4]

In light of the widespread expectations for convergence, this study reveals a puzzling result: systematic diversity underlies the veneer of the convergent VC policy trend. Policies do not converge on replicating the Silicon Valley VC policy model. Policymakers do not replicate the American tax and regulatory policies to enable the private supply of investment capital into local venture capital funds. Even states of similar population and economic sizes, that are geographically proximate and at comparable levels of industrialization, do not pursue VC policies similar to one another. In fact, no two of the countries studied in this book pursued identical VC policy paths. This book explains why policymakers, who meticulously study the Silicon Valley model in an effort to build their own VC market, come to pursue distinctive—and interventionist—VC policy formula. It reveals why they use different "means" to reach the same "end"—a Silicon Valley–like venture capital cluster.

Argument

This book argues that this result—of varied, interventionist strategies—is not puzzling at all. Diffusion frameworks expect convergence because they are designed to explain similarity, not variety. They emphasize the strength of the model, not the importance of local context, in explaining why policies diffuse. In so doing, this scholarship depicts policy information diffusing into contextless realms. This results in diffusion's analytical tools only being able to explain part of an interesting phenomenon: the occurrence of interdependent, but diverse, policies (Klingler-Vidra and Schleifer 2014). Diffusion theorization is ill equipped for investigating the occurrence of variety within patterns of diffusion. It, instead, excels in explaining top-line convergence.

Diffusion research's quantitative bias contributes to this insufficient ability to articulate how, in actuality, the diffusion process leads to only limited degrees of convergence (Dobbin et al. 2007, 463). Research designs and methodologies consist of Large-N studies that impute explanations for the occurrence of broad but shallow patterns of convergence (Levi-Faur 2005a; Levi-Faur et al. 2011). They reveal correlation—that states adopt policies at the same time—without tracking the causal process by which the policy information diffused and, then, the local policymaking process that shaped its implementation. Diffusion studies only rarely employ qualitative case study examinations to trace causal processes (Poulsen 2014).[5]

For example, in her research on the diffusion of liberal market reforms, Meseguer (2009, 1) acknowledges that there were "differences in the timing of reforms, in their speed and intensity, and in their results," but states that the aim of her study was "not to explain those differences." Research on norm internationalization has also not been oriented toward explaining "variation in state behavior"; it has instead been "puzzled by the degree of similarity or 'isomorphism' among states and societies" (Finnermore and Sikkink 1998, 904–5). Focused on surface trends, diffusion scholarship does not delve into the causal chain by which elements of the diffusion process contribute to the pursuit of varying policies (Weyland 2006, 14). Simply said, they don't pay "attention to diffusion itself" (Solingen 2012, 631). In fact, to date only a few scholars have systematically examined the role of domestic factors in driving variation in international diffusion processes (Yeo and Painter 2011; Acharya 2009; Lenschow et al. 2005).

State-of-the-art diffusion scholarship has formulated expectations about the degree of convergence based on properties of the model (the level of specificity of the model and the number of models) and the mechanisms (see Klingler-Vidra and Schleifer 2014 for a review of the literature). The existence of multiple policy models and vague policy ideas are expected to drive diverse outcomes (Falkner and Gupta 2009; Weyland 2006). In contrast, the diffusion of models that are precise blueprints are expected to result in policymakers closely mimicking the source model, and therefore the universe of adopters converging on a similar policy strategy. Competition, coercion, and emulation mechanisms are expected to propel high degrees of convergence (Simmons et al. 2008). Conventionally rational learners converge on replicating the most consistently successful policy; they undergo full Bayesian updating processes, meaning that their prior beliefs (about the consequences of a policy) are overridden such that all policymakers come to hold the same posterior beliefs (Meseguer 2009), and therefore choose the same policy. Boundedly rational learners converge on replicating the "anchor" policy models of the countries they deem to be leaders and peers (Weyland 2006).

These analytical approaches constitute progress in the theoretical tools available to sources of variance in the diffusion process. However, they still leave much to be desired in terms of systematically accounting for whether, how much, and in what way policies vary. They do not offer analytical tools sufficient for investigating how the diffusion process results in adaptation and simply not enough analytical muscle for exploring the local context's role in the process.

Contextual, Not Conventional or Bounded, Rationality in Learning Processes

This book addresses this lacuna by developing a "contextual rationality" approach for exploring diversity amid convergence, which elucidates how local normative contexts shape rational learning in international diffusion processes. This approach—which conceptualizes rationality as contextually based—posits that learning is rooted in policymakers' constitutive and regulative norms rather than in some acontextual environment. How policymakers see themselves (constitutive norms inform their identity) and the appropriate policies available to them (regulative norms) shapes their preferences. Norm-rooted preferences, rather than exogenously derived preferences, inform how they value policies in the diffusion process, and then, how they design policies for local use.

The premise is that political economy scholars need to focus on the local normative contexts in which diffusion occurs in order to understand patterns of policy diffusion. The contextual rationality approach builds on the work of scholars who argue that domestic contexts are not "black boxes" into which models diffuse (Yeo and Painter 2011). It takes seriously the contention that "state identity fundamentally shapes state behavior, and that state identity is, in turn, shaped by the cultural-institutional context within which states act" (Finnemore and Sikkink 1998, 902). The approach taken here presumes that cultural similarities and differences across local contexts affect the "rate and form" of diffusion (Hall 1993; Strang and Soule 1998; Lenschow et al. 2005, 799), rather than result in a binary acceptance or rejection of the diffusion model. It holds that local environments transform the object being diffused in a similar way to what Acharya (2004, 240–41; 2009) refers to as the "local-ization" process in which adopters reinterpret an external model in order to increase its "fitness" with prevailing local norms. It extends our understanding of how the relationships between foreign information and local contexts affect the result of diffusion (building on work by Radaelli 2005).

The contextual rationality framework does not posit that norm-based explanations are at odds with conventional accounts of rationality; instead, it contends that *rational learning processes should be understood as rooted in normative contexts*. It does not suggest that politics do not matter, or that formal institutional constraints do not shape the form that policies take. The contextual rationality framework instead heeds the call of Finnemore and Sikkink (1998, 911) by modeling "social context as a background for rational choice." To address this gap, the approach draws on the rich analytical tools in rationality and contextualism scholarship. It posits that policymakers are guided by "logics of appropriateness" (March and Olsen 1998; Axelrod 1986). Their logics of appropriateness are normatively dependent; rationality does not mean operating as a "technical, rational" and "culture-neutral" actor (Finnermore 1996, 328).

A key ontological difference underpins contextual rationality as compared to bounded or conventional forms of rationality. Contextually rational actors are not conceptualized as learners with limited computational skills dependent on cognitive biases (as in bounded rationality, see Kahneman and Tversky 1983) or with preferences based in material interests, susceptible to full Bayesian updating as in conventional rationality.[6] Even institutional economics—that does consider the constraining role of norms in individual choice—treats "actor identities and interests themselves as preexisting and fixed" (Kowert and Legro 1996, 458). The approach developed here presumes that locale-specific norms about actor's identity (constitutive norms about "selfhood" as mutually constituted and evolving) and socially accepted policy practices (regulative norms) shape rational policy learning processes (Fearon and Wendt 2002).[7]

This book employs the following conceptualization of "norm": the "collective expectations about proper behavior for a given identity" (Jepperson et al. 1996, 54). There are three types of norms—regulative, constitutive, and evaluative—two of which, constitutive and regulative, I focus on in this book. The differences in the norm types are further discussed in chapter 2; for now, I note that constitutive norms inform the identity of an actor while regulative norms—sometimes referred to as social laws, habits, and customs—regulate actor behavior. Together, they "prescribe and regulate the practice of agents in international politics" (Kowert and Legro 1996, 453). Contextual rationality guided empirical investigations, such as this one, investigate how policymakers' constitutive and regulative norms shape the valuation and adaptation of existing models in learning processes. Policymakers do not "choose the policies that are expected to yield the best result" in a distanced, objective way as asserted by Meseguer (2009, 3). Instead of some acontextual efficacy, norms lead policymakers to value policy options that fit their "logic of appropriateness" (March and Olsen 1998) even as they rigorously study proven policy models.

The book's point of departure from the bounded rationality framework is fundamental to its argument: it critiques the theoretical grounding for how little policy models are expected to be adapted. Bounded rationality is "identified with an imperfect ability to perform calculations, to remember or envision states of affairs," or said another way, *a limited form of rationality* (Fearon and Wendt 2002, 55). According to bounded rationality scholarship, convergence occurs precisely because actors' cognitive heuristics leave them beholden to replicate the "anchor" that they study (LeBoeuf and Shafir 2006; Jacowitz and Kahneman 1995). Revered models of leaders and peers become anchors from which policymakers cannot deviate (Weyland 2006). Rather, this book's contextual rationality approach expects policymakers to undergo fully informed and distinctive learning experiences that reach different conclusions about policy values. Contextually rational policymakers are not "limited" or "bounded" in their rationality; they are rational learners whose local normative context forms the basis of their rationality. Contextual rationality, in light of this central analytical role of local norms, has a fundamentally different expectation than the bounded and conventional rationality scholarships: diversity, not convergence. It expects policymakers to adjust even core elements of much studied and highly regarded policy models, such as the Silicon Valley VC policy model, to optimally suit their local context.

In a critique of bounded conceptualizations of the learning process, Meseguer supports the book's expectation. She argues that although the bounded learning framework is: "used to explain policy convergence, what one would actually expect is the opposite—that is, *policymakers arriving at very different conclusions* about the *consequences of policies,* and *hence choosing divergent policies*" (Meseguer 2009, 19, italics added). Following from this logic, normative environments should lead to policymakers coming to different conclusions rather than replicating anchors. With this view, the occurrence of diversity in VC policy diffusion is not a puzzle but the expected outcome. Distinct constitutive and regulative norms fuel local policymakers' studying experiences that result in the pursuit of locally appropriate policies. Across a set of policy adopters, this leads to variety rather than convergence.

States Can, and Should, Support Market Development in Different Ways

This book asserts an important policy implication: failure to copy the American model does not mean that local VC policy efforts fail. This study reveals that several states with exceptionally different policy contexts—to that within which the Silicon Valley venture capital market emerged and from one another—fostered vibrant local venture capital markets. Taiwan's tax credits catalyzed both the most successful government-engineered venture capital market as well as "the most Silicon Valley–like" VC industry in Asia (Gulinello 2005, 845). Israel's funding of an initial cohort of venture capitalists propelled the growth of the world's largest venture capital market in per capita terms (Baygan 2003). Such state-led approaches can—and do—facilitate local venture capital clusters if the policies are appropriately calibrated for local contexts (Klingler-Vidra et al. 2016).[8] Unlike the effective Weberian bureaucrats who are "technical, rational and therefore culture-neutral," it is precisely the policymakers that deploy contextually rational policies that prove effective (Finnemore 1996, 328; Weber 1968). Policy effectiveness, therefore, is the product of the extent of "localization" (Acharya 2009), "embeddedness" (Evans 1995), and "institutional fit" (Radaelli 2005) of the policies with local context, not policymakers' ability to meticulously reproduce Silicon Valley's model.

This argument echoes the conclusions that "Silicon Valley can't be copied" (Wadhwa 2013), claiming instead that customized paths need to be followed. It offers a contemporary validation of Polanyi's assertion that "whatever principle of behavior predominated" was compatible with the market pattern (2001, 71). Policymaking that attempts to suppress the local context in favor of a Weberian contextless way, by copying an international "best practice," does not outperform. There is not, therefore, a universal best practice that all actors should hold as "most efficient and effective" (Finnemore 1996, 329) for supporting market development. A variety of public policies can engineer local VC activities—so long as they fit the local environment (and so long as there is a baseline level of demand for venture capital (Avnimelech and Teubal 2006). As an example, the 1980s Taiwanese tax credit proved effective because of its *fit* with regulative norms. Taiwanese policymakers' adaptation of the Silicon Valley model into a tax credit and an inverse of the LP structure—though making it very different from the acclaimed model—was a precise fit with their logics of appropriateness for supporting local firms.

Building on this premise, this book argues that states can "pick winners" to promote entrepreneurship and innovation. This runs counter to prevailing wisdom about the role of the state purported by neoliberal thinkers. Milton Friedman famously criticized the state's ability to promote productive activity, saying, "If you put the federal government in charge of the Sahara Desert, in five years there'd be a shortage of sand." In a 1986 speech, Ronald Reagan asserted that "the nine most terrifying words in the English language are: I'm from the government and I'm here to help." Criticism of the state's involvement in markets and entrepreneurship is not only relegated to the zenith of free marketeers or to devoted neoliberals or policy wonks. A 2014 study by the Small Enterprise Association of Australia and New Zealand concludes that states "should avoid trying to 'pick winners'" and should instead support entrepreneurship "through the reform of legal, bureaucratic and regulatory frameworks" (Mazzarol 2014, 3).

This book's finding about the essential, purposive role of the state in venture capital is consistent with that of recent, influential scholarship that portrays an effective, necessary role for the state. This includes influential works such as the "entrepreneurial state" (Mazzucato 2013), "innovation and the state" (Breznitz 2007), and "the politics of innovation" (Taylor 2016). This scholarship contends that states' constitution of private market activity is not relegated to traditional sectors. The state can, and often does, have an essential (if not widely publicized) role in forging the competitiveness of innovative sectors.[9] Weiss (2014) offers contemporary "high-technology" proof of Polanyi's argumentation. She argues that the state has been an integral force to the emergence and continued success of the American technology sector. This shatters the "stateless" depiction of the environment within which U.S. technology companies achieved success, and by extension, the neoliberal rise of Silicon Valley.

Venture capital markets need the support of the state. As Polanyi (2001) argued, the idea of a liberal market utopia is a fallacy as even laissez faire is planned. The reality is that, behind the veneer of the supposedly neoliberal Silicon Valley VC market, the U.S. government intervened to support the onset and growth of a VC market. The myth is that VC financing synonymous with Silicon Valley is merely "an invention of the U.S. market" (Weiss 2014, 51). The U.S. government was a key proponent of Silicon Valley's brand of early-stage financing. Public money was given in the form of loans to VC managers from 1958, via the Small Business Investment Company (SBIC) program. Then, beginning in the 1970s, the national government made venture capital more profitable and accessible for institutional investors. The NASDAQ stock market was launched in 1971, the Employee Retirement Income Security Act (ERISA) reinterpretation of the Prudent Man Rule in 1979 allowed institutional investors (especially pension funds) to invest in the VC asset class, the capital gains tax rate (to which VC profits are subject) was lowered in 1979, and the lighter touch regulations were introduced via the Small Business Investment Incentive Act in 1980 (Lazonick 2009).

The Silicon Valley VC policy model is not, in fact, neoliberal. The U.S. government has acted as a "hidden developmental state" (Block 2008) and has epitomized the "neoliberal paradox" (Wade 2016) through its provision of definite support for select sectors while maintaining that it is dedicated to the neoliberal approach. The hands of the American government were visible in allowing and enabling (profitable) VC investment activity as a means of supporting Schumpeterian entrepreneurship (see Weiss 2014 for an analysis of U.S. VC support as a component in the American "national security state"). Internationally, VC markets have not spontaneously appeared. In Israel, the chief scientist invested in ten would-be venture capital firms as a means to create a domestic class of venture capitalists in the early 1990s (Avnimelech and Teubal 2008). In Europe, particularly in the Nordic and Baltic states, public funding bodies such as national governments, the European Investment Fund, and the U.S. Agency for International Development, invested in venture capital managers before start-ups in the region had achieved success (Sabaliauskas 2015).

There is a multitude of approaches to supporting venture capital market building—and different models have worked. Taylor (2016, 5) similarly argues that "there is no single 'best' institution or policy design" to effectively promote innovation. If VC policy diffusion is seen as a binary of whether or not states deploy policies, as typical quantitative approaches do, it would miss the variety of ways VC can be supported. Studies would assume that it is the Silicon Valley VC policy approach that is diffusing and that convergence on the Silicon Valley model is driving success. But the successful policies invest in, tax, and regulate venture capitalists in ways distinct from the U.S. government approach.[10] Contextually rational policy approaches, not conformation to the Silicon Valley template, underscores instances of effective VC support.

Evidence

This study's evidence is presented in two parts: a dataset of forty-five countries' VC policies and deep investigations of diffusion to three East Asian cases. The dataset informs the book's narrative: numerous policymakers deployed purposive action in an effort to build their own Silicon Valley–like venture capital cluster, but did so in different ways from each other and from the model they aimed to replicate. Variation depicts the VC policies utilized within each and every geographic and cultural cluster; no cluster of states adapted the Silicon Valley model in the same way. Early adopters began employing tax, regulations, and funding efforts in the 1980s while some others only attempted their first initiative in the post–global financial crisis era. Because the large dataset revealed pervasive diversity, the lion's share of the book is dedicated to investigating the precise causal drivers of policy adaptations through analytical narratives.

The large dataset identifies the VC policies deployed in forty-five countries that compete in the global information and communications technology (ICT) sector. The dataset specifies the funding, tax, and regulatory components of each state's VC policies from the first launch of a VC policy effort. For the funding category, the dataset details government funds' launch dates, names, assets under management, repayment (and other) terms, and international versus domestic venture capital manager requirements. In addition, it indicates whether each country directly managed venture capital funds or operated a fund of VC funds structure. The section on tax policy specifies the tax rate that venture capital managers are subject to, as well as any tax credits or exemptions for VC managers or investors in each country. The regulatory section identifies the legal structures (e.g., limited partnership and private company vehicles) used to structure VC funds as well as any variations on the Anglo-American limited partnership model. The regulatory component also identifies restrictions on private investors' ability to invest in the venture capital asset class (e.g., if pension funds and insurance companies are able to able to allocate to VC funds) as well as nonpecuniary incentives, such as residency in exchange for VC investment.

This book challenges existing diffusion expectations by exploring diffusion to a cluster of states that are similar in terms of population size, ethnicity, and development. This case selection is motivated by diffusion scholarship's typical research design, which examines how policies diffuse to and within geographically or culturally proximate clusters (see Simmons and Elkins 2004; Weyland 2006). Spatially organized diffusion analyses contend that policies diffuse in a similar manner to clusters of states precisely because of their colocation (Solingen 2012). In effect, diffusion scholarship assumes that mechanisms such as competition and coercion explain similar policy choices. However, like Ruggie's (1982, 382) critique of realist international relations scholarship's emphasis on power rather than "social purpose," this book contends that diffusion mechanisms are blunt instruments that may predict the *form* (e.g., the adoption of VC policy) but not its *content* (e.g., the regulatory, tax, or funding instruments used). Given that this book aims to extend diffusion theory to account for variety, the case studies are chosen in a similar manner: as a culturally, economically, and geographically proximate cluster of states.[11] Rather than proximity somehow contributing to convergence, this study's research design aims to show how even among a cluster of peers, policymakers' norms underpin context-rooted learning processes, which propel variation among clusters of otherwise similar states.

The East Asian cluster "analytical narrative" (Bates et al. 1998) research design enables the study to include many factors that are typically used to explain convergence. By controlling for other variables, it explicitly investigates the differences in norms as the driver of variety (following case study methodology as depicted by King et al. 1994; Ragin and Becker 1992). Moreover, differences in constitutive and regulative norms are not simply expected to lead to variance across the cluster; policymakers' norms are expected to drive adaptation in line with their national normative environment. Although there are expectations informing the analysis of the case studies, this study shies away from invoking predictive typologies. This investigation of "contextually rational human behavior" allows for a view of human behavior as "something intermediate between perfect clouds and perfect clocks" (Almond and Genco 1977, 491) and between "order and disorder" (Steiner 1983). To borrow Almond and Genco's words again, this book seeks to understand probabilistic logics about how a nonphysical thing (in this case, norms) can bring about a physical change in the physical world (the deployment of specific forms of venture capital policy). In so doing, it strives to develop a theory of human behavior that tries to account for actual behavior (typically the work of "descriptive" theories) aimed at achieving optimal choices (rather than "prescriptive theory" that prescribes optimal behavior; see March 1978, 588, for further distinction of the two theoretical frames).

The analytical narratives constitute a regional cluster that is economically and (in many ways) culturally similar, but whose policymakers possess different constitutive and regulative norms: the East Asian states of Hong Kong, Taiwan, and Singapore. Each of these states have largely ethnically Chinese populations of less than 25 million people (between 6 and 23 million) and relatively small, but highly successful, economies with gross domestic product within a range of US$250 billion to US$475 billion. The three island states are "late industrializers" that developed in the same era by plugging into various sectors of the global economy, especially ICT and manufacturing (Fuller 2010; Breznitz 2007).

The impact of norms on VC policymaking is investigated through primary interviews and extensive reviews of government communiqués. Background expectations were formulated based on deep research into economic policymaking in each state (for example, Gold 1986; Huff 1994; King 2006; Greene 2008; Whitley 1999; Walter and Zhang 2012; Witt and Redding 2013). Though political economy literature often groups the East Asian states together as "developmental states" (Woo-Cuming 1989) that "govern the market" (Wade 2004), the region offers normative variety in terms of how states envisage their role in the economy; after all, it includes the most free economy in the world—Hong Kong.[12] The cases' interventionist orientations range from laissez-faire Hong Kong, to Taiwan's reliance on tax supports for local SMEs, to Singapore's focus on financing to attract international firms. The study examines the role of constitutive and regulative norms in shaping how each state's policymakers learned about and subsequently designed VC policy. The longitudinal study begins with Taiwan's VC policy learning in the early 1980s and concludes with VC policies implemented in 2017.

Historically, East Asian states' financial systems have been broadly characterized as bankcentric; debt—not equity—instruments have been crucial to corporate financing (Pempel 2015, 23–24; Walter and Zhang 2012, 11). The development of venture capital markets in East Asia is part of capital market development throughout the region, particularly since the East Asian financial crisis. Public equity markets have grown, in absolute terms as well as a percentage of financial transactions, as East Asia's financial centers are among the world's largest (The Money Project 2016). The growth of equity markets has been driven by market forces and by policies aimed at supporting capital market development, including private equity, public equity exchanges, bond markets, and money markets (Rethel 2010, 493–94). In this respect, the role of the state in venture capital is consistent with this broader equity story: East Asian policymakers have demonstrated their commitment to ensuring the availability of long-term capital to help private companies grow, by being shielded from the vagaries of volatile public equities markets (Pempel and Tsunekawa 2015). State support of venture capital markets is also consistent with East Asian developmental states exhibiting a contemporary form of "financial activism" in their bid to support industrial activity (Thurbon 2016).

Despite the rise of equity financing in East Asia, there is sparse research into the policies that have supported venture capital markets (Da Rin et al. 2013). Kenney et al. (2002) and Dietrich (2003) described the VC policies deployed across Asia Pacific countries. Their studies were conducted fifteen years ago, so they necessarily miss recent policy developments. Furthermore, their studies detail the policy differences but do not analytically explore the reasons *why* the East Asian VC policies constitute "scattering geese." The states' innovation policies have been examined by numerous scholars, including Alice Amsden in her (2001) "rise of the rest"; Douglas Fuller's (2010) edited volume that explores the limits of Hong Kong's laissez-faire approach; Dan Breznitz's 2007 book on *Innovation and the State*; and J. Megan Greene's *The Origins of the Developmental State in Taiwan* (2008). Even these accounts of innovation policy development do not investigate the learning behind East Asia's pursuit of a variety of VC policies.

Exploring how an American policy model diffuses to East Asia is equally fruitful for political economy scholarship reasons. There are only a modest number of studies on the diffusion of Western models to the region (e.g., Yeo and Painter 2011; Klingler-Vidra 2014a). Diffusion research tends to investigate global diffusion trends (e.g., Simmons et al. 2008; Solingen and Borzel 2014) or focus on diffusion to, and within, the Americas (e.g., Weyland 2012; 2006; Meseguer 2009; Swank 2008) and Europe (Radaelli 2005; Checkel 1999).

Finally, the rise of East Asia's VC markets motivates this study. Hong Kong has the second largest VC market in Asia (HKTDC 2016), and Singapore is increasingly lauded for its attractiveness as a Silicon Valley–like VC hub (Wood 2014). Taiwan became the world's third most active VC market (behind only the United States and Israel) by 2000 and is said to be the Asian venture capital market that is "most Silicon Valley–like" (Gulinello 2005, 845). Through varied policies, Hong Kong and Singapore advanced their positions as preferred domiciles for international venture capital funds while Taiwan succeeded in constituting a locally focused, early-stage VC market. This study contributes novel insights into the drivers of success in these VC clusters.

Approach of This Book

This book reveals how policymakers' contextual rationality repudiates pressures to converge on a singular form of VC policies. It exposes how policy diffusion does not occur in a normative vacuum, and instead, how policy learning and the resultant policy choices are "subject to a complex array of *constraints* and *opportunities*" (Almond and Genco 1977, 492). In an aim to build local Silicon Valley–like venture capital markets, even proximate states pursue varied policies. Free market economists would expect the state's intervening to hinder the performance of market-enabling policies (as Friedman thought the federal government's management of the Sahara would lead to the depletion of sand). Industrial policies in which the state directs market activities, according to neoliberal orthodoxy, should torpedo the emergence of vibrant capitalist markets. Institutionalist scholars within the "varieties of capitalism" approach, argue that science and technology policy efficacy is "determined by the degree to which free markets are allowed to structure the incentives" of actors (Taylor 2016, 11). This book's finding embodies the opposite of this expectation; policymakers do not need to sit back and allow market forces to work in order to develop their local venture capital markets. Even the Silicon Valley VC cluster is the result of government policy, not merely the outcome of unfettered capitalism at work.

In venture capital, a supposedly quintessential neoliberal construct, the state is a needed actor—with room to move in terms of policy choices—in the constitution of markets central to financing innovation and entrepreneurship. This is an important takeaway for today's policymakers who are eager to promote innovation, economic growth, and job creation. The lesson is clear: do not follow the same path that others took. Even if it means diverging from highly regarded models, policymakers should ascertain their "aim"—e.g., a locally focused VC industry—and design policies in line with their normative context in order to get there.

The book is organized as follows. Chapter 2 develops the book's contextual rationality framework that places norms at the center of diffusion analysis. In so doing, it presents the understanding that rational policy learning is rooted in constitutive norms that construct the self-identity of policymakers, and that those identities are accompanied by regulative norms that inform logics of appropriateness about policy actions. This normcentric approach contends that policymakers do not complete Bayesian updating of prior beliefs, nor do they simply rely on cognitive shortcuts. In order to understand policy diffusion, it is essential that we understand the normative context within which policymakers are situated. The chapter also synthesizes state-of-the-art diffusion scholarship's expectations about sources of diversity in the diffusion process. This is done so that existing diffusion expectations can be explored alongside the contextual rationality approach in the case study narratives. Given the lack of coverage of venture capital in political economy scholarship, chapter 3 provides an introduction to the asset class and VC policy.

Chapters 4, 5, and 6 are analytically guided accounts of VC policy diffusion in Hong Kong, Taiwan, and Singapore. The contextual rationality analyses canvas the full policy diffusion process. In these chapters I begin by studying how policymakers came to believe that they should aim to build a local Silicon Valley VC market. Policymakers' orientation toward interventionist or neoliberal strategies emanates from their constitutive norms; whether they identify themselves as necessary providers of "positive non-intervention," promotion, or financing and direction. Regulative norms—fitting with these conceptions of self-identity—then inform which policy tools are deemed appropriate. The contextual rationality approach's focus on constitutive and regulative norms allows the investigation to move further back in the causal argument than rationalist frameworks allow; it explores how the self—from which interests flow—is rooted in normative context, rather than only material surroundings.

Chapter 7 offers a comparative analysis of the case study findings. The final chapter concludes the book by applying the findings to larger political economy debates and outlining areas for further research. Chapter 8 also presents the contextual rationality approach in a bid to reinvigorate research agendas that combine rational approaches with contextualism. Empirically, the concluding chapter makes the case for the continuance of the "planning of laissez-faire." Even in areas characterized as bastions of innovative activity, there is not a "retreat of the state" (Strange 1996) or imposition of a "golden straitjacket" (Friedman 1999, 86). The book closes with a critical discussion of the virtues of venture capital market support and shares expectations for the future of venture capital states in East Asia and beyond.

2

Contextual Rationality

Rationality cannot be separated from any politically significant episode of normative influence or normative change, just as the normative context conditions any episode of rational choice.
—Martha Finnemore and Kathryn Sikkink, "International
Norm Dynamics and Political Change"

Contextual rationality is defined according to its two parts; "contextual"
refers to policymakers' locale-specific norms and "rationality" means "the
structuring of action in terms of ends and means" (Finnemore 1996, 331). Rationalism assumes agents possess complete information; exogenously given,
consistent, and stable set of preferences; and a "perfect ability to perform
calculations" (Fearon and Wendt 2002, 55). Together, the phrase *contextual
rationality* means that policymakers are rational in that they have excellent
computational ability *and* that their preferences are rooted in their normative context.[1] Policymaking—an instrumental behavior as it is intended to
accomplish a goal—is therefore both a rational and cognitive exercise. The
conjoining of the terms comes as follows: policymakers value information
about the optimal means to achieve an end in light of their contextual position, rather than some acontextual environment. In contrast to the presup-
position that intersubjectivity or context dependence thwarts rationality, this
approach contends that actors can be both—in fact, must be both—rational
and rooted in context. It builds on the contention just stated that normative
context conditions rationality rather than subverts or opposes rational decision making.

The contextual rooting of rationality positions the "self"-identity as essential to knowing actors' preferences and self-interests. We must know what

an actor's identity is before we can know their preferences and interests (as consistent with Jepperson et al. 1996, 53). This priority is consistent with that taken by sociological institutionalism in which "social structure is ontologically prior to and generative of agents" (Finnemore 1996, 333) and with Jeffrey Legro's (1996) "two-step," which first explains preferences, and then behavior. This premise stands in contrast to the direction of causality between norms and preferences, as delineated by neoliberal institutionalists, who

> continue to treat actor identities and interests themselves as preexisting and fixed. And to the extent that they *are* considered, norms (embodied in institutions) derive exclusively from rational egoistic choice. Their origins are thus limited to the preexisting preferences of agents, and their consequences tend to reflect this constraint. Identity thus remains marginalized, even in more expansive neoliberal institutionalist arguments. (Kowert and Legro 1996, 458–59)

To be sure, rationalist scholarship positions preferences as prior to, and above influence from, norms. The contextual rationality approach developed here contends that norms—especially constitutive norms—inform actors' identities, which have regulative norms informing their appropriate behavior, and, as a result, shape their preferences for policy choices.

Learning—of the conventionally and boundedly rational varieties—explains cases of international convergence while political economy scholarship has made substantial analytical progress in unpacking why states (continue to) differ (see Lenschow et al. 2005; Hall and Soskice 2001; Evans 1995; Katzenstein 1978; 1985; Zysman 1983). These analytical achievements have not been adequately transported to diffusion literature, particularly to scholarship that posits learning as the primary mechanism responsible for diffusion. In diffusion research, scholars largely conceptualize the diffusion of foreign models as resulting in a binary accept or reject decision (Rogers 1995, 364). Some state-of-the-art scholars criticize this "black box" treatment of domestic environments in the diffusion process (Yeo and Painter 2011, 379). They argue that the local context—the prevailing normative context, political institutions, and economic structures—need to be investigated for their impact on how practices are received and adapted (see Lenschow et al. 2005; Acharya 2004).[2]

The analytical muscle for explaining the persistence of cross-national variety still emanates from institutionalist frameworks.[3] Comparative institutionalist scholars argue that global economic forces are "crucially intermediated by social and political institutions and by policy discourses" (Walter and Zhang 2012, 60). Institutional research programs offer important insights into the role of domestic institutions and path dependency in the policymaking process (Skocpol and Weir 1985). Yet they dedicate limited analytical space to accounting for the role of international factors in ushering in policy change (Knill 2005).[4] More broadly, "exclusively domestic explanations are no more satisfactory [than internationally focused explanations] in their failure to recognize the interconnected nature" of the political economy (Pempel and Tsunekawa 2015, 6). Comparative institutionalist frameworks therefore struggle to account for the occurrence of interdependent policy actions that diffusion scholarship excels in explaining (Streeck and Thelen 2009).

This book posits that norm-based accounts of policy diffusion can help address this challenge. To build on the definition of norm given in chapter 1, we place norms in a broader context of institutions. In his classic text, *Institutions, Institutional Change, and Economic Performance* (1990), Douglass North defines three categories of institutions as informal institutions, formal institutions, and organizations.[5] His term informal institution is used in the same parlance as norms in political economy research. The term "norm" is sometimes interchangeably used with that of "social convention," "culture," "custom," and "social practice." The working conceptualization employed in this book is consistent with that of Katzenstein (1996, 5), that norms constitute "collective expectations for the proper behaviour of actors with a given identity." Other definitions of norms similarly emphasize appropriateness and identity. For example, Finnemore and Sikkink (1998, 891) assert that a norm is a "standard of appropriate behavior for actors with a given identity." They are "shared templates and understandings that serve as guides for economic interpretation and interaction" (Nelson and Katzenstein 2014, 362).

The driving reason that this book adopts the term *norm* is because of the precision by which types of norms are involved in constructing identity and in regulating behavior. Norms can be regulative (in that they order and constrain behavior), constitutive (as they constitute new actors, ideas, and actions), and evaluative (stressing morality) (Finnemore and Sikkink 1998, 891; Katzenstein 1996, 5). In this study, two types of norms are investigated: constitutive and regulative. The use of both constitutive and regulative norms helps to bridge the rationalist and constructivist divide, as in "rationalism the main explanatory role of norms is 'regulative' of the behavior of the exogenously given agents, whereas in constructivism norms are 'constitutive' of actors' identities and interests in the first place" (Fearon and Wendt 2002, 61).

Constitutive norms are essential in "defining actor identities," and in constructing national identities (Katzenstein 1996, 4–5). Constitutive norms inform how policymakers see themselves and then, in light of that identity, how they should behave. As an example, policymakers in Hong Kong have defined themselves according to their decidedly laissez-faire approach; they are dedicated to their provision of "positive non-interventionism." As the Heritage Economic Freedom Index results confirm, the modus operandi in Hong Kong is to provide conditions in which market forces thrive, rather than to direct market actors. This laissez-faire identity is accompanied by logics of appropriateness about how they should intervene in a way that is both minimal and positive.

Regulative norms then order and constrain behavior; they are policymakers' "logics of appropriateness" (March and Olsen 1998). Regulative norms inform the range of acceptable policy actions. The normative contexts inform varied but stable preferences, which means that when the states "face similar constraints, they may respond in different ways," as Kowert and Legro (1996, 461) posit in their assessment of studies on the role of culture. As such, constitutive and regulative norms explain variation in policy diffusion (via learning) outcomes and are the key causal concepts in the "contextual rationality" framework.

The next section explores the theoretical underpinnings and expectations of conventional and bounded rationality in order to distinguish and develop the contextual rationality approach. It also further elucidates the three norms that shape policymakers' contextual rationality in the empirical area of VC policy. Policymakers' norms shape identities as interventionists or hands-off, as well as inform the appropriateness of private sector financing and international or local-firm support. The following section elaborates on the formal institution and norm dialectic. Building on the understanding that norms are core to the investigation, I will depict the normative contexts of the three East Asian analytical narratives and articulate expectations for their diffusion outcomes, according to the contextual rationality approach and state-of-the-art diffusion scholarship. Diffusion expectations are based on "intrinsic characteristics" (Finnemore and Sikkink 1998, 906) of the policy model (number of models and the level of specificity) and the diffusion mechanisms (emulation, learning, competition, and coercion). The chapter closes by detailing how the contextual rationality framework guides the analytical narratives.

Contextualism and Rational Learning

Contextualism and rationality are often construed as diametric opposites. Finnemore and Sikkink (1998, 909) assert that there is an "opposition of constructivist and 'rationalist' arguments" that implies that "the issues constructivists study (norms, identities) are not rational, and similarly, that 'rationalists' cannot or do not treat norms or identities" in their research. Fearon and Wendt (2002, 58) present the ideational versus material divide as a core contention between constructivism and rationality; "rationalists believe that people are always acting on material self-interest, and constructivists believe that people are always acting on the basis of norms or values." As an illustration, Nelson and Katzenstein (2014, 361) explain that "policymakers substitute other methods of decision making for rational calculations; specifically, actors' decisions are rooted in social conventions." Elsewhere in their article, Nelson and Katzenstein (2014) assert that expectations are either intersubjective or rational, and that "optics" available to understand decision making are either rationalist or sociological—but not both. Miriam

Steiner (1983, 379) conceptualizes policymakers as having either rationalistic or nonrationalistic worldviews, the nonrationalistic view accounting for an epistemology presuming "subjective awareness" and "sensitivity to subjective contexts." In effect, scholars hold that context-rooted worldviews and decision making are the opposite of rationality. Rationality is subverted by, rather than informed by, contextual inputs.

Scholarship that examines context, such as norms, culture, and institutions, as the core analytical object seeks to explain why locales pursue specific actions, whether it be policy decisions or the adoption of a norm. Explanations emanating from context as the analytical inroads, in light of this orientation, reveal variance, diversity, and specificity through qualitative research methods. To illustrate, Thurbon (2016, 5) explains that "nationally distinctive and temporally contingent developmental strategies necessarily imply the existence of varied, and variable, institutional arrangements and policy practices that are nonetheless directed towards achieving the same end goal." Stephen Bell (2005) repudiates the strict convergence thesis by focusing on the institutional (and structural) situation of agents, which gives them room to maneuver in the face of international pressures. Said simply, ideational and institutionalist accounts tend to expect diversity as their starting point. The rationalist approach, on the other hand, is rooted, epistemologically, in the bedrock of the modern economics discipline, which expects patterns, and often, convergence.

This book's contextual rationality framework fuses contextualism and rationality, rather than conceding to the depiction of the two as ontologically and epistemologically irreconcilable approaches. Contextual rationality assumes actors are rational; they are computationally able to process information, they access large swathes of information and their system of preferences is consistent and stable. Their rationality is contextual because preferences are based in norms that inform how the policymakers see themselves (e.g., identity) and what policy behavior is valued and appropriate in their local context. This assumption that normative context is a priori to rationality is consistent with the depiction by Katzenstein et al. (1998) of constructivists as scholars who "seek to understand how preferences are formed and knowledge generated, prior to the exercise of instrumental rationality." As suggested by Finnemore and Sikkink (1998, 910), actors' utility "could be specified as social or ideational as easily as they can be material." Hall and Taylor similarly attest to valuations occurring "within a broader cultural environment" (1996, 16), meaning that actors can be both "strategic" and influenced by "a familiar set of moral or cognitive templates" (1996, 22).

The assumption here is that rational learning processes necessarily occur in normative contexts, rather than acontextual locales or in only physical materiality. This emphasis on the social aspect of structure addresses a weakness of international relations scholarship, which has placed a "far greater emphasis" on material aspects of structure, such as the "relative position of subgroups within a society and the distribution of material capabilities among them" (Kowert and Legro 1996, 459). In fact, norms are shared by policymakers in a national context and are "instantiated in practices," giving them a form of materiality (Fearon and Wendt 2002). The focus on national norms places the determination of preferences between that of individuals and world levels. Weber's "intrinsic" rationality presumes that actors are individualistic and "highly idiosyncratic" (Kaplan 1976). At the other extreme, "world society" (Meyer et al. 1997) and "international norm" orientations assert that (at least some) norms are universally held (Streeck and Thelen 2005). The contextual rationality's approach holds that norms are exhibited at a national level.

Learning is understood, in diffusion terms, as "a process of reflection on the part of the adopter" (Meseguer and Gilardi 2009, 17–19). In international political economy scholarship, the learning process is largely conceptualized as a Bayesian one (e.g., the rational updating of beliefs underpins the process of reflection). As an illustration, Nelson and Katzenstein (2014, 369) explain that learning constitutes new information, causing "agents to update earlier beliefs and revise their behavior in ways that were consistent with the rules of rational decision theory." Learning involves "observation and interpretation" in light of the "acquisition of new theories or behavioral repertoires" (Simmons et al. 2008, 25). This conceptualization distinguishes two levels of learning—simple and complex. Simple learning refers to new information leading to a change in preferred "means" (e.g., particular policy instrument) while complex learning involves new preferences for the "ends" (e.g., the overall goal) (Levy 1994).[6] Peter Hall further differentiated policy learning into three levels: "The overarching goals that guide policy in a particular field, the techniques or policy instruments used to attain those goals, and the precise settings of these instruments" (Hall 1993, 278). Lenschow et al. (2005) applied Hall's conceptualization to the field of environmental governance. For them, the overarching diffusion idea is the concept of human stewardship over nature; the second level, that of instruments, are governance techniques such as direct regulation, fiscal instruments, or voluntary agreements. The most specific level, the precise settings, are the levels of emission standards or taxes (ibid., 803).

Others have distinguished policy goals from specific strategies. Weyland (2006, 18) draws out different levels of specification: principles are "general and vague on details" whereas a model is a "concrete, specific blueprint." He suggests that the Bismarckian welfare state and the Chilean-style pension system are examples of models; the more general principles include the notion of capital account liberalization or central bank independence (Weyland 2006, 17). Taking a more ideational tact to the differentiation of ends and means, Thurbon (2016, 16) distinguishes between shared goals and ambitions of the elites, in terms of national techno-industrial transformation and "shared ideas about how these goals might best be met (involving strategic interventions in the market)."

Drawing these conceptualizations together, the approach taken here recognizes that learning occurs at varied levels, across broad policy goals or aims and at a more tactical-instrument level. Linking these different levels of abstraction together with the conceptualization of forms of learning, we can depict the first form of learning as being about overarching policy goals, which is understood as complex (the "ends"), while learning about policy instruments and settings is conceptualized as simple learning (the "means"). Policymakers' simple and complex learning processes are triggered by a variety of sources, including their own policy experiences, experiences within their region, and information they gather on policy experience from the rest of the world (Lee and Strang 2008). Complex learning can bring a new policy aim on the agenda, while simple learning will inform the means adopted to achieve that goal. Radaelli (2005), for example, revealed that the diffusion of the regulatory impact assessment idea across the European Union did not produce convergence in the more tactical design of impact assessment practices. The contextual rationality approach's depiction of learning focuses on the simple learning level: learning about the means available in order to achieve an end (not about the end in and of itself).

In the diffusion of new policy areas—or policy innovations (Rogers 1995)—policymakers may come to accept that a new end is desirable (e.g., complex learning). But complex learning does not trigger the abandonment of norms about appropriate means in the simple learning process. The contextual rationality approach contends that policymakers' existing "logics of appropriateness" (March and Olsen 1998) are crucial determinants of cost-benefit analyses about which policies are optimal for local use. Normative context informs how different means are evaluated for reaching an aim—such as how to build a local VC market akin to that of Silicon Valley. In the face of compelling evidence of a successful policy model, norms are not displaced, as "cultural legitimation rather than task demands or functional needs" continues to characterize policymakers' learning and policy design processes (Finnemore 1996, citing the work of Meyer and Rowan 1977). To illustrate, policymakers come to believe that the Silicon Valley model is the ideal model of an innovation ecosystem. Concomitantly, their existing logics of appropriateness shape their evaluation of which strategies are optimal in their quest to build a Silicon Valley–like VC cluster. Because each national context has its own, historically informed constitutive and regulative norms, policymakers come to the conclusion that a distinctly national policy form is optimal. Across a universe of policy adopters, this explains the occurrence of variance amid convergent trends.

Conventional Rationality

Conventionally rational learning processes involve policymakers conducting comprehensive scans of available models. Economics depicts man as rational, meaning that he has "impressively clear and voluminous," if not absolutely complete, knowledge; exhibits a well-organized and stable system of preferences; and possesses a strong computational skill (Simon 1955, 99). When the rational man learns, he chooses optimal policy according to a cost-benefit analysis that maximizes utility by minimizing risk associated with implementing a new policy.[7] Rational actors' choices are the result of computational efforts to "maximize their satisfaction (utility) by efficiently matching available means to their desired ends" (Kowert and Legro 1996, 456). When presuming policymakers as rational actors, scholars assume that policymakers' preferences are based on their institutional and material position. Policymakers' preferences are stable and consistent, and the information they seek is "orderly and empirically available," helping them to "identify and select optimal courses of action" (Steiner 1983, 375). In light of these restrictive assumptions, Kowert and Legro (1996, 457) assert that orthodox economic accounts of rationality "can only provide an extremely sparse account of behavioral variations in the actors facing similar constraints."

Rationalist scholars assume that actors hold some prior beliefs about the expected outcomes of various policies, which inform their preference formation. As Bayesian learners, policymakers are expected to fully update their prior beliefs about the expected results of alternative policies. The updating occurs in line with the "consistency of the information [on the policy experience] and the strength of prior belief" (Carlsnaes et al. 2012). The rational learning process drives the Bayesian updating, and thus the value and rank order of their preferences (Simmons et al. 2008, 28). Inundated with evidence of policy performance, the "impact of the prior beliefs vanishes rapidly in the [Bayesian] updating process" (Meseguer 2009, 47). Meseguer (2009, 67) goes on to explain that "no matter what their initial beliefs . . . if confronted with a good deal of information, all policymakers will converge in their beliefs about the outcomes of policies, and will also, I hypothesize, converge in their policy choices." To be sure, exposed to the same information, policymakers come to hold the same posterior beliefs. In line with this Bayesian convergence, policymakers then choose the same policy, because they believe that the same (effective policy model) is optimal. As Nelson and Katzenstein (2014, 369) assert, the rational process causes actors to "revise their behavior."

Figure 2.1, below, illustrates the causal pathway imputed by the conventionally rational characterization of learning. Prior beliefs are updated most completely when a policy has been implemented in a highly successful case, and when success is achieved on many occasions. The consistency of policy performance reduces the perceived risk associated with implementing a policy; the reduced risk helps drive policymakers' full updating of prior beliefs (Simmons et al. 2008, 26–27). This is represented visually in figure 2.1. In the top row, policymakers experience full Bayesian updating due to the strength, and consistency, of the evidence of the successful impact of the policy model. Policymakers then, regardless of their preexisting beliefs, design a close

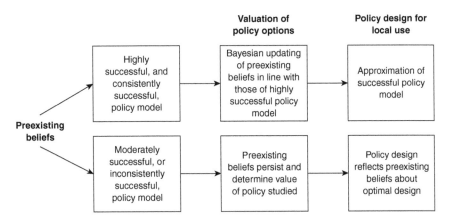

Figure 2.1 Conventional rationality learning causal pathway

approximation of the studied policy, and as a result, states converge on the revered model. In the bottom row, however, beliefs persist as the policy information is only moderately successful, or is inconsistent in its performance spatially or temporally.

Figure 2.1 has two rows to illustrate the core tenet of the conventionally rational conception of learning: the more, and more consistent, evidence of success, the more complete the updating of prior beliefs. With inconsistent evidence, Bayesian updating is less complete; with consistently positive evidence, is it more complete.

In addition, conventional rationality scholarship expects several factors to propel and confound the full Bayesian updating process. Policymakers are less likely to experience Bayesian updating when learning from their own experience. Meseguer (2009, 47) argues that prior beliefs are "expected to be more persistent in the updating of own experience." To be sure, "own experience" is less likely to propel Bayesian updating. The involvement of intermediaries such as international organizations is expected to inhibit Bayesian updating as they "shape and filter" the lessons drawn during policy learning processes (Simmons et al. 2008, 30).

Across this scholarship, adherence to an ideology is presented as irrational behavior. Ideology and culture oppose, rather than shape, rationality. Some assert that adherence to an "ideology" or "dogmatism" can thwart rational learning. Carlsnaes et al. (2012) contend that the extent of Bayesian updating is determined by the "strength" of prior beliefs. Freeman (2006) explains that firmly held ideologies reduce the risk that policymakers associate with a policy choice. The use of ideology, however, is not associated with optimal policy choice. As Meseguer (2009, 61) explains, "Even if a policy performs comparatively worse, it may not be abandoned if it is ideologically preferred." In foreign policy analysis scholarship, Steiner (1983) explains

that the presumption was that decision making based in feeling and intu-
ition, rather than rationality, led to "bad decisions." For these scholars, the
existence, and persistence, of culture and ideology thwarts rational processes
and the selection of optimal choices.

Conventional rationality does not sufficiently allow for social context as a
plausible, productive determinant of policymakers' rationality. This is where
contextual rationality comes in. It builds on Kowert and Legro's assertion that
"social prescription often supersedes material self-interest" (1996, 451–52)
and that a rejection of rationalism does not mean that authors espouse "ir-
rationalism" (1996, 457) or "nonrationalism" (Steiner 1983). The contextual rationality framework presumes that context-rooted norms inform actors' preferences and self-interests, and that the studying of foreign policy
experience does not trigger the updating of constitutive or regulative norms.
Policymakers rigorously study policy experiences elsewhere. In so doing, they
do not become contextless actors. Even in the face of the most consistent,
conclusive evidence of positive policy performance elsewhere, they do not
lose their norms guiding who they are or how they *should* act. Their norms
persist, determining their cost-benefit analysis of policies, and ultimately, the
policies they pursue.

Research on rational learning focuses on policymakers' assessment of
economic optimality, not on what is politically optimal, or even saleable
(see, for example, Meseguer 2009). This is a critical flaw in the depiction of
the conventionally rational learning process as policymakers evaluate and
design policies in socially appropriate ways (see Hall and Taylor 1996, 16).
Experimental studies have repeatedly found that people do not behave "axi-
omatically rational in the presence of uncertainty" (Nelson and Katzenstein
2014, 366; Kahneman and Tversky 1983). If actors take social prescription
or uncertainty into account, conventional rationality holds that learning is
therefore irrational. Thus, while "material factors matter at the limit . . . *how*
they matter depends on ideas" (Fearon and Wendt 2002, 58). Different from
conventional conceptualizations of rationality, the contextual rationality approach holds that rationalization processes are based in "value rather than
in interests" (Kalberg 1980, 1145). In light of policymakers' identities and
what they know "to be acceptable"—not simply their material endowments
or some exogenously given preferences—they act rationally.[8] The base of rationality is context rather than materialism, which means that "interests are
constructed through a process of social interaction" (Katzenstein 1996, 2).

Bounded Rationality

While this book's contextual rationality approach critiques conventional rationality, it also constitutes a departure from understanding policymakers as
boundedly rational. Bounded rationality posits that rationality is somehow
limited or incomplete, as actors' learning and decision-making processes are

abbreviated by their cognitive biases (see work of Gilovich et al. 2002; Kahneman and Tversky 1973, 1983; March 1978; Simon 1955; 1957). Steiner (1983, 376) explains that bounded rationality scholarship presumes that "human beings are biologically and psychologically limited in their capacity to consider, calculate and compare." More than humans' ability to process information, this limitation impedes the orderliness of preferences, such that actors have "unstable, inconsistent, incompletely evoked, and imprecise goals" (March 1978, 595).

In light of their limited resources, boundedly rational actors rely on cognitive shortcuts to learn and to make decisions, and these shortcuts help them to skirt the rational analytical process. Comprehensive learning about optimal—or in Simon's (1957) words "satisficing" rather than optimal—choices is replaced by cognitive heuristics that make learning and decision making "easier." Cognitive biases point actors toward studying and replicating models that are representative and available (Kahneman and Tversky 1983). Their "anchor" bias then leads them to approximating the models they study rather than adjusting them (LeBoeuf and Shafir 2006). The starting information—the anchor—exerts "drag on the subsequent adjustment process," leaving final formulations close to the original (Epley and Gilovich 2006, 311).

Drawing on cognitive psychology tools, Weyland (2005; 2006; 2010; 2012) blazed a trail for using cognitive bias conceptualization to explain policy diffusion outcomes in international political economy research. Weyland (2006, 50–51) asserts that Kahneman and Tversky's three cognitive biases—availability, representativeness, and anchoring—inform policymaking in diffusion processes. The availability bias refers to "people's reliance on vivid, concrete, salient examples, which remain disproportionately cognitively 'available'" (McDermott 2008, 2). Peer countries with "similar policy orientations and legacies (i.e. shared traditions of political development and form of state interventions) framed within shared histories of political development, institutional patterns, and cultures" are expected to learn about each other's policies (Swank 2008, 78). The availability heuristic leads policymakers to study the policy experiences of leaders (e.g., the United States or European Union) or peers that are geographically or culturally proximate to their existing belief system, political development histories, or institutional patterns (Volden et al. 2008; Swank 2008, 78; Gilardi 2010, 651).

Representativeness, bounded rationality's second cognitive bias, is the tendency to assume that one country's (positive) policy experience is likely to be representative of how the policy will perform elsewhere (McDermott 2008, 2). This heuristic impacts the valuation stage of the learning process (Weyland 2006, 50) as it leads policymakers to conclusions about the expected local performance of the policy models (Knill 2005). The representativeness heuristic, as argued here, fails to make a critical distinction between whether policymakers value the means (e.g., the policy instruments) or the end (e.g., the successful outcome). Policymakers can deem the end (e.g., the creation of a local Silicon Valley VC industry) to be highly desirable, while finding little value in the means (e.g., a reinterpretation that allows public pension funds to invest in the high-risk asset class).

The third heuristic, anchoring, describes actor's tendency to "focus on the 'anchor' of the original model" (McDermott 2008, 2). Anchoring posits that policymakers are "reluctant to diverge radically" from the model (Weyland 2006, 51). This is why, according to bounded rationality scholarship, we see patterns of policy convergence. Policymakers deviate only superficially from the anchor as they contend that it is optimal to implement the "core" of the studied model. The anchoring heuristic critically undermines bounded rationality's capacity for investigating how policymakers adapt models. Because policymakers are beholden to reproduce the anchor, bounded rationality scholars are left unable to explain why they would adapt (or even reject) elements of a highly successful model.

I critique this notion that the foreign model is an anchor for two reasons. First, even cognitive psychology studies struggle to demonstrate the impact of the anchoring heuristic outside of the laboratory. Epley and Gilovich (2006, 311) conclude that "process-tracing procedures have yielded no evidence of adjustment in the standard anchoring paradigm." Second, anchoring falters by arguing that it is policymakers' constitutive and regulative norms that anchor the policy, in light of what is held as locally appropriate means. The primacy of norms—rather than the foreign model—as anchor dovetails with conventional rationality's presumption that existing ideology or dogmatism limits Bayesian updating.

As figure 2.2 illustrates, boundedly rational learning posits that models are selected according to their availability and representativeness. These two heuristics are involved in the selecting of policies to study (as depicted

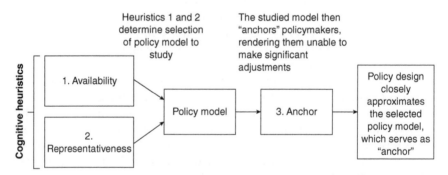

Bounded rationality posits that there are three cognitive heuristics:
(1) availability, (2) representativeness, and (3) anchor.

Figure 2.2 Bounded rationality learning causal pathway

in how boxes 1 and 2 appear, analytically, before the policy model), as well as the value assigned to them. Not only are the policies that are representative due to some form of affinity, they are said to be valued because of their relevance.

Then, the third cognitive shortcut—depicted in "3. Anchor" in figure 2.2—limits the extent to which the policy is adapted. In this book's contextual rationality approach, it is the locale-specific conceptions of identity and appropriate policy paths (stemming from constitutive and regulative norms) that act as an anchor from which behavior cannot deviate, rather than an external model limiting the range of acceptable policy choices.

Differentiating Contextual Rationality from Conventional and Bounded Rationalities

Contextually rational policymakers are expected to systematically adapt even highly successful models in line with their normative frameworks. This contextually rational depiction posits that actors can be both rational in their computational capacity and orderly in their system of preferences. In this view, unlike conventionally rational assumptions, rationality is rooted in normative context, so that policymakers do not become blank canvasses, holding acontextual "posterior beliefs" as the result of their extensive studying of highly revered models. Their local norms persistently inform their cost-benefit analysis of optimal policy means.

At the same time, policymakers' capacity to process information is not limited, nor are their preferences unstable; the contextual rationality approach does not presume that policymakers rely on cognitive shortcuts in the same way that psychologists observe the role of heuristics in casual experiments about snap decisions in the lab. They acquire extensive information about the policy models they study over the course of months or years. They strive to wholly understand the function of the original model rather than quickly "self-generate" an understanding of the anchor (Epley and Gilovich 2006, 312). They maintain stable preferences for which policy forms are optimal. As a result, they are not beholden to mimicking the anchor. Instead, the normative context in which they operate shapes their preferences and, as a result, the rank value of acceptable policy choices.

Norms are the essential conceptual unit, as policy information is sought out, received, and valued in normative (rather than fundamentally material or institutional) contexts. Norms, similar to "social conventions,"[9] help actors to reduce the risk associated with policymaking by shaping how policies are valued. There is an "interlocking web," or "two-level" depiction of constitutive norms, that inform identities and regulative norms that affect assessments of appropriate behavior (Kowert and Legro 1996, 468), as depicted in steps 3 and 4 in figure 2.3 below (constitutive norms are causally prior). Then regulative norms, which flow from the constituted identities, operate as "templates for understanding how to operate in contexts that are experienced as shared and common" (Nelson and Katzenstein 2014, 367). Contextually rooted appropriateness, not technical efficiency, underpins the cost-benefit calculations performed in the learning process. This contradicts the conceptualization of learning by rational choice scholars. As Fearon and Wendt (2002, 60) explain, an economically rational actor's cost-benefit analysis prioritizes the most efficient means to the end, whereas a sociological view of actors is based in questions of appropriateness ("how is a person in my role (or with my identity) supposed to act in this circumstance?"). When policymakers are conceptualized as operating in context, the presumption is that they need "an ability to discern actions that are appropriate or 'fitting' in a particular subjective context" (Steiner 1983, 382).

In light of the logic of appropriateness being at the core of the learning process, the contextual rationality framework expects a diversity of means pursued by policy adopters—based on context-specific norms—rather than convergence on a single policy as the result of full Bayesian updating or cognitive heuristics. This is a profoundly different expectation than both conventional and bounded rationalities. Conventional rationality assumes full Bayesian updating. Policymakers' posterior beliefs about optimal policies converge due to the strength of evidence acquired in the learning process. They are, therefore, expected to converge in their policy choices by replicating the policy formula that has most consistently resulted in successful outcomes in an effort to maximize their utility (by reducing performance risk). To be sure, conventionally rational learning assumes that policymakers reduce risk by pursuing consistently successful policies, while the contextual rationality approach holds that they reduce risk by employing policy means they know to be locally appropriate and thus designing distinct policies. Bounded rationality expects convergence, but through a different causal path than conventional rationality. It expects policymakers to shortcut the Bayesian updating process by relying on cognitive heuristics. Their prior beliefs are not fully updated because they do not hold stable preferences and choose to study policies effectively implemented by their self-determined leaders and peers. The "anchor" heuristic limits the deviation away from replicating the proven policy models of leaders and peers.

Table 2.1 compares the rationalities across the following dimensions: nature of their search for information, determinants of policy valuation, sources of policy change, expectations of convergence or variance, and forms of policy choices. The table compares the function of the three forms of rationality in the context of simple learning processes, summarizing the discussion in the previous sections. The first row illustrates the differences in the way in which information is sought out; ranging from full and rigorous searching (in conventional and contextual conceptualizations) to limited searches for what leaders and peers have done (according to bounded rationality).

TABLE 2.1
Comparing rationalities

	Conventional rationality	Bounded rationality	Contextual rationality
Nature of search for information	Full and rigorous search for existing models	Limited search for information on models of leaders and peers	Full and rigorous search for existing models
Preference formation	Exogenously given and orderly, consistent	Unstable and inconsistent	Stable and consistent with normative context
Determinants of policy value	Preferences updated by consistency and extent of external policy's success	Preferences updated by cognitive heuristics	Preferences based on identity and logic of appropriateness
Expectation: convergence or variance	Convergence	Convergence	Variance
Form of policy choices	Replica of most consistently successful policy	Replica of the policies of leader or peers	Varied forms, each reflecting context-specific norms
Sources of policy changes	New (foreign) evidence	New (foreign) evidence	Critical junctures, policy experience and new (foreign) evidence

It also depicts the primary determinants of policy valuation, which is essential to determining how optimal policies are to be designed for the local context. Row 2—Preference formation—accounts for the different approaches' presumption of how preferences are formed as well as their consistency. In conventional accounts of rationality, preferences are assumed to be stable and predictable and are exogenously given. Bounded rationality, in contrast, expects human beings' preferences to be unstable and inconsistent given the limited capacity for information processing. Contextual rationality situates itself differently; actors' preferences are presumed to be stable and consistent, but rooted in normative contexts (rather than exogenously given).

Row 3—Determinants of policy valuation—shows that the value of policies stems from their performance elsewhere (driving full Bayesian updating in a conventionally rational learning process), from cognitive shortcuts (relying on representativeness), or from local norms informing appropriateness. Through these different expectations for what policy is acquired and how it is valued, the table's fourth row depicts the overall expectation of whether diffusion will result in convergence or variation. Because of the expectation that external evidence will result in Bayesian updating or in being anchored, conventional and bounded rationality expect convergence. The contextual rationality approach, in contrast, expects variation (the table's fourth row depicts the way that variation is expected to manifest in VC policy). The fifth row—Form of policy choices—offers a more granular expectation for what policy forms will result from diffusion, via learning, in light of the different conceptualizations of rationality.

The final row—Sources of policy changes—identifies what can drive policy change over time. For conventional and bounded rationality, the causal power lies with the availing of foreign policy evidence, whereas for contextual rationality, it is local events, conceptualized as critical junctures and local policy experiences, that can cause normative shifts in addition to new (foreign) policy information potentially triggering change. Meseguer (2009) contends that, over time, all policymakers are conventionally rational. I disagree. More external policy information does not necessarily supplant appropriateness in the long run simply because the game is longer. Policymakers' norms persist throughout the learning process; they offer a means to reduce the risk inherent in designing policies for a new aim by continuing to act in locally appropriate ways. Sugden (1989) revealed that social conventions lead to differing outcomes across iterative games, pointing to the continued role of socialization in actors' decision-making processes. Similarly, the presumption here is that policymakers do not lose all trace of prior norms about optimal policymaking just because time passes. It is, rather, changes in the local context—through critical junctures and (poor) policy performance as identified in the contextual rationality column in table 2.1 above—that increase policymakers' openness to updating their norms. The result is greater openness to alternative policy approaches and identities.

Figure 2.3 visualizes the causal pathway behind contextual rationality. The first step—a dialectic between formal institutions and constitutive and

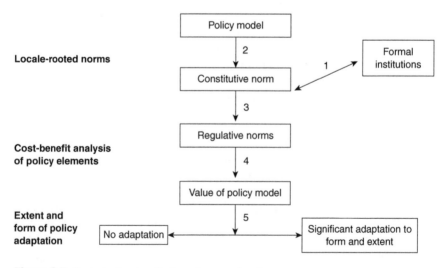

Figure 2.3 Contextual rationality learning causal pathway

regulative norms—depicts the ongoing feedback loop in which norms and formal institutions reinforce and update one another. Norms do not operate in isolation. Rather, norms and institutional structures are mutually constituted, as Jepperson et al. (1996, 63) explains: "Cultural and institutional structures have no existence apart from the ongoing knowledge of actors . . . cultural and institutional structures cannot be divorced analytically from the processes by which they are continually produced and reproduced and changed." Then, the figure shows how policy model information is met by light of constitutive norms (point 2) and regulative norms (point 3). The normative environment informs the identity and expectations of proper behavior. These context-based norms inform the value of the policy model, as represented in step 4. Based on the value assigned to various policy models, policymakers adapt the policy model to a certain extent and form (step 5).

Figure 2.3 illustrates the presumption of this contextual depiction of rationality, that "human behavior is driven by a normative logic of appropriateness" (Fearon and Wendt 2002, 65). Policy values, and then the resulting policy choices, are informed by the processing of policy information in local normative contexts.

How Contextual Rationality's Norms Shape VC Policymaking

Three norms are expected to shape policymakers' learning about Silicon Valley VC policies. The first norm is the constitutive norm that informs policymakers' view of self as having an interventionist or hands-off role. This informs how policymakers see themselves in terms of what extent to which they should intervene in the economy. The constitutive norm—their "interventionist orientation"—identifies the extent to which policymakers understand they should intervene in the economy. Policymakers' interventionist orientation can range from an aversion to getting involved to their penchant for seeing their role as an essential director of private sector activity.[10] As an illustration, Chalmers Johnson (1982) revealed that Japan's MITI members felt that it was their job to tell the private sector what to do. The constitutive norm driving cost calculations in VC policy diffusion are policymakers' broad interventionist orientation norms. This refers to policymakers' conceptualization of their role in the market, particularly the *extent* to which they, as responsible for economic policy, should intervene in promoting or directing market activities. As VC policy information diffuses, constitutive norms imbue value on the policy model, in line with the policy's neoliberal or interventionist character.

How policymakers constitute their role in the economy informs their valuation of VC policies. There is, of course, no singular interventionist orientation in East Asia. Some East Asian policymakers, according to Johnson's work on Japan, contend that the private sector would not know what to do unless told. Others, such as the colonial Hong Kong government, felt markets could better manage production and the allocation of resources than the state. Acting in line with their conception of the appropriate role of the state, Hong Kong's colonial era policies minimized state involvement in markets whereas Japan's MITI promoted national champions and drove the development of specific sectors. The interventionist orientation speaks to whether, and how, policymakers value models that direct market activity (e.g., funding) and those that enable the market to lead (e.g., regulations). For example, in laissez-faire Hong Kong, neoliberal policies that achieved success abroad may be adopted with few alterations; policymakers' constitutive norms affirm that a hands-off approach is appropriate. In contrast, more interventionist approaches are likely discounted or adjusted due to their lack of fit with Hong Kong policymakers' identity as adherents to positive nonintervention.

As illustrated in figure 2.4, the constitutive norm shaping actor identity—the extent to which they are interventionist or laissez-faire—"shapes prevailing rules for behavior," the regulative norms (Kowert and Legro 1996, 464). Then, regulative norms inform policymakers' preferred *form* of intervention. In VC policy diffusion, the regulative norms are (3a) private sector financing norms and (3b) norms dictating how to support international or local

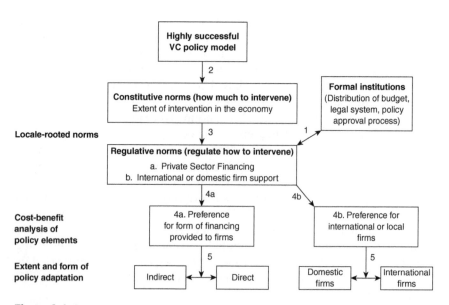

Figure 2.4 Contextual rationality's VC policy learning causal pathway

firms. Regulative norms effectively "order and constrain" (Finnemore and Sikkink 1998, 891) policymakers by "defining standards of appropriate behavior" (Katzenstein 1996, 5). The first of the regulative norms dictates how policymakers should use public finance to promote private activity—whether it is appropriate to directly finance specific firms, or to provide financial support in more indirect ways. The second regulative norm guides the logic of appropriateness for designing policies that solicit international firms or support local ones.

Regulative norms inform preferences for policy forms (represented in 4a and 4b in Figure 2.4). These preferences are then manifested into specific forms and extents of policy adaption, specifically whether the target firms are domestic or international and whether policymakers prefer direct or indirect financing approaches (designated as "5," the outcome of the contextually rational learning process, in figure 2.4).

Private sector financing norms—the regulative norm designated 3a in figure 2.4—informs policymakers' logic of appropriateness for financing private sector activity. They determine how models that deploy public money are valued and adapted; they can lead to the pursuit of policies that either use loans, grants, or equity investment funds, or policies that avoid funding all together. These norms range from contexts in which policymakers contend that directing large sums of financing is best, to the opposite extreme, in which policymakers are vehemently opposed to directly giving money to any private firms. Thus, these regulative norms range from "direct" to "indirect" forms of private sector financing. Direct funding norms lead to the creation of a fund of VC funds, in which a cohort of venture capitalists are financially supported. In states where policymakers' private sector financing norms dictate that indirect finance is appropriate, they tend to support VC markets through tax support, pooled financial resources, and nonfinancial incentives.

The second regulative norm investigated (3b in figure 2.4) is the logic of appropriateness dictating whether to support international or local firms. This norm informs whether policymakers support local companies or foreign firms. States adapt the Silicon Valley VC policy model differently depending on which of these two classes of firms they tend to support. Policymakers that deem it appropriate to support international firms are expected to adopt Silicon Valley's LP structure more or less intact as their norms value policies that please international investors. The adoption of the widely used LP structure signals an interest in complying with international practices. In states where policymakers' norms dictate that they should support local firms, on the other hand, the LP structure will be adapted to support local VC managers. Regulative norms that prioritize local investors tend to value policies that adapt or reject the LP structure, among other aspects of the Silicon Valley model (as in 4b in figure 2.4).

Norms and Formal Institutions: A Dialectic

Norms, and the policy choices they shape, do not exist in a vacuum, and both the constitutive and regulative norms can, and do, change over time. One driver of normative change is the dynamic whereby local formal institutions affect the prevailing constitutive and regulative norms, and vice versa (as illustrated in figure 2.4 as "1"). The dynamic between constitutive and regulative norms, and formal institutions, is what Hall calls a "relational character" (Thelen and Steinmo 1992). There is a "dialectical interplay" between the norms held by policymakers and the institutional environment in which they operate (Thurbon 2016, 6; Bell 2005). This dialectic is designated as the two-directional "1" because of its constant reproducing nature, working regardless of the introduction of policy model information.

Formal institutions are the laws and rules guiding economic and political interaction, as individuals know, ex ante, what is acceptable (Sobel 2012). This book's investigation of formal institutions focuses on processes of policy approval, legal systems, and the distribution of budgetary power.[11] In the VC policy area, this includes the distribution of budgetary power and the structure of legal systems, accountability, and processes of approval. These formal institutional elements are explored for their impact on the constitutive and regulative norms as delineated in the previous section.

Private sector financing norms, for example, are influenced by the distribution of budgetary power to policymakers. In contexts where power over budgetary use is subject to cross-departmental review (e.g., Taiwan) or even legislative approval (e.g., Hong Kong), policymakers' norms dictate that financing private sector activity is not desirable. Because of the difficulty of obtaining approval for funding, policymakers in these formal institutional contexts possess regulative norms that lead them away from formulating policies that require significant funding. The opposite is true for states in which policymakers simply need to ask their direct manager for access to funding (e.g., Singapore) (Klingler-Vidra 2015).

To be sure, the process of policy approval and the distribution of budgetary power affect policymakers' regulative norms around financing private sector firms. For example, in Hong Kong's case, policymakers need to seek legislative approval in order to deploy funding. In the process of seeking legislative approval policymakers are exposed to public scrutiny. This exposure has a dampening effect on their norm regarding the desirability of formulating policies that require budget. The result is that finance-laden policies are not held as appropriate due to this formal institutional dialectic (the origins of this institutional design are briefly discussed in the Hong Kong chapter). In Singapore, on the other hand, those responsible for creating and implementing economic policies do not need sign-off from other entities to secure funding. Their ease of access to funding informs their logics of appropriateness such that they embrace direct financing. Thus, the greater ease of access to funding—due to formal institutions—engenders norms that hold finance-focused policies appropriate. Thus, access to budget informs policy-makers' preference for direct funding to private firms, indirect funding via tax credits, or policies that avoid budgetary requests all together.

Legal frameworks are examined for their impact on how Silicon Valley–inspired regulations are adapted. Legal systems affect which, and how, policy models can be implemented. Each state's existing legal treatment of investment vehicles affects the starting point for policymakers considering adopting foreign legal and regulatory structures. The issue of liability provides an instructive illustration. Some states do not, or did not, have legal structures that allow limited liability for investors. Legally speaking, policy models, such as the LP structure emanating from Silicon Valley, which limit liability, would be novel. In order to adopt a local version of the LP structure in which the investor is not wholly liable, there would need to be a change in the understanding of who—investor or manager—should incur financial responsibility of the business risk. Without such a change, policymakers would not find it appropriate to adopt an LP structure that limits the responsibility of investors.

Continuity and Change: The "Stickiness" of Norms

This book differentiates between policy change and normative change; not every episode of a policy change is the result of a normative change. This presumption is consistent with Ruggie's seminal findings on the role of "embedded liberalism" in economic policymaking in the postwar era: "much of the observed change has been at the level of instrument rather than norms" (1982, 412). In longitudinal accounts of policy, such as the investigation of VC policy diffusion over the course of fifty years as in this book, it would be unreasonable to infer that each and every specific policy-level change follows from an underlying normative change. Thurbon (2016, 3) similarly expects policy-level change over time in her analysis of the persistence of the developmental mindset in Korea.

Norms go further back into the conceptualization of self, and this conceptualization is less susceptible to change, whereas policy instruments are expected to change more regularly.

Normative "stickiness" is characteristic of patterns of continuity and change rather than frequent switches.[12] The problem of trying to simultaneously account for continuity and change is one that accompanies much comparative historical institutionalist scholarship (Mahoney and Thelen 2010; Goldstein and Keohane 1993; Thelen and Steinmo 1992). In varieties of capitalism research, for example, criticisms abound that the logic of historically derived institutional complementarities can explain the persistence of a given path but cannot account for change (Breznitz 2007, and others, make this critique). Constructivist and institutionalist scholars grapple with how to analytically account for, and empirically identify, normative change. Berger (1996) explores how incremental changes in collective identities can drive changes in state policy. In the same edited volume on culture and national security, Risse-Kappen (1996) reveals how concepts can be internalized as part of state identities, and Acharya (2009) uses the lens of "constitutive localization" to explain norm evolution over time.

For many institutionalist researchers, "critical junctures" or "exogenous shocks" are employed to overcome this conceptual impasse (Mahoney and Thelen 2010). Critical junctures are "moments in which uncertainty as to the future of an institutional arrangement allows for political agency and choice to play a decisive causal role" (Capoccia 2015). Critical junctures can take the form of crises, wars, or other fundamental disequilibria, and they account for short-term fluidity in what is otherwise stable periods of institutional—and in this case, normative—constellations. The shock can act as an "increase in the uncertainty" about the optimal policy that "makes policymakers' automatically more receptive to new information" (Meseguer 2009, 47). Crises, as a form of critical junctures, can "elicit new narratives, signal the obsolescence of the status quo" (Nelson and Katzenstein 2014, 362). According to Thurbon (2016, 9), South Korea's revival of financial activism was supported by increasing competitive pressures vis-à-vis China, which "led policymakers to question the desirability of freer financial markets." Critical junctures—whether they take the shape of an economic or security crisis, or a spike in competitive pressures—are not simply capable of triggering a policy shift. As these scholars argue in their various empirical applications, critical junctures drive openness to changes to the underlying normative framework.

Policy output, or performance, affects the persistence of the norms with which they are associated. Scharpf (1997) and Bernstein (2011) explain that there are both input and output determinants of legitimacy.[13] Extending their argument to norms, norms have input legitimacy because they fit within the broader context of what is socially appropriate and this affects output legitimacy, the performance of the policies associated with norms. When the policies perform well, the performance reinforces the normative environment from which they emanate. When they perform poorly, then actors can come to question the norms. The logics of appropriateness are critically examined, and there is an opportunity to formulate new norms.

Constitutive and regulative norms are susceptible to contestation as a result of policy output (e.g., poor policy experience) and shocks in the national political economy context (e.g., economic crises and spikes in national security concerns, among other critical junctures). Constitutive norms are most entrenched when related economic outcomes are strongest; the ends (e.g., the economic performance) justify the means (e.g., the optimal way to intervene). If strong state leadership vis-à-vis national champions helped to catapult the economy to the forefront of the global technology sector, for example, policymakers continue to hold tight to state-led norms. If, however, the state's support of national champions no longer seemed to propel competitiveness at the global frontier, or was failing to meet economic objectives, policymakers question their normative foundation. This leads to a crucial determinant of norm-guided learning: the strength of the economic performance associated with the normative context shapes the extent to which policymakers are open to normative updating.

This emphasis on local performance dovetails with similar assertions made by political economy scholars. Almond and Genco (1977, 492) note that "actors in politics have memories; they learn from experience." Steiner (1983, 378) explains that "adaptive" rationality involves actors learning "through their actions as they go along by observing their consequences, making inferences about them, and drawing implications for further action." Similarly, Hall (1993, 277) asserts that policy "responds less directly to social and economic conditions than it does to the consequences of past policy." Thurbon (2016, 8) also explains there is a performance contingency to norms; in her case study, "the negative economic and social impacts of Korea's "growth first" strategy began to fracture the developmental consensus." In effect, over time, policymakers' norms informing what is appropriate is eroded through the "bad consequences" of the policies that were employed in their name (applying the logic of normative interactions as discussed by Fearon and Wendt 2002, 62).

Specific to VC policymaking, critical junctures primarily manifest as economic crises, which force policymakers to reconsider what is the optimal form and extent of intervention in the economy. In the depth—or wake—of an economic crisis, a need to find a new way of organizing economic activity can emerge. Policymakers who had been fervent advocates of hands-off approaches become less certain that that is the way forward. Perhaps a laissez-faire tactic was appropriate in the past, but—they would reason—would it be enough going forward? In the face of this economic turbulence, policymakers open themselves to valuing approaches that they would have previously dismissed. Previously devout neoliberals could, for example, come to value the state's greater, more direct role of instigating activity. Their norms informing how, and to what extent, they should intervene are open to reinterpretation and updating.

Changes in formal institutions can drive normative change, and vice versa. The issue at hand is delineating which formal institutions are expected to inform a dynamic relationship with constitutive and regulative norms. Shifts in the distribution of budgetary power could drive normative change. For example, a change to the policymaking process whereby policymakers can no longer easily access funding may reshape the regulative norm that direct financing is appropriate. Regime type changes can act as critical junctures that drive normative change. Shifts from authoritarian to democratic functioning can accompany similar moments of reframing how the state should intervene. The book investigates whether, and how, increased scrutiny or regime type shifts affect policymakers' logic of appropriateness for VC market purposive action.

The East Asian Analytical Narratives

This section depicts the normative contexts that enable the investigations of contextual rationality in the East Asian case narratives. Identifying each state's normative context ex ante endows greater analytical power for investigating the role of policymakers' norms in VC policy diffusion to Hong Kong, Taiwan and Singapore. For this reason, I do not employ existing comparative capitalism typologies, whether they be specific or encompassing delineations of national institutional arrangements in East Asia.

Political economy, business systems, and innovation systems scholars have produced carefully delineated, and descriptive, East Asian types (Whitley 1992; 1999; 2007; Johnson 1982; Walter and Zhang 2012; Wong 2003; Witt and Redding 2013). Such accounts describe central aspects of individual states. Whitley (1992), for example, develops characteristics of the business systems in Japan, South Korea, Taiwan, and Hong Kong; Thurbon (2016) explores financial activism in South Korea, while Witt and Redding's (2013) edited volume goes even further by mapping thirteen different types of East Asian business systems. Now classic developmental state literature also tends to focus on individual countries, as Johnson (1982) did in his seminal study of the Japanese developmental state. Woo-Cumings (1999) and Amsden (1979; 2001) explore the different strategies and institutional settings in Korea and Taiwan. Evans (1995) and Kohli (2004) develop typologies and causal logic through their examinations of the cases of Korea, Brazil, India, and either Zaire or Nigeria, respectively. Other typologies articulate institutional subsets (business systems, financial architectures, and labor market regimes) for several East Asian settings (such as cogoverned, state-led, networked, and personalized) in a subset of empirical areas (Walter and Zhang 2012, 8–17). While this scholarship helps to inform the ex-ante normative context for this study, these types do not fully delineate the normative contexts that are central to this book's research.

Globally applied comparative capitalism coverage—notably the varieties of capitalism (VoC) approach—that attempts to bring East Asia into the fold does not offer germane normative depictions for these analytical narratives. In fact, in several cases this literature has depicted a singular type, based on analyses of Japan, Korea, or China (see Amable 2003; Aoki et al. 2007; Lechevalier 2011; Storz and Schafer 2011). Amable (2003) developed comparative capitalism's singular Asian model that effectively describes the Korean and Japanese models while Soskice offers a group-coordinated East Asian economies type (Crouch 2009, 85). These scholars assume that East Asian policymakers promote specific sectors and national champion firms (*keiretsu* or *chaebols*) (Pempel and Tsunekawa 2015). Most recently, Henry

Wai-chung Yeung (2016) offered a depiction of the contemporary developmental state and national champion firm relations in Korea, Taiwan, and Singapore, which he calls "strategic coupling" in light of the large firms disembedding from their home developmental states and embedding in global production networks. These approaches overcorrect for the accuracy of the country-specific studies underpinning the developmental state literature. However, they have overlooked how East Asian systems that long fostered start-ups rather than only state-owned enterprises, such as in Taiwan, and laissez-faire practitioners, especially Hong Kong. Storz et al. (2013) edited a special issue of *Socio-Economic Review,* in which they strived to remedy the incongruence with VoC's assumption of an Asian model with the empirical reality of diverse forms of institutional complementarities. While a broadly important contribution to the literature, their accounts focus on institutional complementarities rather than normative contexts, and are therefore not sufficient for this project.[14]

This book's analytical depictions draw most closely on the approach of economic sociologist Peter Evans (1995).[15] In Evans' *Embedded Autonomy,* he develops four ideal types of the ways in which the state is involved in market activities: custodian (focus on regulation), midwife (supporting new enterprises), husbandry (promoting domestic firms) and demiurge (state as producer). My analytical depictions are in many ways a more normative version of Evans's types, focusing on policymakers' identity and conceptions of appropriate policy action, rather than mapping out their strategies for intervening. His custodian is aligned with my "positive nonintervention" and "nightwatch-man state" depictions of Hong Kong; his midwifery, and this book's characterization of Taiwan as the private sector promoter refer to similar approaches to supporting entrepreneurs; and in some respects, my Singaporean financier and director type is akin to his husbandry.

My analytical narratives differ from Evans's types in two primary ways. First, my depictions focus on delineating the *normative settings* that shape policy learning and design in specific East Asian cases, whereas Evans developed typologies intended to offer hypotheses for a wide set of industrial strategies and relationships between state and society. For Evans, the custodian state refers to activities in which the state provides enabling or restrictive laws and rights while my night watchman policymakers are conceptualized for the norms that guide whether and how they finance domestic or international private firms. Evans's types can be simultaneously expressed by the same state because they ultimately refer to activities. My contextual rational conceptualizations inform analytical narratives, and thus depict norms exhibited by policymakers in a given context (at a particular time). A policymaker cannot, therefore, concurrently identify herself as a night watchman and a private sector promoter for venture capital, whereas in Evans's approach, a policymaker could pursue both midwifery and husbandry practices simultaneously.

Second, Evans's types are interested in state-society relations within the domestic arena whereas contextual rationality captures how policymakers' regulative norms inform their strategies aimed at international and domestic firms. Husbandry, for example, explores how the state promotes domestic firms competing in international (technology) markets. While this type allows for reverberations between domestic support and international competitiveness—particularly how international pressures may prompt further state support—it is focused on support of domestic entrepreneurs. My depictions are interested in whether policymakers' norms dictate whether they should support local or international firms as a means of advancing the domestic market. This is an important distinction given the increasingly international character of capital markets and entrepreneurship in the contemporary political economy since Evans's book was published.

This study conceptualizes the East Asian cases in an effort to strike a "Goldilocks balance" of getting parsimony and comprehensiveness "just right." To do this, it depicts a neoliberal to interventionist range of policymakers' constitutive and regulative norms in the less conceptually treaded parts of East Asia (meaning non-Japan, China, or Korea). The East Asian normative contexts conceptualized here include the night watchman state, the private sector promoter, and the financier and director, and they reflect key differences in constitutive and regulative norms, specifically policymakers' interventionist orientation, private sector financing norms, and local versus international company focus in the economic policy arena.

The purpose of these conceptualizations is to inform the analytical narratives that the study focuses on (in chapters 4 through 6). Table 2.2 summarizes the constitutive and regulative norms pertinent to entrepreneurship and innovation policy. This characterization of norms does not attempt to broadly depict all policymaking arenas for each state (e.g., they may not also be true for agricultural, health, or education policy areas). As Finnemore (1996, 327) explains, "Particular norms matter in particular issue-areas" rather than holding true across all issue areas even within a single country. They are, instead, presented as the normative baseline for innovation and entrepreneurial policymaking in each case. The name for each case encapsulates the identity by which the constitutive norms impute on the policymakers—for Hong Kong, an identity as a night watchman (and guardian of positive nonintervention); for Taiwan, they identify as promoters of

TABLE 2.2
East Asian analytical narrative conceptualizations

		Hong Kong	Taiwan	Singapore
Constitutive norm	**Interventionist orientation**	Night watchman	Private sector promoter	Financier and director
Regulative norms	**Private sector financing**	Indirect	Indirect; matching funds	Direct
	International versus local	International	Local	International

private sector activity; and for Singapore, policymakers identify as financiers and directors of market activity.

The first East Asian case depicted here—Hong Kong, the night watchman state—is the most laissez faire. Night watchman state policymakers' constitutive norms dictate that the state should allow the market to operate freely. Policymakers' adherence to "positive nonintervention" forms the basis for viewing their role in market operations. Policymakers' norms hold that their actions should focus on "protecting individual rights, persons and property, and enforcing voluntarily negotiated private contracts" (Buchanan et al. 1980, 9). They believe it appropriate to leave market operations to private sector actors, so regulative norms confer that indirect financing is best. As a vivid illustration of norms constraining behavior to a laissez-faire approach, the last governor of Hong Kong quipped, "The words 'industrial policy' make me curl up inside" (Patten 1998, 243). In line with its long, esteemed history as a trading hub, policymakers second regulative norm—whether it is appropriate to support international or domestic firms—emphasizes attracting international firms. As summarized in table 2.2, Hong Kong policymakers' norms assign value to policy models that invoke a hands-off approach, using indirect financing means to attract international firms.

In the private sector promoter, Taiwan, policymakers' constitutive norms hold that they should have a more active role in encouraging private firms. Their identity takes the shape of a needed promoter of market activity. Their norms are consistent with Karl Polanyi's *The Great Transformation* (2001) assessment that state encouragement of private activity is a prerequisite for markets to occur. These policymakers' norms presume governments must act to constitute markets. In this way, the private sector promoter is expected to value policies that position the state as a "midwife" to industry by offering overt support and direction in addition to a broadly enabling regulatory arena (Evans 1995, 80–81). Then, their regulative norms collectively hold that it is appropriate to organize and support, but not finance, local firms. They assign value to policy instruments that indirectly finance local firms by conceding revenue, such as tax credits, as a means of encouraging a certain activity. Taiwanese policymakers' norms that found it appropriate for the state to develop domestic skills and opportunities by advancing the competitiveness of local firms. One way this norm has been historically expressed is through the central bank's focus on "recycling foreign reserves to local firms wishing to internationalize but agreeing to 'keep their roots' " (Thurbon 2016, 14), rather than in attracting international firms to the island. Altogether, Taiwanese policymakers' norms dictate that they play a critical role in the market and that the appropriate ways of intervening are through indirect finance for local firms.

Singaporean policymakers, conceptualized as the financier and director, hold a different view of the state's role in the market. For these policymakers, their constitutive norms inform their identity as financiers and directors of market activity. They provide capital directly to, and organize the activities of, private firms. Their normative orientation is akin to Gerschenkron's vision of the state's role as one of investing in private activity and in organizing financial markets (Forsyth and Verdier 2003). Gerschenkron (1962) contended that the embedded state had to go beyond constructing an enabling environment. Their regulative norms then hold that it is appropriate for the state to "serve as investment banker, bringing together the necessary funds and encouraging their application in transformative activities" (Evans 1995, 31). This direct financing was deemed an appropriate means of attracting international firms. Singapore is cited as the "foremost example" of the late developmental model in which states "lured multi-national corporations with incentives and then encouraged them to progressively build up local competencies" (Fuller 2016, 4). Financier and director policymakers' regulative norms value funding-centric approaches more than the Taiwanese private sector promoter, and certainly more so than laissez-faire Hong Kong. For Singaporean policymakers, it is appropriate to direct funding to foreign, rather than domestic, firms as a means of intervening. In sum, Singaporean policymakers' norms inform their identity as necessary providers of direct funding efforts aimed at attracting international firms.

The conceptualization of the states' normative contexts highlights how they differ from one another. Moreover, the focus on norms moves the examination away from tracking specific policies, and toward a greater understanding of the approach of the state, similar to Thurbon's (2016) emphasis on developmental mindset, rather than precise policy prescriptions as the measure of a developmental state. Importantly, none of the three cases under investigation here—Hong Kong, Taiwan, and Singapore—are consistent with the national champion approach to development. In these three cases, policymakers' norms do not hold it appropriate to build state-owned enterprises, or aid national champions such as the Korean *chaebols* or Japanese *keiretsu*, as their competitive strategy. They prefer small, local firms in the case of Taiwan, or attracting multinational firms to set up locally in order to build domestic capacity across firms as in Hong Kong and Singapore. The different normative frames of policymakers across these states are evidence of the variety of domestic institutional contexts in East Asia. Distinctive normative contexts are, therefore, essential to explaining the variety of Silicon Valley VC policy adaptations.

Expectations Based on State-of-the-Art Diffusion Scholarship

Diffusion Mechanisms

The contextual rationality framework places the role of policymakers' norms at the center of the East Asian analytical narratives. This pride-of-place positioning of norms is taken in order to explain policy diffusion as propelled by the learning mechanism. Learning occurs when policymakers study a set of policies that have been successfully implemented in their locale or elsewhere (Gilardi 2010; Berry and Baybeck 2005; Rose 1991). The contention is that learning processes drives convergence, due to the updating of Bayesian beliefs or adherence to the cognitive heuristic of the "anchor" (Weyland 2006; Simmons et al. 2008, Meseguer 2009). As previously developed, this book's point of departure from existing scholarship on diffusion and learning is the presumption that the learning process is one in which rationality is understood as contextually based; meaning that policymakers' cost-benefit evaluations and decisions are shaped by their norms rather than the product of Bayesian updating of beliefs (conventional conception of rationality) or reliant on cognitive short-cuts (as bounded rationality contends). This difference drives the expectation that diffusion leads to diversity amidst convergence, rather than broad patterns of convergence.

The other three diffusion mechanisms—competition, coercion, and emulation—are the alternative paths by which policies and organizational structures diffuse across states and transnational organizations (Shipan and Volden 2008). Some policy diffusion research clearly pits policy diffusion mechanisms against each other, such as Meseguer's (2006) analysis of the spread of neoliberal policies, which tested for evidence of learning, imitation, and coercion. Research projects that delineate and test the role of multiple diffusion mechanisms can bear greater analytical weight than studies that simply show that policies diffuse across borders. While it is valuable that diffusion studies are able to specify the mechanism responsible for diffusion, the mechanisms are not so distinct from each other in practice (Kogut and Macpherson 2008). Instead, the diffusion mechanisms may drive one another or occur simultaneously (Meseguer 2009).

When policymakers design policies for new issue areas, with which they are not yet familiar, emulation can occur. The successful deployment of a policy in one locality may create an "information externality" (Swank 2008, 77) or "public good" (Kogut and Macpherson 2008, 110) for other policymakers. This essentially means that by virtue of a policy's employment in one locality, other policymakers may attempt to replicate the policy model. Whereas learning involves researching the merits of other policies, emulation occurs when policymakers imitate other policies merely in an effort to appear similar (Shipan and Volden 2008). Emulation constitutes policymakers "mindlessly" duplicating policies from other states without researching the precise attributes and choices (Meseguer 2009, 4).

The emulation mechanism is highly conductive to convergence. Policymakers simply copy the proven policy models. Imitation is more likely to occur in contexts where actors hope to gain legitimacy and, ultimately, enhance their survival prospects in uncertain environments. For example, Sylvia Maxfield (1998) found that developing country politicians push for central bank independence in an effort to imitate policies in industrialized countries. By appearing similar to key industrialized states, the developing country policymakers strived to signal credibility to international investors. In emulation, adaptation is absent as policymakers aim to reproduce what has been successful or what will help them to signal credibility. Though emulation can occur, my contention is that policymakers are likely to undergo a learning process rather than adopting an external model "as is." As such, this book conceptualizes policymakers' learning as the primary diffusion mechanism in which policymakers "pull in" policy information.

The remaining two diffusion mechanisms—competition and coercion—describe external forces that place policy information on the agenda. Depending on their strength, these pressures lead to the deployment of similar policies across adopters. In the case of competition, the globalization thesis posits that states converge on the model that appears to enjoy the competitive advantage (Simmons et al. 2008). In the East Asian environment, in particular, the competitive pressures experienced in the wake of the East Asian financial crisis led to expectations that the "homogenizing pressures of globalization" would reduce the capacity of the developmental state to a regulatory role (Thurbon 2016, 11). These expectations are underlined by the presumption that states—due to their need to attract capital—will converge on policies that successfully attract capital holders. As an example of how the competition mechanism works, Simmons and Elkins (2004) found that the adoption of capital account liberalization policies in one state changes the competitive landscape for its peer states and that this, in turn, constrains policymakers' policy choice sets (this pressure intensifies as more peers liberalize their capital accounts). The strength of economic competition is investigated by measuring policymakers' concerns that capital would be redirected elsewhere (Berry and Baybeck 2005). When faced with increasing competitive pressures, policymakers are pressured to adopt internationally orthodox, market-friendly policies. As a consequence, policymakers dealing with heightened competitive pressures are expected to converge on the most successful policy form.

Coercion occurs when power asymmetries create conditions in which policy actions are forced by external actors. Empirical investigations of coercion strive to demonstrate the impact of formal conditionality or "persuasive opportunities" on policy choices (Simmons et al. 2008, 13; Kogut and Macpherson 2008). Diffusion via coercion takes place when an international organization, such as the International Monetary Fund, requires economic reforms as a condition for funding. Such requirements are construed as "hard coercion," whereas other less direct (but no less powerful) modes of "soft coercion" are less explicit in stating their power. Klingler-Vidra and Wade (forthcoming) reveal how the money the World Bank lends to aid recipient countries, such as Vietnam, helps shape the range of acceptable policies. The strength of coercive forces is often determined by the financial need of the less powerful state, as well as the capabilities of its policymakers. In this way, policymakers most in need of external financing and least capable of formulating policies are most susceptible to an external actor coercing the use of a policy.

Pulling this discussion of the diffusion mechanism expectations together, state-of-the-art diffusion literature expects a high degree of convergence on proven policy models. None of the diffusion mechanisms are expected to produce radical and pervasive adaptation. The contextual rationality expectation, however, expects substantial and widespread adaptations as policymakers necessarily come to different conclusions about the value of a particular version of a model through their learning processes.

Diffusion Models

This study also tests state-of-the-art diffusion literature's ability to account for how attributes of diffusion models impact outcomes. The level of specificity of policy models fosters different degrees of convergence. Essentially, less convergence is expected to occur when vague principles are diffused and more convergence is expected when specific models diffuse (Klingler-Vidra and Schleifer 2014). When vague policy models are diffused, they leave greater room for interpretation (Weyland 2006). With interpretation comes different conclusions about what the model actually is, and so greater variety in the forms of local policies implemented in an effort to reproduce the model. The existence of multiple models also undermines convergence as adopters either focus on reproducing models akin to different nodes (Drezner 2005), or choose to construct hybrid combinations of the models (Falkner and Gupta 2009).

Applying these diffusion model expectations to the Silicon Valley VC policy diffusion context leads us to expect certain degrees of convergence. For example, if the highly specific Israeli or Taiwanese policy models are diffused, the expectation is for more convergence across the cases. However, when the less specific Silicon Valley policy environment is diffused, states are expected to adapt the model to fit their norms, resulting in low degrees of convergence across adopters. By testing diffusion scholarship's state-of-the-art expectations alongside those of contextual rationality, this study advances political economy scholarship's ability to explain why diffusion does not often result in convergence. Moreover, it provides insights into *how* context shapes the diffusion process.

Venture Capital and VC Policy

Silicon Valley, Singapore, Tel Aviv—the global hubs of entrepreneurial activity—all bear the marks of government investment.
—Josh Lerner, *Boulevard of Broken Dreams*

In contrast to the extensive coverage of venture capital in the popular
press and policy circles, there has been limited conceptualization or empirical
investigation to date of this phenomenon in political economy scholarship.[1]
Even in research that explores the nature of SME financing, venture capital
is dismissed because of its small size in relation to other financial services sectors (Deeg 2009).[2] When it is addressed in comparative capitalism research,
venture capital receives superficial analytical engagement. In the foundational
varieties of capitalism text, Hall and Soskice (2001, 29) note venture capital as
a "qualification" to liberal market economies financiers' short-termism and reliance on public information: "New firms in high-technology fields can often
secure funds from venture-capital companies that *develop the resources* and *technical expertise to monitor their performance directly* and trade ownership stakes in
these firms for the high risks they take" (italics added). As a means of remedy-
ing this lacuna in the literature, and at the same time providing better context
for this book's investigation of the venture capital state, this chapter conceptualizes the venture capital industry and VC policy in political economy terms.

Venture Capital

Venture capital is a form of private equity that provides early-stage, non-
publicly traded companies with financial capital in exchange for equity or

equity-related stakes (Mathonet and Meyer 2007). The money that venture capitalists invest has, except for corporate venture capital funds who manage company money, been entrusted to them by institutional investors, such as pension funds, endowments, insurance companies, and sovereign wealth funds. In line with their investment mandate agreed with these investors (e.g., "limited partners" in the fund), venture capitalists allocate the fund's money into start-ups that often have small revenues and negative profitability (Casper et al. 2009, 200–8; Kortum and Lerner 2000). To invest at these early stages, rather than rely on public data, venture capitalists obtain information through their "dense networks" in order to get comfortable with the risk (Hall and Soskice 2001, 23). They follow an investment process that includes the following stages: deal sourcing, due diligence, and deal management through to divestment (which is referred to as "exit" in venture capital vernacular) (Lerner et al. 2014, 4–5).

To source potential start-ups for investment, venture capitalists rely on desktop and personal network-focused methods. Desktop methods include having associates comb publicly available sources (such as TechCrunch's "CrunchBase") or paid information services (e.g., Dun and Bradstreet). The more common sources of venture capitalists' potential deals, however, are active professional networks in the sectors in which they invest (e.g., entrepreneurs in the video gaming space) and with fellow investors (e.g., other VC managers and angel investors). These networks help them to hear about new start-ups, or to identify when a start-up is planning to fundraise. Venture capitalists attend industry events and conferences that continually develop and reinforce their networks. The reputations of venture capitalists in these networks is a key factor in accessing deals, consistent with how nonfinancial companies' reputation helps them access patient capital (see Hirschman 1970 and Deeg et al. 2016 for a conceptualization of patient capital and Hall and Soskice 2001, 23, for a discussion of purported national differences in the availability of patient capital).

As a start-up is identified as a potential investment, venture capitalists include the start-up in their veritable pipeline of companies that undergo due diligence. The due diligence process, which begins when the idea of investing is initially broached and continues until well after the term sheet has been drafted, is extensive (Kortum and Lerner 2000). Venture capital investment teams initiate the due diligence process by requesting and reviewing numerous documents from the start-up, including financial statements, business plans, and intellectual property offerings.[3] They rely on their dense networks to triangulate the information provided by the start-up. For example, venture capitalists speak with a number of individuals to check that the start-up's growth assumptions are valid. A venture capitalist commented that a start-up had made it "far in the process" but a conversation with a potential customer revealed that their sales projects were "completely unrealistic as this supposed anchor customer said they would never give them so much business" (author interview, London, 6 February 2015). As a result of this

TABLE 3.1
Venture capital in the start-up funding life cycle

Financing stage	Period (years)	Risk level	Activity to be financed	Typical investor
Initial financing	7–10	Extreme	Supporting an idea or R&D for product development	Friends, family, government grants
Seed round	5–9	Very high	Initializing operations or developing prototypes	Angel, government grants, VC seed funds
A round	3–7	High	Starting commercial production and marketing	VC funds
B round	3–5	Medium to high	Expanding market and growing working capital need	VC funds
Later stage (growth capital)	1–3	Medium	Marketing expansion, acquisition, and product development	Private equity and follow-on rounds from VC Managers
Buy out-in/ mezzanine/ IPO	1–3	Low to medium	Acquisition financing	Multinational companies, private equity, and IPOs

Source: Adapted from Klingler-Vidra 2016.

feedback, the venture capitalist decided to halt the due diligence process and, more broadly, the prospect of investing.

Venture capitalists invest in companies across a range of maturity, from the seed stage (supporting a team with just an idea or prototype) to later stages of growth capital (which constitutes more mature companies seeking funding to expand their product line, geographic reach, etc.) (Klingler-Vidra 2016). Table 3.1 specifies how venture capital investments fit into start-up funding in terms of the length of investment tenure, risk level, the activities that are financed, and the types of investors who typically participate at each stage.

Once they invest, venture capitalists are believed to provide "smart money." This positive connotation comes from the fact that, in addition to money, they bring technology savvy, product development expertise, and a Rolodex of potential customers and acquirers.[4] By taking board seats in the start-ups they invest in, venture capitalists have "oversight privileges, which range from the approval of budgets and advice on product development to the right to replace the management team" (Lerner et al. 2014, 2). Venture capitalists provide value on management boards because of their experience in guiding other start-ups, but also because the backgrounds of venture capitalists tend to be that of technically trained, experienced entrepreneurs themselves. This close operational relationship stands in contrast to the oversight of a loan: "Unlike bank loans, where the entrepreneur receives money and is left alone as long as the payments arrive on the pre-arranged schedule, venture capital investments add the quality of active investing to the cash infusion" (Lerner et al. 2014, 2).

Venture capitalists are incentivized to play such an active role through the significant equity stakes they take in the start-ups in which they invest. Equity stakes of up to 30 percent motivate them to provide these nonfinancial resources that other types of investors, particularly banks, are not able or willing to offer (Gompers and Lerner 1999). They are motivated for the start-up to succeed as a business (and the bigger the better!) rather than simply hoping to earn a few percentage points' return on their distribution of capital.

In 2014, the distribution of venture capital globally across these stages was as follows: 22 percent went to seed stage, 32 percent to A and B rounds, and only 7 percent to growth capital (Preqin 2015b, 11). Between the run-up to the global financial crisis and 2014, seed stage deal numbers surged—in absolute and relative terms—across markets (see Klingler-Vidra 2016 for analysis of the rise of seed).[5] VC investments, especially those made at the early stages, have the potential for producing outstanding returns. However, VC is a risk-laden asset class given the lack of collateral, the illiquid nature, and the high failure rates endemic to start-up investing (Mathonet and Meyer 2007).

Their revenue comes from selling their equity stakes through one of the four exit routes (Espenlaub et al. 2011; Cumming 2010; Mathonet and Meyer 2007; Kortum and Lerner 2000):

1. Initial public offering (IPO): sale of ownership through the listing of ownership shares on a public equity market (e.g., stock exchange such as NASDAQ),
2. Trade sale (also referred to as merger and acquisition, M&A): sale of ownership to another company (e.g., Facebook's acquisition of WhatsApp for $19 billion),
3. Sale to financial institution: sale of ownership to a financial institution via a leveraged buy-out or other transaction, and,
4. Stock buy-backs: the management team buys back the equity held by venture capitalists and other investors.

The first two exit paths—IPO and trade sale—entail the management team and investors selling their shares for (an optimal) profit. The second pair of exit paths—sale to financial institution and stock buy-backs—gives venture capitalists liquidity, but they are not the preferred exit routes for investors trying to maximize their return on investment. The value of a company at any one of these exit paths, relative to the value at the time of investment, determines venture capitalists' profits on their investment. As an example, a venture capital firm that owns a 20 percent stake in a company that completes an IPO for $1 billion earns $200 million for their share in the company. Their profit comes from the difference between the size of their initial investment and this $200 million. If they invested $10 million for a 20 percent share in the business four years before, they turned $10 million into $200 million—twenty times their return on investment (assuming no dilution occurred).

The investors in venture capital—the "limited partners"—include pension funds, endowments and foundations, banks, corporations, and government (Gompers and Lerner 1999). Venture capital offers these limited partners a return that is not highly correlated to other asset classes, such as bonds and public equity markets, contributing to portfolio diversification. They invest in VC funds for portfolio diversification purposes as well as the large returns that top tier VC funds have reaped (Mulcahy et al. 2012). To produce outstanding returns, VC funds seek to invest in companies that can disrupt industries and change the way businesses or consumers behave. Such disruption often occurs through technological developments that bring buyers and sellers together in new ways (think Uber) and solve complex problems (health issues). Because of technology-focused businesses' ability to produce disruptive businesses, the technology sector is the largest recipient of venture capital, with healthcare and life sciences next in line (Klingler-Vidra et al. 2016). In 2014, for example, more than 65 percent of VC deals were in technology sector firms, across the Internet, software and related firms, telecoms, other IT, clean technology, and semiconductors and electronics categories (Preqin 2015a, 110).

Facebook provides an illustrative example of both the high risks that VC managers take when investing in high-technology start-ups and the huge returns they can earn when their investments are successful. Shortly after Mark Zuckerberg formed Facebook, he needed capital to hire staff, buy servers, and further develop the technology. After raising money from angel investors in 2004, Zuckerberg secured a US$12.7 million VC round led by Accel Partners (a Silicon Valley-based VC manager) based on a US$100 million valuation. Their investment paid off: within five years, Accel sold an estimated one-fifth of its Facebook equity at a US$35 billion valuation—earning them a 350 times return on their investment (Arrington 2010). Of course, not all the start-ups that venture capitalists invest in achieve such outstanding returns. Instead, VC managers diversify their portfolios of companies, expecting approximately 10 percent of the start-ups they invest in to outperform (Zider 1998). This low success rate persists even though venture capitalists on average invest in only 1 percent of all the start-ups they have received business plans from (Fenn et al. 1995).

Spectacular returns earned in cases such as Accel's investment in Facebook, Kleiner Perkins Caufield & Byers's investment in Google, and one of American Research and Development (ARD)'s investments that turned US$50,000 into US$350 million, brought significant attention to the VC asset class. In addition, some of today's most ubiquitous global companies, including Facebook, Google, and Genentech, were aided by VC financing, network introductions, and operational expertise in their ascent (Lerner 2009, 28). In the contemporary era, the motivation to invest in the next "unicorn"—a privately held start-up that achieves a valuation in excess of US$1 billion—draws institutional capital into the asset class. As more and more VC-backed start-ups have achieved unprecedented valuations and highly successful exits via IPOs or acquisitions, the VC market's public profile and allure has grown.

Origins of the VC Industry

The formation of the first professional VC management firms first took place in the United States and the United Kingdom around the time of World War II. The two entities most often cited as the first VC managers were in the United States: ARD and J. H. Whitney and Company (Lerner 2009, 9–12). On the other side of the Atlantic Ocean, in 1945, a VC investment firm called 3i was formed by the British government with GBP15 million in capital in response to the MacMillan Committee Report in 1931, which identified the "MacMillan Gap"—a "chronic shortage of long-term investment capital for small and medium-sized businesses" (3i 2017). It is critical to note that the first American VC funds were not government-funded, as was the case with Britain's 3i.[6] The early successes of the private VC firms in the United States contribute to the perception that the American VC industry is a product of private market forces. As Weiss (2014, 54–55) explains, the U.S. government's investments in high-tech military security projects had a "formative" rather than "direct role" in the early days of VC; for example, the leadership of ARD were former military generals who strived, through ARD, to finance "unexploited military innovations" emerging from World War II.

These pioneering American and British VC entities represent the first time that the financial support of start-ups shifted out of the hands of high-net worth individuals (what we would today call "business angels") and into organized investment management businesses.[7] Following in the footsteps of those early VC management firms, in 1958, Draper, Gaither, and Anderson launched the first fund with a LP structure (Gompers and Lerner 1999, 7). Though VC investment activity started to take place on both sides of the Atlantic around the time of World War II, it was the VC market centered in the U.S. Silicon Valley that achieved world-renown "exceedingly attractive" returns by the 1970s (Lerner 2009, 29). The success achieved by VC managers in the United States came in tandem with the global high-technology industry's growth and high-technology companies' unprecedented IPO valuations.

Although it is conceptualized as an American institution, the venture capital industry is increasingly international. By the late 1990s, there were "more than 250 venture capital funds operating in Eastern Europe and Asia and as many as 400 operating in developing countries worldwide" (Aylward 1998, 5). More recently, the rate of international growth has increased (Ha 2009). Through 2008, 70 percent of the venture capital industry's funding activity took place in North America, but by Q1 2015 the value of deals in North America accounted for only 60 percent of the global total (Preqin 2015b, 11). While Silicon Valley still constitutes the most significant concentration of VC funding in the world, Israel is the largest VC market on a per capita basis, and key venture capital hubs now include China and India. Speaking to the scale of these international venture capital clusters, in 2015 U.S. VC managers invested US\$72.3 billion, China-based VC managers invested US\$49.2 billion, and European VC managers US\$14.4 billion (Ernst & Young 2016, 3). The growth of venture capital markets around the globe has been the result of a rise in cross-border investments as Western investors seek investment opportunities in high-growth markets (OECD 2014). International VC investment activity is also the product of the effective VC policies across a number of states (Lerner et al. 2014).

VC Policies

VC policies are motivated by policymakers' perception that the industry has a strong, positive macroeconomic contribution.[8] The venture capital industry is purported to drive innovation, employment, and economic growth through the financing, networks, and operational expertise that VC managers bring to the start-ups in which they invest (National Venture Capital Association 2011; Lerner 2009; OECD 1996). Given its investment in technology-centric start-ups, venture capital is linked with innovation and economic growth (Kortum and Lerner 2000; European Commission 1995). The logic flows as follows: start-ups are thought to be more innovative than large (traditional) firms, so in supporting (technology-focused) start-ups, venture capitalists are investing in innovation-generating technology companies that will aid greater productivity. Further productivity enhances economic growth as more output comes from the same amount of inputs (e.g., the same amount of land, labor, and capital). Venture capital facilitates the potential of these innovative start-ups by filling the "equity gap" that early-stage start-ups face (Lerner et al. 2014). The term *equity gap* refers to the (perceived) inability of early-stage start-ups to find funding, particularly from banks (OECD 1997; UNCTAD 1997).[9] The equity gap can be detrimental to start-up's ability to develop its product, hire staff, or expand geographically. In short, venture capital policy is pursued due to venture capitalists' purported ability to drive innovation and the growth of high-technology firms, which can support economic growth.

Often, the American VC market is touted as a triumph of neoliberal market forces. However, researchers have convincingly argued that Department of Defense contracts and the launch of the Small Business Investment Company program were major drivers behind the creation of Silicon Valley VC from the 1950s, and then its exponential growth (in funds under management and profitability) from the 1970s (see Weiss 2014; Mazzucato 2013;

Lazonick 2009). In this way, Lerner (2009, 41) contends that the "Silicon Valley was far from a creation of unfettered capitalism." The interventions that Lerner, Lazonick (2009), and other scholars point to within the Silicon Valley model are the favourable tax treatment and regulatory changes, as well as funding, which supported technology entrepreneurship across the United States, not Silicon Valley specifically. The remainder of this section details the three elements of VC policies, beginning with those deployed in the United States and including the variations on each aspect as the policy model has diffused: regulation, taxation, and funding.

The American regulatory environment enabled the growth of the Silicon Valley VC cluster. National regulatory contexts and improvements, such as the LP structure, the 1979 relaxing of the national Employment Retirement Income Security Act (ERISA) Prudent Man Rule, and the 1980 Small Business Investment Incentive Act, fueled the exponential growth of private capital into Silicon Valley's VC market (Kenney 2011; Lazonick 2009; Avnimelech and Teubal 2004).[10]

The limited partnership (LP) is the legal structure overwhelmingly employed by Silicon Valley venture capitalists. The LP structure is attractive for several reasons. First, it ensures that the maximum that VC investors can lose is the money they invest in the venture capital fund. The LP structure ensures that personal assets are not legally considered collateral should the fund management company and its portfolio companies encounter financial difficulty. Another benefit of the American LP structure is its tax treatment. The carried interest (carry) of the VC fund is transparent, or passed through to its investors, instead of being "double taxed" on the management company level. As a result, returns on a LP fund are taxed as capital gains, instead of higher income tax rates, for the investors (e.g., not at the company level and then again by the investors). Finally, LP structures make venture capital a potentially lucrative career as it allows for the distribution of equity in underlying investments across the venture capital management team. It is not only the limited partners, or the managing partners, who profit from large exits—so can associates and other more junior team members.

While the LP structure is widely employed in Silicon Valley and numerous international jurisdictions, other legal forms, such as company structures, have been used in states such as Japan and Taiwan. Company structures, in contrast to the LP structure, do not shield the personal assets of investors or managers and do not correspond to a capital gains tax rate (Liang and Wang 2010). This study differentiates between these two different types of structures—the LP and the corporate structure. It also distinguishes variations of these structures. For example, in 2002 Australia launched an adaptation of the LP structure. In an effort to limit the potential for foreign firms to exploit the LP structure's favorable tax treatment, Australian policymakers adjusted the LP structure to require that "each company backed by a venture partnership have at least half its assets in Australia" (Lerner 2009, 158).

Regulatory changes in the United States in 1979–80 enhanced the fund-raising and operational environments for Silicon Valley venture capitalists. In 1979, the U.S. Department of Labor's reinterpretation of the ERISA "Prudent Man" rule allowed American pension funds, university endowments, and foundations to invest in more speculative asset classes, including VC (Lerner 2009, 39; Gompers and Lerner 1999). The ERISA reinterpretation had an extremely positive impact on the funds available for Silicon Valley venture capitalists. Pension funds became a major funding source for American VC funds (Lazonick 2009). Also in 1979, two bills were introduced in Congress—the Venture Capital Company Act and the Venture Capital Investment Act—which aimed to improve SMEs' fundraising abilities by "promoting uniformity in securities regulation and reducing paperwork" for investors (Public Law 96–477 1980). The bills proposed to exempt venture capital managers from the reporting requirements of the 1940 Investment Advisers Act (e.g., having to register and be regulated), as long as the venture capital funds did not raise funds from more than fourteen investors. They also strived to facilitate venture capitalists' earning of performance fees of no more than 20 percent of realized gains, which was a departure from previous interpretations of the 1940 Advisers Act. These bills were formalized into law via the Small Business Investment Incentive Act of 1980, which collectively ensured that venture capital firms did not have to register and could earn performance fees (Talmor 2015).

The American policy environment includes a generally attractive tax rate for venture capital profits: VC fund profits ("carried interest") are taxed at the capital gains tax rate. In the same era that regulatory changes were implemented with the objective of supporting venture capital, the U.S. capital gains tax rate to which venture capital profits are subject was lowered; in 1979 the rate was reduced from 35 percent to 28 percent for assets held more than one year (Adam Smith Institute, 2009).[11] Moreover, in an attempt to encourage investments in small businesses, U.S. tax code 1202, in Title 26, the "Qualified Small Business Stock," reduced the amount of capital gains tax liability for investors (e.g., venture capitalists) when exiting from their positions (e.g., only on 50, or 50 percent of a US$10 million position) in qualifying companies (Wallen 2017).[12] Profits are not necessarily taxed at the capital gains tax rate outside of the United States. There is a variety of ways in which venture capital profits are categorized for tax purposes across national jurisdictions—either as capital gains, income, corporate, or tax exempt. The rates associated with these tax categories range from zero (tax exempt), to capital gains (typically from 15 to 20 percent), to corporate or income tax rates in excess of 40 percent.

Tax policies also take the form of tax credits. Governments incentivize investment by offering credits commensurate with the amount of capital invested. The UK's Venture Capital Trust Scheme relieves income tax and capital gains tax liabilities for individuals investing up to GBP200,000 in an approved Venture Capital Trust (HMRC 2015). This means that investors in approved trusts benefit from a reduced income tax liability when they make their investment, and they also stand to benefit from exemption from capital gains tax if their investment proves profitable. Another illustrative example is the Taiwanese VC tax policy, where 20 percent of the amount invested in Taiwanese start-ups was given as a tax rebate for individuals (from 1982) and corporations (from 1991). This credit ensured that investors could only lose up to eighty cents on the dollar they invested (Kenney et al. 2002). Foreign investors in VC funds are, in many countries, exempt from paying local capital gains taxes (they are only liable for capital gains tax liabilities in their home jurisdiction). Switzerland has a distinctively local spin: Swiss residents that invest in VC funds with at least 50 percent of the fund's capital in Swiss start-ups are eligible for tax benefits.

Public money is directed to specific venture capitalists. Even in the United States, significant funding flowed (in the form of loans) to VC firms via the Small Business Investment Corporation (SBIC) scheme beginning in 1958 (Weiss 2014), and many American city and state governments run their own venture capital funds of VC funds (see Lerner 2009, 138–142 for examples).[13] Funds of VC funds allocate investment capital to VC managers when private investors (e.g., pension funds, insurance companies, and high net worth individuals) are not allocating sufficient amounts to venture capital funds. They often strive to correct a market failure: inadequate volume or quality of venture capital activity. Funds of VC funds can address these issues by investing in venture capital funds alone or alongside private investors. In the case when funds of VC funds invest alongside private investors, policymakers require that a certain amount of funding comes from private investors before the government money is available to the venture capital manager. By requiring private sector participation, the funds of VC funds incentivize venture capitalists to raise capital from private investors. This design aims to decrease future dependence on state funding by pushing the venture capitalists to be competitive enough to raise funding from private investors (Lerner 2009). Ultimately, this is meant to ameliorate the risk of the state crowding out private investors.

Public funds of VC funds vary in five primary ways. They differ according to their (1) structure, (2) repayment terms, (3) duration, (4) coinvestment involvement, and (5) sizes. First, fund of funds provide capital to VC funds in different ways. They can be structured as investments in VC funds, providing capital as an LP (e.g., investor) in the fund, or they can offer leverage to VC funds. A fund of funds can be launched as a fund that invests in VC funds (mimicking the LP-GP structure), or they can offer loans that are viewed as a portfolio, rather than structured as a fund of funds (e.g., the U.S. SBIC). Second, repayment terms (on equity investment) differ as they either give venture capitalists the option to buy out their investment at a nominal interest rate (e.g., 5 percent) or as a share of the investment return (e.g., equal to its equity stake). Third, funds vary in their duration as some are deployed with set end dates (such as the five years given to Israel's Yozma Fund), while others are structured as "evergreen funds" that do not close (such as Finland's FoF Growth structure that reinvests exit proceeds for future investments). Depending on their duration, they act as a one-time jumpstart or ongoing aid to local VC industries. Fourth, funds of VC funds vary in terms of their involvement of coinvestors. They may require matching funding from international investors or coinvest alongside local investors, while others may act as the lone investors in the VC funds. The Finnish FoF Growth funds, for example, address the issue of VC investments being individually too small and work-intensive to warrant dedication of money and due diligence resources by local pension funds. They do this by having the pension funds invest in the FoF Growth's fund of VC funds; the FoF Growth team is responsible for due diligence as well as relationship management with the VC managers (author interview, Helsinki, 22 June 2011). Last but not least, funds of VC funds differ in size. Fund sizes range from as little as US$6 million in some American states up to the Singaporean and Russian US$1 billion funds of VC funds (Lerner 2009; NRF 2014).

In sum, the U.S. VC model includes the direct distribution of capital, through the SBIC loans from the late 1950s, to the encouragement of private funding for the asset class through the ERISA reinterpretation, lowering of the capital gains tax rate, and the advantages of the LP structure. While the U.S. government directly supported VC in myriad ways, the framing of the American VC model is often one of market forces triumphing. In addition to domestic VC activities, the venture capital construct has been propagated internationally through USAID and its activities in promoting VC investments as part of aid packages (see Fox 1996 for early evaluation of USAID's experience with venture capital in developing countries).

This presents the paradox. Neoliberal norms are regularly touted by American policymakers, yet they have pursued interventionist means to create and enhance innovative capacity, including the venture capital market centered on the Silicon Valley. Fred Block (2008) coined this the "hidden developmental state." Robert Wade (2016) took the incongruence a step further, by arguing that American policymakers willfully exhibit a "do what we say, not what we do" approach; the U.S. government intervenes in innovation capacity, but projects a neoliberal approach and promotes neoliberal strategies in its interactions with other countries and through its role in international organizations. As Gestalt psychologists revealed in their work on illusions; even when someone knows "the trick," they are still tricked into seeing the illusion.[14] The supposedly neoliberal U.S. model could operate according to a similar logic: American policymakers, and those viewing U.S. policy from the outside, know of the various interventions that are made, but still broadly believe the projection that the approach is, instead, neoliberal.

Second, the prominence of external security concerns can explain the pursuit of interventionist approaches to promote innovation (as explained by Weiss 2014 and argued by Taylor 2016). Both Weiss and Taylor argue that external security imperatives motivate governments to promote mission-specific innovation. Applying the "national security state" and "creative insecurity" argumentation to this book's normative approach, we can say that American policymakers see themselves, above all else, as supporters of national security, even if they also identify themselves as laissez-faire policymakers. In this normative mode, they intervene to support innovation and technology to ensure the security of their liberal democracy. The primacy of the national security identity in the 1950s, in this logic, would explain the generous SBIC funding ($4 of government money for every $1 of private money invested by the VC). Then, over time, the neoliberal identity would reassert itself as primary, along with the uptake of private investment in VC funding and the performance of American high-technology sector. The security concerns in the 1950s constituted a critical juncture, enabling fluidity in constitutive and regulative norms in the short run. By the 1970s, the neoliberal identity was again at the fore, and accordingly, the state reduced the scale of government funding (down to 1:1) and focused on regulatory and tax levers to encourage private activity (e.g., ERISA reinterpretation, capital gains tax rate reduction, and the launching of NASDAQ).[15]

These two approaches on the more-interventionist-than-expected role of the U.S. government in the venture capital industry warrant further empirical investigation. Has it been a quite purposive disconnect between what policies are pursued and what is projected to the public and the international community? Or, have policymakers' efforts reflected the primacy of a national security norm? This second line of questioning and argumentation underscores the potential for normative change to occur over the course of this longitudinal study; just as in the U.S. model, critical junctures in the form of economic crises impact the normative composition of the three East Asian case studies as the following chapters will reveal.

Additional Models: Israel, Japan, and Taiwan

The forty-five countries included in the Large-N dataset here have all deployed some form of VC policy. As a result, there is a range of models available for study. The VC policy experiences most often cited as models for East Asian policymakers interviewed for this study were Taiwan's 20 percent tax incentive, Japan's regulatory environment, and Israel's Yozma (Hebrew: "initiative") Fund. The following paragraphs detail these policies in turn.

The Japanese VC industry began with financial institutions setting up VC funds in the 1970s. Japanese VC funds, as bank subsidiaries, were not structured as LP funds, as that entity type did not yet exist in the Japanese legal context. VC funds were subject to unlimited liability until the 1988

Investment Responsibility Association Law limited investors' liability (Kenney et al. 2002, 54–55). Regulators did not adopt the Anglo-American LP structure until 1998 (via the Limited Partnership Act for Venture Investment in 1998) (Walter and Zhang 2012, 144). Prior to the LP structure being available, Japanese VC investors risked their personal assets given the lack of a limited liability structure (Liang and Wang 2010). Their use of a corporate structure for venture capital investment provided an alternative model to the orthodox LP structure, one that incentivized low(er) risk investments by corporations.

Taiwan launched a tax credit in 1983 as the Ministry of Finance issued the Regulations for the Administration of Venture Capital Enterprises. This included a 20 percent tax deduction to first-time investors in venture capital, as long as they maintained their high-tech VC investment for a minimum of two years (TVCA 2006). In addition, tax exemptions were offered for earnings from VC investments that were reinvested in another company (Koh and Wong 2005, 26). Taiwanese policymakers were innovators in their use of tax credits to spark VC market activity; though the U.S. government encouraged venture capital activity via a lower long-term capital gains tax rate for VC profits, a tax rebate was not part of the Silicon Valley VC policy model. The Taiwanese tax innovation contributed to the creation of Asia's most active and most "Silicon Valley-like" venture capital market (Gulinello 2005, 845).

Israel's Yozma Fund is a widely studied policy. In June 1992, Israel's Office of the Chief Scientist created Yozma Venture Capital Ltd. (which launched in 1993) with US$100 million in assets under management (Lerner 2009, 155–156). Yozma was led by Yigal Erlich, Israel's former chief scientist, with the goal to build an internationally linked, professional venture capital market (author interview, Tel Aviv, 6 October 2013). Yozma invested via ten drop-down funds and also made direct investments in start-up companies (Avnimelach and Teubal 2004). The Yozma Fund required the local Israeli VC managers to have foreign partners (i.e., Walden, an American private equity firm and Kyocera in Japan) before they were eligible to receive the money in an effort to "bring foreign venture capitalists' investment expertise and network of contacts to Israel" (Lerner 2009, 156). The Yozma Fund was designed to be privatized within five years, so as not to become a subsidy to the VC market; it was privatized in 1998 (Erlich 2002). The fund's participants were given the option to buy out the government investment at cost plus a nominal interest rate and a 5–7 percent share in the future profits of portfolio company exits (Mathonet and Meyer 2007, 268). Through this onetime injection, the Yozma Fund initiated the growth of the Israeli venture capital market, which became the second biggest venture capital market in the world on an absolute basis and the world's largest in per capita terms by 2000 (Baygan 2003).

In light of the book's emphasis on the fit of policy determining performance, it is instructive to examine the case of Israel's failed VC policy: the

Inbal Fund. The Inbal Program, launched in 1991 by the Ministry of Finance, was a domestically oriented government insurance scheme that provided a 70 percent guarantee to four VC funds listed on the Tel Aviv Stock Exchange (Avnimelech and Teubal 2004). Its domestic orientation did not fit its policymakers' normative environment; Israeli policymakers' norms are decidedly foreign capital focused. They value policies that solicit financing from foreign firms rather than domestic firms (Klingler-Vidra et al. 2016), yet the Inbal Fund was squarely focused on Israel's domestic stock exchange. Owing to its misfit, when the program did not produce returns, it was quickly wound down (Author interview, Tel Aviv, 6 October 2013). To be sure, the combination of the mismatch with Israeli policymakers' norms that international—not local—capital should be prioritized, and the resultant slow uptake of the program, led to its expedient demise. The next year the Office of the Chief Scientist's externally focused Yozma Fund went on to catalyze an internationally linked VC market for Israel. The contrast in the performance of the Yozma and Inbal funds in Israel dovetails with the core argument of this book: policy fit with local normative context shapes a policy's performance.

Conceptualizing VC Policies on a Neoliberal to Interventionist Continuum

To aid the comparability of international VC policies, the three VC policy elements (regulation, taxation, and funding) are conceptualized to correspond to different levels of state intervention: regulation (low), taxation (medium), and funding (high). Of the three components, the lowest level of state intervention is regulation. The "low" categorization of regulatory policies comes as regulatory changes enable markets, but do not direct or concede state resources in order to encourage specific activity. As an illustration, the LP structure and the Small Business Investment Act of 1980 both facilitate venture capital activity by reducing bureaucratic responsibilities and offering a platform within which private investors can profit. They engender private sector activity by providing an institutional framework that enables the constitution of a market, but do not offer further incentives.

The tax instrument is categorized as medium-level interventionism because this tool encourages venture capital activity by conceding government revenue. VC tax efforts include offering low tax rates specifically to venture capitalists or extending tax credits for private investment into the venture capital asset class. Whereas regulation only provided the legal infrastructure, tax incentives explicitly encourage and reward VC investment activity. Tax rates and tax credits are medium-level interventions as they are forms of indirect financing; the state concedes revenue to encourage venture capital investment and fundraising activity. Through tax policies, the state is not giving financial resources directly to VC managers as it does when it distributes funding (e.g., via a fund of VC funds structure) to select venture capitalists.

VC funding constitutes the top end of the interventionist spectrum as the state is giving money directly to specific VC managers. Here, the state directly allocates capital to firms and therefore risks crowding out private sector investment. Funds of VC funds grant policymakers the power and budget to pick winners (e.g., selected VC managers), rather than fostering the entire sector as tax policies do, or enabling markets to act as regulations do. It is important to note that although the state does pick VC managers to invest in, funds of VC funds invest in several VC managers in an effort to support the sector, not to build national champion fund managers. Public funds of VC funds are therefore highly interventionist, but not state-promoted national champions nor state-owned enterprises, which would be a greater intervention.

Together VC policies range from regulation (low), to ratcheting up the statist nature of involvement by offering tax incentives (medium) or funds of VC funds (high). The analytical cases are expected to pursue VC policies that are different from one another in each arena (e.g., within the regulatory category) and in concert (e.g., the composition of policy tools pursued across the regulation, taxation and funding categories). Given the long time frame explored, the performance of a state's venture capital policy is not viewed as a binary success or failure. VC policy performance is examined on an individual initiative basis and within focused periods of time. Taiwan's 1983 tax credit, for example, is lauded as effective in jumpstarting the number of Taiwanese venture capitalists through the 1990s. Singapore's Technopreneurship Investment Fund increased the number of firms in the early 2000s, and Hong Kong's enabling regulatory environment steadily supported the rise of local VC markets.[16] The Taiwanese tax policy had the greatest positive impact on VC activity among the lot, whereas Hong Kong's hands-off approach saw the private sector build its local VC market from the 1980s. Performance is not even consistent across the deployment of similar instruments within each case (e.g., Singapore's TIF and ESVF had different experiences), let alone across various policy instruments (e.g., tax and regulatory policies) within a case. In chapters 4–6 I investigate the role of norms in driving the use of varied forms of regulatory, taxation, and funding policy tools in Hong Kong, Taiwan, and Singapore, and identify the performance of various policy instruments, particularly whether they produced output legitimacy.

4

Hong Kong

Night-Watchman State

The words "industrial policy" make me curl up inside.
—Chris Patten, *East and West*

Hong Kong has been ranked the freest economy in the world by the Heritage Economic Freedom Index for more than fifteen consecutive years (Miller and Kim 2016).[1] The city-state boasts one of the world's leading financial centers,[2] across banking and capital markets sectors, in line with its openness. Patten's colorful statement, as quoted above, about industrial policy making his stomach "curl up inside" is representative of Hong Kong politicians' opposition to interventionist approaches until the British handover of Hong Kong to China in 1997. Policymakers have long identified as protectors of laissez-faire, contending that the private sector better allocates resources than the state (GIS and Roberts1992; Info HK 2002). Think tanks have reinforced their identity; the Heritage Foundation and the Cato Institute have given the number-one global ranking to Hong Kong for economic freedom for fifteen plus and thirty-five years plus, respectively. However, scholars have been increasingly critical of the notion that Hong Kong's government follows a truly neoliberal approach (Latter 2007; Youngson 1982, 132–36; Choi 1994, 42), particularly in the name of supporting innovation (Fuller 2010).

The Hong Kong VC industry, like the broader economy, is effectively entrepôt. Hong Kong's open nature was established during a hundred years of British colonial rule. It continues today as the city-state remains a low-tax, open trading post and a top global economy (Latter 2007).[3] Its venture capital market similarly functions as an entrepôt hub as funding comes from abroad and investments are made into SMEs based across Asia (HKVCA 2013). The remarkable growth of the VC market has come as Hong Kong maintains a formidable position as a global financial center and exceptional access to the mainland Chinese market (author interview, Hong Kong, 3 January 2012). Its VC industry has also grown as the result of policies that have explicitly aimed at promoting Hong Kong as an internationally competitive VC hub.

In line with the neoliberal narrative, Hong Kong's large and internationally inclined venture capital industry formed in the absence of purposive VC policy. For some observers, its growth also came without intervention (see Dietrich 2003; Kenney et al. 2002). However, as will be revealed in this chapter, this study's research found that there has been more government intervention in Hong Kong's venture capital market than recognized by academics and industry analysts. Venture capital strategy was consistent with Hong Kong's broader positive nonintervention approach (Mole 1996, 1). However, by the 1990s, the approach changed as its policymakers began to feel the "limits of laissez-faire" and increasingly viewed themselves as essential supporters of innovation activity (Fuller 2010). Feeling ever-greater competitive pressures and (psychologically) reeling from the East Asian financial crisis, in the late 1990s policymakers learned about the Silicon Valley model as a means of diversifying the local economy. They were concerned that private investors might not shoulder the necessary risk of financing early-stage (high-technology) companies. Therefore, policymakers studied ways in which they could help drive venture capital market activity (Wong 1996, 29). Venture capital investments would spark entrepreneurial activity in the local technology sector and would be a means toward maintaining Hong Kong's position as the investment gateway to China (see Hong Kong Trade and Industry Bureau 1998). With this "end" in mind, policymakers sought to learn about VC policies, starting with the Silicon Valley model.

Beginning with the impact of competition in motivating learning, this chapter examines the diffusion of VC policy to Hong Kong. I explore how learning processes are based in the normative context of the Hong Kong policymakers. Policymakers initially saw themselves as neoliberal, but then over time, took on the constitution of innovation-supporting agents. Policymakers' norms and their interaction with (changes in) formal institutions informed a distinct set of VC interventionist policies in the name of laissez-faire. Hong Kong policymakers pursued a variety of VC strategies—across the regulatory, tax, and funding categories—in the name of mere market enabling. The last section assesses how contextual rationality drove Hong Kong policymakers' set of VC policy choices from when they first began in the mid-1990s through to 2017.

Normative Context

Before VC policy entered the agenda, Hong Kong government's self-proclaimed role in promoting market activity was described as merely "one of facilitation" as the state "neither protects nor subsidizes manufacturers" (GIS and Roberts 1992, 79). As former governor Patten's quote at the beginning of the chapter suggests, policy elites prided themselves on their laissez-faire approach. They identified as defenders of the "positive nonintervention" mantra, which meant that it is their role to provide services that are "good for business," including education, health, housing, and infrastructure, without unnecessary interference in business and without high tax rates (Mole 1996, 4). They embody the adage that "small government, big market" is best (author interview, Hong Kong, 21 December 2011).

In the colonial era, Britain ruled Hong Kong with little involvement in economic activity (Au and White 2009, 8). This normative approach fit the formal institutional arrangements of the time; small state expenditures helped Britain minimize its financial obligations and maintained Hong Kong as an export-oriented trading post within the empire (Choi 1994, 40–41). Accordingly, policymakers refrained from implementing sector-specific policies. Growth, particularly of the financial sector, was expected to continue without the colonial government paying for it.

From the 1980s policymakers became aware that if Hong Kong was to maintain its competitiveness, more government support, perhaps via an institute like the Japanese MITI, might be needed (Hong Kong Legislative Council 1987; Youngson 1982, 147).[4] Policymakers felt that Hong Kong was experiencing an industrial hollowing out and loss of a competitive edge in technological innovations (Fuller 2010). The laissez-faire model was failing to deliver in light of technological advancement. Policymakers began to conceptualize the use of financing as necessary in order to advance their "technology sector and further build out its financial services sector offerings" (author interview, Hong Kong, 20 December 2011). They continued to see their identity as one of positive intervention, merely doing what was necessary, in the contemporary economy, to enable private sector actors to compete in global innovation-centric activities. In this way, "positive nonintervention" included selective intervening in the name of enabling—not directing—innovation-promoting activity. In order to drive innovative activities, the government would need to provide greater incentives to encourage entrepreneurship and risk-laden investments, but this did not mean that Hong Kong's laissez-faire policymakers were interventionist.

Local VC Activity Begins

Hong Kong's venture capitalists began operating two decades before purposive policies were implemented. Venture capital activity was initiated by the private sector in the 1970s as part of the island's overall financial services sector growth (author interview, Hong Kong, 3 January 2012). The first local venture capitalists were corporate subsidiaries (Citicorp Venture Capital and

Inter-Asia Venture Management) that launched operations in 1972 (Kenney et al. 2002). Venture capital activity initially grew as the Hong Kong Stock Exchange (which was launched in 1986) produced exceptional returns for investors, which brought international attention to equity investments in pre-IPO companies in Hong Kong (Au and White 2009, 9).

For the early participants, venture capital was conceptualized as another banking service offered by large banks in Hong Kong. In the mid-1980s, the Hong Kong Association of Banks set up a working group to assess "the demand for venture capital as a source of investment funds alternative to bank loans, examining how venture capital operations might be facilitated" (Hong Kong Legislative Council 1987, 742). Local venture capitalists viewed their investments as "pure play, late-stage financial transactions" as opposed to long-term financial and operational partnerships with early-stage start-ups (author interview, Hong Kong, 21 December 2011). Venture capitalists came from banking backgrounds, as opposed to having start-up or operational experience in the technology sector, as they would in the United States (Au and White 2009, 30).

The idea that VC activity could contribute to Hong Kong's economic and technological upgrading was mentioned in the Hong Kong Legislative Council's 1987 proceedings. In a January 14, 1987, LegCo meeting, a participant suggested a new category of investment dealers he called "venture capital investment dealers." He explained that venture capitalists' use of equity investments, as well as VC managers' ability to "provide managerial, technological or professional support," could help promote start-ups (Hong Kong Legislative Council 1987, 714). But, the very next person to speak reiterated the role of noninterventionism in Hong Kong's economic success, effectively rebuffing further discussion of state support of the venture capital sector. For the time being, deliberations over the government's role in promoting VC activity ended. Hong Kong's leadership stated that its "continuing success" was "due to a simple tax structure and low tax rate" (GIS and Roberts 1992, 80). Sector-specific promotion of VC was not yet on the docket.

Rising Competitive Pressures Motivate VC Policy Learning

In the 1990s, rising competitive pressures vis-à-vis Singapore and mainland China motivated the diffusion of VC policy information into Hong Kong. Competition mattered since, as a quintessential entrepôt trading post, Hong Kong relied heavily on its leading position as a world financial center. Throughout the 1990s, it competed for capital particularly hard against Singapore. In line with China's economic rise, both states vied to be the preferred hub for venture capitalists investing in the mainland (author interview, Hong Kong, 3 January 2012). But, as Singapore and Chinese mainland cities gained as regional financial hubs, Hong Kong's position as the gateway to China's "dragon's head" (Yeh and Xu 2006), the institutionally friendly, open, and market-oriented part of China, was increasingly contested (Kenney et al. 2002, 105). As China's financial centers—in Shanghai and then Shenzhen—advanced their size and international orientation, Hong Kong policymakers felt increasingly insecure about their distinct advantage. This left Hong Kong policymakers feeling ever-greater pressure to compete in attracting venture capital managers investing across East Asia. The threats of VC managers opening offices in China and companies executing IPOs on Chinese exchanges "helped to motivate the Hong Kong government to support venture capital" in the 1990s (author interview, Hong Kong, 3 January 2012).

Suddenly, "the government had to get involved [in] early stage R&D," and policymakers felt that "risk [equity] investments would not have been picked up by the private sector" (author interview, Hong Kong, 21 December 2011). Policymakers wanted to strengthen "technology development and application, build up a critical mass of fine scientists and engineers, skilled technicians and venture capitalists" (ISD 2000, 103). They felt they needed to play a role in furthering "innovation and technological improvement" in order to shift Hong Kong's economy in the direction of SME technology activity and as a means of extending the financial services offering (ISD 2005, 107).

In response to these competitive pressures and in line with their identity as laissez-faire supporters of innovation, Hong Kong policymakers studied what other countries had done to support successful innovation ecosystems. They learned about policies to support technological development, particularly those of Singapore, Taiwan, and South Korea (author interview, Hong Kong, 21 December 2011). The following argument was made in the Legislative Council (LegCo)'s proceedings:

> In South Korea, Taiwan and Singapore, there are officially sponsored organizations which have been set up to give support to small and medium-sized factories, but in Hong Kong there is as yet no such organization. *This is an area which the Hong Kong Government should study carefully as to what is being done in the three places mentioned, and establish a similar type of organization adapted to Hong Kong circumstances* (Hong Kong Legislative Council 1987, 715, italics added).

This LegCo quotation illustrates policymakers' intention to study peer countries and, simultaneously, their intention to adapt what they learn to the Hong Kong context.

Hong Kong's studying of the Silicon Valley VC policy model was facilitated by its cosmopolitan capitalists (Hamilton 1999) who have long-established *guanxi* (Chinese for "networks"). Leveraging these networks, Hong Kong policymakers were "keenly aware of Silicon Valley" and were importing "information on how to build a Silicon Valley–like cluster" at home (author interview, Hong Kong, 21 December 2011). Their admiration for Silicon Valley has been expressed in numerous ways by innovation policymakers. The chairman of the Hong Kong Science Park said that the creators of the park "looked to the U.S., particularly Silicon Valley, and their incubation model" when designing the science park (author interview, Hong Kong, 20 December 2011). Policymakers learned that "a major factor behind the success of Silicon Valley as a leading R&D hub is the availability and contributions of private capital, in particular from *venture capitalists*, to support projects with good realization" (Hong Kong Legislative Council Panel on Commerce and Industry 2010, 6). Policymakers shared the overarching aim of helping to foster Silicon Valley–like activity in Hong Kong.

They institutionalized ways to acquire knowledge on the Silicon Valley policy model. Policymakers with Silicon Valley experience were preferred in the Innovation and Technology Commission (ITC)'s hiring process. The ITC's senior manager for technology entrepreneurship funding (as of 2012) is a salient example of this. While working for IBM for more than twenty years he "was sent to Silicon Valley to spend time researching the incubation model" (author interview, Hong Kong, 21 December 2011). Upon his return to Hong Kong, he was hired by the ITC to be the manager for its entrepreneurial funding initiatives. He won the highly competitive position due to his Silicon Valley knowledge, networks, and entrepreneurial experience. These internationally experienced policymakers helped the ITC acquire information on the Silicon Valley VC policy model. The ITC was keen to support the advance of Silicon Valley–like venture capital in Hong Kong and needed these first-hand insights to begin to formulate their strategy.

A Fund of VC Funds as a Way of Indirectly Financing Firms

As a result of these shifting interventionist orientations, in the 1990s the government launched "a special fund for projects which enhance the territory's technological and industrial development" (GIS 1995, 103). They also went on to create the Cyberport and Hong Kong Science and Technology Parks Corporation initiatives and the government commission (the ITC) that focused on advancing innovation and technology (Shih and Chen 2010, 114).

Holding it appropriate to support innovation-centric, private-sector activity, policymakers launched the Applied Research Fund (ARF) in 1993 (GIS 1995). The ARF was originally called the Applied Research and Development Scheme and its funding totaled HK$200 million (Hong Kong Legislative Council Panel on Trade and Industry 1999a, 3).[5] The ARF came in the form of loans and grants administered as a private entity wholly owned by the state and its goal was to produce a 5 percent return on investment (Kenney et al. 2002, 104; Hong Kong Trade and Industry Bureau 1998, 2).

However, by 1997 the LegCo contended that the ARF was not a success, and as a result, there was a call to produce a new management strategy for a future version of the fund (ISD 2005). The critique was that the government did not have the sources to manage such investments so a new model was needed (author interview, Hong Kong, 21 December 2011).

To this end, the 1997 administration review of the ARF recommended that "professional venture capital firms with the experience in technology investments" should manage the ARF. With professional venture capitalists making the decisions about which start-ups to invest in, the LegCo hoped that the fund would "promote technology ventures" and "fill a gap in the local capital market" (Hong Kong Legislative Council Panel on Trade and Industry 1999a, 1). It would also "further promote the capital market's interest in technology projects" in the long term (Hong Kong Trade and Industry Bureau 1998, 2). Legislators and policymakers were more comfortable with this structure; the second version of the ARF was given three times the amount of money to manage (author interview, Hong Kong, 21 December 2011). The Finance Committee of the LegCo approved the recommendation for the altered structure in March 1998, and then the ITC set out to appoint three VC firms to manage the investment activity.

Three VC managers were hired to manage investments for the ARF II in November 1998, making it a fund of VC funds, rather than a government managed VC fund. When explaining why more than one VC manager was selected to manage the ARF II, the Trade and Industry Bureau commented that "we believe the involvement of more venture capital firms will create more synergy between the Government and the venture capital industry, and will gradually build up a culture of technology investment in Hong Kong" (Hong Kong Trade and Industry Bureau 1998, 3). The selected venture capital managers were responsible for achieving set investment targets and providing "management and network advice to the investee companies" (ISD 2000, 111). The VC managers were Walden Technology Management, HSBC Private Equity Management, and AsiaTech Ventures. Walden and HSBC were each entrusted with HK$300 million while HK$150 million was given to AsiaTech (Hong Kong Legislative Council Panel on Trade and Industry 2000, 1). In November 1999, a fourth venture capital firm was added (Softech Investment Management Ltd) with HK$250 million to manage (Hong Kong Legislative Council Panel on Trade and Industry 2000, 2). All of the venture capitalists included in the ARF II scheme were remunerated through a 3 to 4 percent management fee—which is well in excess of the standard 2 percent management fee—and a formula-based share of the profits (Hong Kong Trade and Industry Bureau 1998, 2). The ARF II did not have a 5 percent return target as the first ARF had; it was instead expected to produce the best return achievable.[6]

In designing the ARF II, Hong Kong policymakers were driven by their regulative norms that prioritized the support of (large) international firms and preferred indirect financing of private sector firms. The international firm regulative norm drove policymakers' preference for the ARF II endowing money to Walden and other international VC managers, rather than to new, local VC managers. The policymakers' private sector financing norms held the state should provide financing for innovation-centric activities, but at the same time, the state should not directly preside over the investment allocations. To be sure, Hong Kong's launch of a fund of VC funds (the 1998 ARF) primarily reflects policymakers' norms not fitting with the (much smaller) 1993 ARF's operations (with the ARC running the VC fund itself) (author interview, Hong Kong, 21 December 2011). They felt it inappropriate for the ARC to manage direct VC investments; a fund of VC funds, instead, would allow professional investors to make these decisions.[7] This fit with their preference for indirect financing of private entrepreneurs.

To be sure, policymakers felt it optimal to intervene to support VC—a driver of Silicon Valley and Taiwan's innovation activities—by hiring multiple, international VC managers in the form of a fund of VC funds. Their decision to select more than one external VC manager was to reduce their role as direct financier; with multiple professional managers that would "diversify the risks involved" and "introduce an element of competition." So, rather than the 1998 ARF being an adaptation of a VC policy diffusion model (namely the Yozma Fund), its structure reflects norm-based assessments of an earlier experimentation with direct VC management (particularly the 1993 ARF).

The normative position that it was best to support innovation activities, but not choose which firms to invest in, was expressed in speeches given by senior government officials at the time. The state was supporting innovation activities in the name of nonintervention. In his 1997 policy address Tung Chee-hwa, Hong Kong's chief executive, set out "his vision of developing Hong Kong into a center for innovation and technology," appointing the ITC to advise him on policies that would enable the private sector to achieve that vision (Hong Kong Trade and Industry Bureau 1998, 4). The 2002–3 budget speech given by Financial Secretary Antony Leung in March 2002 serves as another example. Leung said that being a believer in a market economy does not mean that the "government should be passive." For him, the role of the state is to provide "infrastructure in which the private sector will not invest" (Info HK 2002).

As of May 2000, the ARF II, via its fund of VC funds structure, had invested HK$230 million in fourteen technology companies (Hong Kong Legislative Council Panel on Trade and Industry 2000). These investments were hailed an initial success. Four of the portfolio companies won awards for technology and innovation and another company was acquired by a public traded company (Hong Kong Legislative Council Panel on Trade and Industry 2000, 2). Despite the initial success, the ARF II went on to lose more than HK$240 million (Au and White 2009, 15). In fact, the ARF II was later described as "something of a disaster" as the fund had to write off over half of the invested amount (Latter 2007, 30).[8] The poor performance of the ARF II was attributed to the "invasive government restrictions on investment opportunities" (author interview, Hong Kong, 21 December 2011). In addition to (quarterly) reporting requirements, the purported failure of the fund of VC funds was alleged to be the result of inappropriate expectations, as the VC managers (Walden, HSBC, AsiaTech, and Softech) were to produce returns within an unrealistically fast time frame (Au and White 2009, 15–16). In 2004 the LegCo Audit Committee forced the ITC to wind down the ARF II (ISD 2005).[9] Hong Kong policymakers—who had primarily launched the fund of VC funds as a means of reducing the government's direct role in "picking winners"—had to wind the fund down six years later, even though the typical lifespan of a VC fund is ten years (see chapter 3 discussion of timing in the VC model).

Concomitant to the ARF II's operations in the early 2000s, increasing competition from other financial centers, particularly Singapore, motivated Hong Kong policymakers to consider further strategies to (re)assert its competitive edge. The financial secretary's 2003 budget speech is evidence of the competitive pressures:

> Hong Kong is facing keen competition from other major IFCs [international financial centers] in attracting foreign investments. Major financial centers, such as New York and London, as well as the other major player in the region, Singapore, all exempt offshore funds from tax. The financial services industry has expressed the view that it is vital for us to provide tax exemption for offshore funds, or otherwise some of these funds may relocate away from Hong Kong (Low Tax 2011).

In line with their regulative norms that indirect financing means were appropriate, policymakers considered ways in which they could make Hong Kong even more attractive, without offering direct funding. They began to consider tax strategies, though the offering of horizontally low tax rates was established by Colonial Regulations and maintained through its Basic Law[10] as a SAR of China. The idea of a generally favorable tax rate environment for all participants in the economy, not for favored industries, had long been entrenched, formally and normatively, in Hong Kong.[11]

Rather than offer a tax credit, as Taiwan had done, Hong Kong policymakers felt it appropriate to simply lower the tax rate to which VC funds' profits were subject. The lowering of the VC tax rate was conceptualized as an overt attempt at attracting international venture capitalists to Hong Kong. It would promote "Hong Kong as an international financial center" rather than "increase the high-tech start-up activity in Hong Kong" (author interview, Hong Kong, 20 December 2011). In 2006, the Inland Revenue Department acted on this preference for lowering tax rates by introducing the Revenue Bill, also known as the Profits Tax Exemption for Offshore Funds, which exempts offshore funds from paying tax (Chen and Lee 2007).[12]

Hong Kong policymakers, interested in attracting international VC managers to its local industry through nonpecuniary means, long relied on the availability of their LP structure. This LP structure was first established by the British colonial government in Hong Kong in 1912 and updated as Capital Ordinance 37, section 4, in 1950 (Hong Kong Legal Information Institute 2013). The generally well-governed Hong Kong financial system, including the provision of the LP structure, paved the way for its financial services sector to expand to VC investment activities in the 1970s (Kenney et al. 2002, 100). As policymakers have deemed the LP structure as the optimal means, regulation-wise, for attracting international capital, Hong Kong policymakers have not deployed further or alternative VC industry regulations.[13]

Prioritizing the attraction of international capital, policymakers have not valued legislation akin to the 1979 reinterpretation of the U.S. ERISA act, or what is known as the Prudent Man Rule, which enabled American pension funds to invest in VC funds. Their aim has not been to increase the pool of domestic funds for venture capital. Hong Kong's regulations stipulate that public funds, such as pension funds that would be investors in the VC asset class, are restricted from investing in VC. They are only permitted to invest in publicly traded equities, debts, warrants, and futures (Au and White 2009, 24–25). As in Singapore, Hong Kong's regulations require mandatory contribution to a retirement savings account (the Mandatory Provident Fund, then the Default Investment Strategy, in Hong Kong; and the Central Provident Fund in Singapore). These compulsory savings mechanisms are oriented toward social protection, to ensure retiring populations have sufficient financial support for their retirement (Kim 2015). In their early days, surpluses from these funds were used to finance infrastructure and state-owned enterprise development (Yeung 2016, 11). Since at least the 1990s they have not been envisaged as a source of money to use for local economic objectives, not least for the purposes of investing in high-risk activities such as venture capital. In this vein, investment capital for Hong Kong's VC industry was expected to come from international investors, not local pensioners' savings.

Intervening to Propel the Free Market

In the name of positive nonintervention, Hong Kong's policymakers have implemented a variety of purposive actions to support the VC industry since the 1990s. This stands in contrast to the findings of a 2003 APEC-sponsored research report on Asia Pacific VC ecosystems, which commented that "all Asian APEC economies in this study, except China Hong Kong, have special laws and special regulatory authority designated by law or regulation for venture capital firms" (Dietrich 2003, 22). While Hong Kong has not deployed

VC-specific regulations, the APEC report's statement is misleading as it suggests that no VC policy action was taken by the Hong Kong state. This has not been the case; at least since the 1990s the government has promoted venture capital. The scope and centrality of Hong Kong's push for innovation-centric entrepreneurship has grown in recent years, with the creation of the Innovation and Technology Bureau in November 2015 bringing the policy area to the bureau level and the April 2017 launch of the Innovation Technology Venture Fund.[14] In her October 2017 policy address, Hong Kong's chief executive, Carrie Lam, reaffirmed the government's high level of commitment in "promoting the development of innovation and technology and the creative industry in Hong Kong." Table 4.1 details the array of policies pursued since 1993, as discussed in the preceding section.

To be sure, Hong Kong's government has not merely provided an enabling regulatory environment. It has been an investor in VC managers and has conceded tax revenues, which rebuffs the (mis)conception that the Hong Kong government has not intervened. The ways in which the state has intervened is, at the same time, consistent with policymakers' constitutive and regulative norms that posit their identity as supporters of innovation activity through indirect finance and by supporting international firms.

Formal Institutions and Norms

The Hong Kong policymaking process during British rule has been described as "executive led" (Cheung 2004). The governor, key business people, and civil servant elites set the policymaking agenda and had decision-making power. In the colonial system, the Executive Council (ExCo) and the LegCo served advisory roles to the governor. They did not have binding power over the governor's policy decisions (Choi 1994, 47); the governor's grasp on power during this era was unrivaled by the LegCo nor ExCo elites (Koehn 2001, 98–99). Colonial policymakers, not beholden to public opinion and without fear of public scrutiny, were able to make swift policy choices in line with their norms. The following passage reiterates these points on the concentration of power:

> The policymaking process in Hong Kong was very much executive-led . . . the Governor and the elite Administrative Officer grade dominated decision-making through the Executive Council . . . while the legislature mainly served to endorse the government's proposals . . . carefully staged public consultation exercises were used largely to legitimize the policy process and civil society was relatively weak. (Cheung 2011, 114)

The governor and top administrative officials had total authority over policy design. That leadership maintained staunchly neoliberal norms. Industrial policy, which made senior officials' stomachs "curl up inside," was not a

TABLE 4.1
Key dates in Hong Kong's VC policies

Year	Policy developments
1993	Applied Research Fund (ARF), a government VC fund managed by the Applied Research Council, with US$32 million in budget, began administering financing (mostly loans) to SMEs with a target annual return of 5 percent
1998	ARF took the shape of a fund of VC funds, following a LegCo review, and received another US$96 million in funding; in November 1998 the ITC appointed three private VC fund managers—Walden Technology Management, AsiaTech Ventures, and HSBC Private Equity Management—to manage the fund
1999	ARF added Softech Investment Management as the fourth VC manager, and the Innovation and Technology Fund (ITF) was launched with HK$5 billion as a means of supporting the transition of local industries to higher value-added activities (the ITF subsumed the Industrial Support Fund, which had been launched in 1994, and the Services Support Fund, which had been launched in 1996)
2000	Applied Science and Technology Research Institute (ASTRI) was created to conduct industry-oriented R&D
2000	The Innovation and Technology Commission (ITC)[1] was formed along with the July 1, 2000, reorganization of the Trade and Industry Bureau into the Commerce and Industry Bureau
2001	Small and Medium Enterprise Fund was set up in 2001 to improve SME financing
2004	The ITF set up the Small Enterprise Research Assistance Program to finance start-ups' R&D; repayment is contingent on their success (producing a profit or exiting); ARF II wound down at the recommendation of the LegCo
2005	Revenue Bill (Profits Tax Exemption for Offshore Funds) 2005 ensures that offshore VC funds domiciled in Hong Kong are entitled to a tax exemption, and China passed its first VC legislative package—Provisional Measures for the Administration of Venture Capital Enterprises
2007	Hong Kong passed the avoidance of double taxation legislation for Chinese investments
2015	Creation of the Innovation & Technology Bureau (ITB), the smallest of Hong Kong's thirteen government bureaus, headed by Nicholas Yang (approved by LegCo)
2017	Chief executive's 2017 budget outlines plans for setting up a US$250 million Innovation and Technology Venture Fund, in which the fund provides matching funding to VC funds as coinvestment partners on the basis of approximately 1:2 for local technology start-ups; the Innovation and Technology Venture Fund does not provide money directly to start-ups

Sources: GIS 1995; GIS and Witt 1993; GIS and Daryanani 1994; 1995; HKVCA 2004; ISD 2000; 2005; 2009; Kenney et al. 2002, 100–105; Au and White 2009, 13; Shih and Chen 2010, 117; Innovation and Technology Commission 2011; *South China Morning Post* 2017b; Berger and Lester 1997.

[1] The ITC, and since 2015 the ITB, is the government entity with oversight for most of the initiatives relevant to VC policy and SME support. Since its creation, public funds for SMEs and VC managers, including the Innovation and Technology Fund, the ARF, DesignSmart Initiative, the Patent Application Grant, and Innovation and Technology Venture Fund, have been under the oversight of this commission, then bureau.

fit with the concentrated, and decidedly neoliberal, colonial policymaking context.

As Hong Kong's transition to a Chinese SAR took shape in the 1990s, public scrutiny increased,[15] along with policymakers' normative shift toward actively supporting innovation. The increased scrutiny that came alongside the rise of a politicized environment contributed to "a risk-averse culture" among policymakers (Latter 2007, 136). In explaining the differences across the two periods, an interviewee went so far as to say that "we never had politics before 1997, until the British left" (author interview, Hong Kong, 3 January 2012). Since the handover, policymakers have had to ask the LegCo for funding and approval to make any substantive changes to existing programs (author interview, Hong Kong, 21 December 2011). This challenge in realizing innovation-promotion action was a crucial force behind the creation of the ITB in November 2015, the hope being that a bureau-level entity would be better able to implement policies than the ITC had been.

By the late 1990s, the LegCo went from being an appointed body that only "rubber stamped" policies to a partially elected group that "controls the choices" of civil servants hoping to pass and maintain budget for policies (author interview, Hong Kong, 21 December 2011).[16] The LegCo played a role in limiting direct finance for venture capital, pushing for the ARF's closing down in 1997 in favor of hiring professional VC managers in the ARF. Then, in 2004, the LegCo's Audit Commission flagged performance concerns and asserted that the ITC Commissioner "should take vigorous actions to strengthen control over the disposal of ARF [II] investments" (Legislative Council Audit Commission 2004; Hong Kong Audit Commission 2004). This critical finding was "the beginning of the end of the ARF [II] initiative" as public pressures recommended that the ITC scrutinize the fund's outputs and reconsider its operations (author interview, Hong Kong, 20 December 2011). The LegCo forced the winding down of the ARF II, a case in point that policymakers' desire to support innovation has been met by increased scrutiny.

A Busy Night Watchman

Competitive pressures propelled policymakers' shift toward finding it more appropriate to intervene in order to support innovation. Hong Kong's continuing bid to be a leading financial center, and more specifically, a hub for international venture capital investment in mainland Chinese start-ups led policymakers to feel increased pressure to compete to attract VC managers. Singapore and China were advancing as fund management locations, and Beijing and Shanghai became preeminent investment and operational destinations.

Feeling the competitive pressures, they felt they had reached the "limits of laissez-faire" and increasingly saw themselves as supporters of private sector–led innovation activity. While in favor of innovation support, they preferred indirect financing and support of international firms. Although it represented a shift from the unadulterated laissez-faire mantra, indirect financing to international firms was seen as the appropriate means of intervention. Policymakers launched the ARF II as the result of their preference for

indirect financing as the VC managers were viewed as a conduit, not the recipients of the money; this was valued over managing a direct VC fund (akin
to the ARF) in order to support innovation. Policymakers maintained their
normative position that they should support international firms through indirect financing means, in line with their view of themselves as neoliberal
enablers, not market makers. The growing power of the LegCo scrutiny since
the 1997 handover has reinforced the regulative norms that the offering of
indirect financing to attract international capital was appropriate—and direct financing was not. This normative position was most recently reflected
in the Innovation and Technology Venture Fund's structure as a passive coin-
vestor rather than a direct investor in start-ups.

Bounded rationality would expect that Hong Kong policymakers replicate the "anchors" that they studied (the United States and Taiwan). Conventional rationality expectations are that policymakers would have determined
some acontextual optimal policy strategy based on their familiarity with the
Silicon Valley model; in light of the success of the American and Taiwanese
policies by the time Hong Kong policymakers came to study them, then they
should have replicated the ERISA reinterpretation or Taiwan's 20 percent tax
credit. But, neither of these paths were pursued. Instead, Hong Kong policymakers designed policies in line with their normative context. They offered
a tax exemption, instead of a tax credit, as they value their broad low-tax
system. Reluctant to use tax incentives to promote specific sectors, they felt it
appropriate to offer a low tax rate for offshore funds, rather than VC-specific
credits. In a similar vein, they deployed a fund of VC funds as it offered them
a way to indirectly allocate money to international firms (through the ARF II)
and a coinvestment model that does not require "picking winners" (via the
Innovation and Technology Venture Fund). They did not pick up the ERISA
reinterpretation because fundraising from local pension funds was not appropriate; mandatory pension savings is seen as critical to social protection,
not for propping up new sectors. In all, Hong Kong synthesized its own mix
of interventionist policies that reflect the persistence of its constitutive norm
(that policymakers identify as purveyors of positive nonintervention) and its
regulative norms that inform policymakers' preference for indirect financing
to attract international firms. As a result, while categorized by Milton Friedman and others as a textbook example of laissez-faire, Hong Kong did not
act as a truly hands-off state in the VC policy area. Its policymakers launched
interventionist VC policy tools, including a tax exemption and a fund of VC
funds, in the name of positive nonintervention for promoting innovation.

Contrary to state-of-the-art diffusion scholarship's expectations that multiple diffusion models drive adaptation, the existence of multiple VC policy
models was not found to account for the form of Hong Kong's adaptation
of the Silicon Valley VC policy environment. Policymakers learned about the
policy approaches employed in Silicon Valley, Taiwan, and Singapore for ways
the state could support high-tech growth. But they chose to not duplicate

what they learned of the highly regarded Silicon Valley policy model (beyond the continued use of the LP structure) or the Taiwanese tax model. Rather, they synthesized their own versions of two policy elements (tax and funding).

Hong Kong's deployment of interventionist VC policies is interesting given its ranking as the freest economy in the world. If even East Asia's neoliberal poster child grasped onto interventionist VC policies, what can we expect of states that held more interventionist constitutive norms to begin with? For one, the behavior of Hong Kong policymakers in market promotion, rather than wholly devolved self-regulation of the market, points to the empirical impossibility of truly free markets. As Polanyi (2001, 155) exclaimed, "Economic liberals must and will unhesitantly call for the intervention of the state in order to establish [the market], and once established, in order to maintain it." The rhetoric of Hong Kong politicians and policymakers has been devotedly laissez-faire, and their conceptualization of the appropriate ways for being laissez faire includes purposive action.

The implications of the Hong Kong findings will be assessed in the analysis chapter, in line with a discussion of the analytical narratives of Taiwan and Singapore. The aim is to determine the generalizability, or broader explanatory power, we can draw from the case. Each analytical narrative will be explored for what it tells us about the form of rationality that underscores learning in international policy diffusion. The cases reveal the centrality of norms in informing policymakers' preferences for particular forms of VC policies. Policymakers intervene to support the venture capital market, a supposedly neoliberal construct, according to spatially—and temporally—dependent logics of appropriateness. Now the analysis moves on to how Taiwanese policymakers' norms shaped their learning of the Silicon Valley VC policy model to fit their domestic context.

Taiwan

Private Sector Promoter

> The successful model of a developed country can be used as a reference but cannot be duplicated as every nation must respond to its own social background and economic conditions.
> —Government Information Office, *Republic of China: A Reference Book*, 1983

Volumes of academic research have examined the mechanics behind the economic miracle achieved in Taiwan, notably research by Robert Wade (2004), Alice Amsden (1979; 2001), Chalmers Johnson (1982), Sanjaya Lall (1996), Juhana Vartiainen (1999), Meredith Woo-Cumings (1999), and Stephan Haggard (1990). This developmental state scholarship provides insights into the industrial policies behind Taiwan's miracle, the importance of economic success to the martial law government, and the drivers of the Taiwanese technology cluster's outstanding performance. However, both Dan Breznitz's *Innovation and the State* (2007) and J. Megan Greene's *The Origins of the Developmental State in Taiwan* (2008) assert that there has been an insufficient examination of the *sources* behind the Taiwanese state's industrial policies. This chapter addresses this lacuna in the literature by exploring why and how Taiwanese policymakers designed their VC policies as part of policy efforts to become a "Silicon Island" (GIO 2001, 161).

There are three reasons why it is important to identify the sources of Taiwanese VC policy choices. First, Taiwan provides the opportunity to examine how policymakers' norms—that favor local firms and indirect finance—affect VC policy diffusion outcomes. Second, despite the VC industry's contribution to the Taiwanese economic miracle, the sources of Taiwan's VC policy choices have not yet been explored. Taiwanese venture capitalists invested in more than three thousand local companies, and VC-backed technology companies constitute approximately half of all technology companies listed on the Taiwanese stock exchanges (Yeh 2006, 22). A 2006 presentation given by Thomas M. F. Yeh, the then vice chairman of the Executive Yuan's Council for Economic Planning and Development (CEPD),[1] attests to the impact of Taiwan's venture capital market: "A substantial contribution to Taiwan's industrial restructuring, SME development, high-tech industry incubation, job creation, and stability of economic development. . . . Its impact on the nation's most significant period of rapid economic boom has been remarkable" (Yeh 2006, 3). In 2014, more than 75 percent of the equity invested in Taiwanese ICT firms came from domestic venture capitalists (TVCA 2015, 4). Local venture capitalists primarily invest local money, as foreign money has historically accounted for less than 7 percent of the investment in Taiwan's VC market (Breznitz 2007, 141).

Third, Taiwan's VC policies are of interest to many policymakers given the achievements of its market. Taiwan's venture capital market has been described as "arguably the most successful engineered venture capital market in the world" (Gulinello 2005, 848). Effective policy helped Taiwan's VC industry become the fourth largest VC market in Asia (behind Japan, Hong Kong, and Singapore) and the world's third most active, in terms of deal volume, behind the United States and Israel, by the early 2000s (AVCJ 2005).

The next section investigates the effect of rising competitive pressures on Taiwan's VC policy diffusion. Attention then turns to exploring how Taiwanese policymakers' constitutive and regulative norms, in a dynamic with formal institutions, drove their valuation and adaptation of policy models. To bring the findings together, table 5.1 offers a chronological summary of Taiwan's VC policies and then the concluding portion of the chapter assesses how the contextual rationality approach can help us understand the shape of Taiwan's VC policy choices (better than conventional or bounded rationality approaches, or state-of-the-art diffusion scholarship, could).

Competitive Pressures

Economic competitiveness has been critical to Taiwan's strategy to survive as a state (Amsden 2001). From October 1971, when the United Nations voted to recognize the PRC and simultaneously expel Taiwan, there had been heightened urgency in the need to be economically competitive. Policymakers valued policies that helped ensure trade continued to flow to the island (Greene 2008). Trade and aid inflows amounted to US$4.5 billion by 1984 (GIO 1986, 237). As its largest trading partner, the United States alone accounted for more than 41 percent of this foreign investment into Taiwan (GIO 1986, 239).[2] American investment played a critical role in Taiwan's economy, leading one interviewee to quip that a local VC industry may have initially been "conceived as a means to attract more investment from the U.S." (author interview, Taipei, 6 January 2012).[3]

Venture capital has been conceptualized as a tool for improving the competitiveness of Taiwan's high-technology sector, and therefore, the state's broader economic development (Wang 1995, 4). Technology-focused SMEs have been the "backbone" of the Taiwanese economy, in contrast to "many advanced nations, where conglomerates dominate the economy" (GIO 1999, 172).[4] Policymaker support has helped turn Taiwan into a top global producer of high-technology products such as personal notebook computers and semiconductors (Tsai and Wang 2004, 65). They have felt that local high-technology entrepreneurs needed venture capital in order to be successful. In turn, for venture capital to be successful, four things were necessary: "capital, entrepreneurial talent, investing talent and functioning stock exchanges—and Taiwan had all these ingredients" (author interview, Taipei, 5 January 2012).

The need for VC came because Taiwan's financial system was bank-dominated. A handful of banks had dominated official financing such that seven banks accounted for nearly 90 percent of all domestic deposits in 1980 (Wade 2004, 159).[5] Taiwan's high-technology SMEs could not secure access to these bank loans. Instead they had to establish credit lines with unregulated and unofficial sources (the grey market). As part of policymakers' efforts to rectify banks' inadequate provision of capital to its fast-growing cohort of technology start-ups, they sought to learn about alternative ways to finance high-technology SMEs. But they were not keen to attract international capital as the solution.

Taiwanese policymakers held regulative norms that favored the promotion of local capital and local firms. These norms stem from policymakers' fear of the "vulnerability of Taiwan's de facto sovereignty" (Pempel and Tsunekawa 2015, 6).[6] The deep-seated fear of foreign influence—in the form of foreign control of capital flows or investment decisions—has informed Taiwanese policymakers' regulative norms that hold local support, and in effect, financial independence, essential.

Studying VC Policy as a Solution for Promoting SME Competitiveness

By the early 1980s Taiwanese policymaking elites set out to learn how a local venture capital market, like that in Silicon Valley, could support its burgeoning high-technology industry and SME-dominated economy. At that time, venture capital was a relatively new asset class that had only achieved success in Silicon Valley and Boston's Route 128. As a result of its newness, hard evidence of the positive impact of venture capital investment activity on technology, innovation, and the broader American economy was not yet available

(Kortum and Lerner 2000). They decided to go to the source; in 1981, senior policymakers and a select set of private sector actors took a study trip to the United States (Silicon Valley and Boston) and Japan in order to learn how to promote venture capital locally (author interview, Taipei, 6 January 2012; Yeh 2006).[7]

Former finance minister Kwoh-Ting (K. T.) Li pushed for the trip. He wanted to learn about the drivers of the technology cluster and venture capital industry successes (Breznitz 2007, 140; Kenney et al. 2002, 36). For Li, a venture capital market could expand Taiwan's incomplete financial services sector, promote its domestic technology start-ups, and advance the local use of modern management techniques (Saxenian and Li 2000, 4). Li and his colleagues studied Silicon Valley venture capital as a means of addressing this funding need; venture capital would "integrate capital, technology, talent, and management for the purpose of upgrading Taiwan's technological developments" (Executive Yuan Development Fund 2013, 1). Because he "promoted the conception of VC long before other Taiwanese policymakers were considering it" (author interview, Taipei, 5 January 2012), Li has been called the "original champion of VC in Taiwan" (Saxenian and Li 2000, 3).[8]

Further learning about the Silicon Valley VC model was facilitated by the so-called "Silicon Valley—Hsinchu Connection" (Koh and Wong 2005, 27).[9] The connection "fostered transfers of institutional know-how as well as capital and market knowledge" by Taiwanese entrepreneurs and engineers at multinational corporations in the United States (Saxenian and Li 2000, 1). Two of the key agents facilitating this learning process were Ta-Lin Hsu,[10] a senior IBM manager and VC investor in California, and Morris Chang,[11] a senior manager at Texas Instruments and later the head of ITRI and founder of Taiwan Semiconductor Manufacturing Company (Kenney et al. 2002, 25; GIO 2001; Saxenian and Li 2000, 3). Hsu is said to have brought "Silicon Valley style venture capital to Taiwan" by helping the American investment bank Hambrecht & Quist (H&Q) set up operations in Taiwan and by initially educating policymakers—especially K. T. Li and the Executive Yuan—about the venture capital asset class (author interview, Taipei, 6 January 2012). Stan Shih, the founder of Acer, the company that launched the first venture capital firm in Taiwan in 1984, was also central to diffusing Silicon Valley venture capital information (Kirby 2002).[12]

Taiwanese policymakers' determination of potential VC policy's value was rooted in their local normative context. As an illustration of the centrality of norms in the process, government communiqués stated that each country has its own model and approach to development, which are intimately related to its cultural, historical, and socioeconomic background (GIO 1983, 159). Policymakers were intent on designing policies that fit the local context. Even the term *venture capital* had to be modified in order to fit Taiwan's local environment. Upon returning from the study trip, K. T. Li did not choose the Chinese translation of "risky investor," which is how the phrase would have been translated. He instead translated it to "start-up investor" so as to decrease the perception of risk in the asset class (author interview, Taipei, 5 January 2012). The promotion of local investment—not the attracting of foreign money—was most valued in the minds of Taiwanese policymakers.

In studying the American model, Taiwanese policymakers found that Silicon Valley's "generally enabling environment contributed to the VC market's success" (author interview, Taipei, 5 January 2012).[13] Their reading of the Silicon Valley model was that market forces—not government funding, regulatory changes, or low tax rates—were responsible for its success. Coming to the conclusion that Silicon Valley was the product of a historically contingent set of market forces, policymakers were emboldened to act differently; their constitutive norms held that it was the role of policymakers to promote market development, so they set out to do just that.

Adapting for Local Context

As a next step, they sought to learn from states that they felt were more proximate in their interventionist approach (Wang 1995; author interview, Taipei, 6 January 2012). In this vein, a CEPD policymaker commented that "Silicon Valley is a good example of liquid human capital and forming business ventures very quickly. In Taiwan we don't have liquidity of human capital talent like in Silicon Valley. So, we learn from Japan, Korea or Germany" (author interview, Taipei, 6 January 2012). Policymakers kept abreast of policies deployed by regional peers and the performance of peers' VC markets, particularly Japan. They studied the VC regulatory environment in Japan due to their "Japanese legal legacy" and affinity for the Japanese approach to managing investment risk (author interview, Taipei, 6 January 2012).

Local regulations, in particular, drew on what they learned about the Japanese VC regulatory environment.[14] Taiwan's policymakers studied how Japanese regulators appeased the risk-averse nature of local investors; Japan, which had a corporate structure that restricts the power that VC managers had over investment decisions, was different from the American LP structure (author interview, Taipei, 5 January 2012). Taiwan's corporate legal structure (or "paper company" structure as translated from the legal term used in Taiwan) drew on Japanese regulations by not limiting liability and by reducing VC managers' power over investment decisions. While Taiwanese policymakers learned from Japan, they did not simply copy their regulations; Taiwan's heir corporate legal structure is not as restrictive as Japan's unlimited liability structure (author interview, Taipei, 6 January 2012).[15]

Thus, though Taiwanese policymakers closely studied the Silicon Valley VC regulatory environment, their "paper company" structure is not at all consistent with the Silicon Valley LP structure and is instead more similar to the Japanese regulatory structure that they valued for its treatment of risk and control.[16] Taiwan's VC structure consists of the VC management firm (the "private company") maintaining a consulting relationship with the fund (the "paper company"). These rules of incorporation afford investors in the fund, rather than the VC manager, to have authority over investment decisions (Yeh 2006, 4). Effectively, the VC management company only does the due diligence and makes recommendations for investments (author interview, Taipei, 5 January 2012). In contrast, in the American LP structure the VC manager makes buy and sell decisions unilaterally on behalf of their investors.

In Taiwan, only the VC management companies' founders have equity stakes in the paper company (the VC funds). As a result, even senior employees do not share in the profit of the fund (Kenney et al. 2002, 42). The Taiwanese paper companies are also different in that they do not have liquidation dates. This "evergreen fund" set-up means that VC managers may run overlapping funds, instead of following the American model of raising, investing, and liquidating funds (Lerner 2009). Taiwanese paper companies, again different from the LP context, were required to invest in registered firms in the high-technology sector in order to be eligible for the tax credits. This requirement decreases the VC managers' abilities to invest in seed opportunities, as very early stage start-ups are often not yet incorporated as firms (Breznitz 2007, 141). Again, this adaptation reflects the value that policymakers gave to policy components that minimized risk, though in ways distinct from the way the Japanese structure achieved this.

Unlike the 1979 ERISA reinterpretation that allowed Silicon Valley venture capitalists to raise funds from pension funds, launching a VC fund in Taiwan involves securing the right percentages of capital from a restricted universe of potential investors. Taiwanese pension funds have not been allowed to invest in VC funds (Wang 1995, 23; author interview, Taipei, 6 January 2012). VC managers need to apply for a recommendation from the Industrial Development Bureau (IDB, previously the Ministry of Finance) if they have capital commitments from banks, insurance companies, or securities firms.[17] What's more, there has been a limit on the percentage of funds that banks, insurance companies, and other financial institutions can invest in VC companies—with banks at 5 percent and insurance companies at 25 percent (Kenney et al. 2002).[18] This means a critical component of the Silicon Valley regulatory environment (the ERISA reinterpretation in 1979) has not been deployed, as local personal savings are to be protected (similar to the social protection mantra that guides the perceptions of the acceptable risk for pension fund assets as seen in the Hong Kong case—and as will be similarly at play in the Singaporean context). Instead, local corporations were conceived of as the right source of high-risk funding for venture capital.

Taiwanese policymakers' regulative norms prefer indirect financing, by way of tax incentives, for local firms in target sectors (Amsden 1979; Wade 2004; Fields 2012).[19] In keeping with these norms, they offered tax credits to the tune of 20 percent for high-technology sector R&D in the 1970s (Breznitz 2007, 100–125; Fuller 2002). Robert Wade, in *Governing the Market*, explains that policymakers' preference for tax incentives stems from "the high priority to economic stabilization [which] reinforced the position of the monetary authorities vis-à-vis the industrial authorities, *limiting the use of selective credit as a primary instrument for steering the behavior of private firms* as compared to Korea. Hence the government's reliance on public enterprises, trade controls, and *tax incentives*" (Wade 2004, 296, italics added). The 20 percent tax credit for start-up and R&D investments provided investors with a five-year corporate income tax holiday for "newly established capital or technology-intensive projects" (GIO 1986, 237). This approach—indirect financing—was widely held as effective and appropriate.

This is all to say that regulative norms favoring the use of tax incentives, rather than the direct transfer of public money, were already firmly established by the time VC policy came onto the agenda in the early 1980s. Tax incentives were considered a "tried and true" strategy (author interview, Taipei, 5 January 2012). Regulative norms held that it is appropriate to deploy a 20 percent tax incentive as the primary effort to constitute a local venture capital market. A similar tax credit had worked in the technology sector over the previous decade. They did not "want to take risks, so felt that it's best to be consistent" with strategies that worked before (author interview, Taipei, 5 January 2012). The 20 percent incentive fit policymakers' norms: policymakers should intervene by indirect finance to local firms. Thus, upon return from the United States and Japan, policymakers began working to draft tax credits to support a new venture capital market.

In line with their indirect financing regulative norm, two years after their 1981 study trip to the United States and Japan, Taiwan's Council for Economic Planning and Development (CEPD) passed a Ministry of Finance (MoF) bill—the Regulations for the Administration of Venture Capital Enterprises—that gave a 20 percent tax credit for first-time VC investors beginning in 1983 (Kenney et al. 2002).[20] The regulations gave a 20 percent tax deduction for local first-time VC investors, as long as they maintained their high-technology VC investment for a minimum of two years. The tax incentive aimed at directing long-term capital from Taiwanese investor toward new, high-growth technological enterprises (Wang 1995, 2).

In 1991, the tax credit was expanded to incentivize local corporations to invest in VC; this helped to expand the size of Taiwan's corporate VC investor base (Kenney et al. 2002). Tax exemptions were also offered on the capital gains earned by venture capitalists investing in high-technology SMEs (Wang 1995) and for earnings from profits that were reinvested in VC funds (Koh and Wong 2005, 26). These tax incentives aided the growth of Taiwan's vibrant VC market (Dietrich 2003, 22).[21]

Policymakers' regulative norm that it is appropriate to support local firms had a formative impact on Taiwan's VC policies. Most notably, to ensure that venture capital money went to local high-technology SMEs, policymakers restricted tax incentives to privately held, Taiwanese technology firms (Wang 1995, 2). In the 1980s, policymakers (in the CEPD in particular) encouraged local corporations, such as Formosa Plastics, to invest in the burgeoning VC asset class. As a result of such incentives, many of Taiwan's VC managers have been successful local technology firms that have invested in local start-ups (author interview, Taipei, 6 January 2012).[22]

Taiwanese policymakers' private sector financing norms dictated that they should not commit large sums of money directly to the high-technology and VC industries. Taiwan's policies for the high-technology sector focused on tax credits, R&D provision, and commercializing SME products (Greene 2008). So that businessmen do not become reliant on public funding, policymakers only gave modest financing to private sector actors (GIO 1983, 160). Private sector financing norms translated into the government offering tax incentives and coinvestment partnerships with "Walden, H&Q and other VC managers, like Intel Capital and GE Capital" (author interview, Taipei, 5 January 2012). They allocate capital to start-ups and VC managers via coinvestment provisions, alongside private VCs in the case of start-up investments, and alongside other investors in the case of VC funds. Through these coinvestments, particularly through the National Development Fund (hereafter referred to as the "Development Fund") activities, the government offers modest financial support without having to "pick winners" on their own.

The decision to use the paper company structure, instead of the Silicon Valley LP structure, was also driven by policymakers' regulative norms that held it optimal to support local, rather than international, firms. Taiwanese VC policymakers adapted the regulatory environment for VC since local investment practices dictated that investors have control over investment decisions. They "learned about the LP structure from the U.S., but they have changed the roles and responsibilities of LPs and GPs since Chinese people like to be involved in investment decisions. Chinese don't like to give their money and then not have the chance to decide about how the money is spent" (author interview, Taipei, 5 January 2012). Policymakers adapted the Silicon Valley LP regulatory structure for VC in Taiwan so that it pleased local investors. It took the form of an adaptation of a Japanese-inspired paper company structure in which, investors, not VC managers, have authority over investment and exit decisions.

The regulative norms informing the preference for indirect financing has contributed to the Taiwanese state not launching a fund of VC funds. Instead, policymakers have offered coinvestment alongside private VC managers (Pandey and Jang 1996) and through a bilateral fund, run in partnership with New Zealand (MoEA 2012). Finding it inappropriate for the state to decide which firms receive investment capital, Taiwanese policymakers have coinvested in start-ups along with private VC managers via the Development

Fund. The Development Fund aims to "strengthen and aid in the development of the *domestic* venture capital industry, foster the continued growth of knowledge economy industries, enhance the *nation's competitive ability*, and accelerate domestic economic development" (Executive Yuan Development Fund 2013, 1, italics added). Through this arrangement, private investors, not the Development Fund, make the decision about which firms to invest in. This shape of funding began in 1985 as the Chiao Tung Bank formed a VC fund by providing capital along with the Development Fund and the Sino-American Foundation, with the other 50 percent of capital coming from the private American investment bank H&Q. The Development Fund and Chiao Tung Bank initiative was renewed in 1991 as the Second VC Investment Program as the US$25 million fund grew to a US$75 million VC fund (Koh and Wong 2005, 26–27; Kenney et al. 2002, 38–39).

Additional government venture capital funding came in October 2001 as the Development Fund participated in the National Development Plan (NDP). Starting in the early 2000s, and continuing until today, the NDP raises 30 percent of its capital from the fund with the remaining 70 percent coming from the private sector (author interview, Taipei, 6 January 2012). The Development Fund invests in VC firms to "augment investment in the venture capital industry" in Taiwan (Executive Yuan Development Fund 2013). Recently, as part of the HeadStart Taiwan initiative, a US$400 million National Development Fund offers matching funds for venture capitalists investing in Taiwanese start-ups (National Development Council 2014). To be sure, across these various VC funding schemes, Taiwanese policymakers assert that they are not making direct investment decisions; instead, these initiatives reflect their regulative norms that hold it optimal to match the funding allocated by private investors, rather than finance directly.

In a similar vein, Taiwan's first fund of VC funds only came into being in March 2012. Taiwan and New Zealand launched a bilateral fund of VC funds via the Strategic Cooperation on Joint Investments in Venture Capital Funds, with assets under management of US$160 million (each state allocated approximately US$80 million) (MoEA 2012). The bilateral fund is the result of a collaboration between Taiwan's Development Fund and the New Zealand Venture Investment Fund (NZVIF), modeled after Israel's Yozma Fund (Lerner 2009, 133–35).[23] The Taiwan-New Zealand fund of VC funds structure—akin to the NZVIF and the Yozma Fund—requires that VC managers raise at least 40 percent of their capital from private sources and half of the investment capital goes to start-ups in each country (Krupp 2012). For Taiwanese policymakers, this bilateral fund took an appropriate form: it provides finance to match the funds that private VC managers had decided to invest in start-ups, so that the Development Fund would not have to directly choose investment targets.

Formal Institutions and Norms

Taiwanese policymakers have strained access to budgetary power. This dialectic has informed and reinforced their regulative norm that it was optimal to use tax incentives, rather than direct financing mechanisms, to support private sector activity. The Ministry of Finance was the main regulating body for the venture capital industry from 1983 until 2005. During that time, the MoF launched the tax credit legislation, and VC managers had to seek "special approval" from the MoF to operate (Wang 1995, 5). Through the new regulatory package (the Scope) in 2005, the Ministry of Economic Affairs's IDB effectively became the venture capital industry regulator. Since then, venture capitalists seek fundraising and registration approval from the IDB. Though the IDB oversees the venture capital industry, it had little authority over financing for the venture capital industry (author interview, Taipei, 5 January 2012). Instead, the IDB had more of a coordinating role as it has organized task forces to bring focus, energy, and expertise to industry-specific policymaking (Breznitz 2007, 100–125).[24] The Executive Yuan's CEPD, and since 2014, the NDC, has had budgetary power. It invested alongside, and in, the venture capital industry via its Development Fund from 1985. Taken together, taxation and regulation were under the purview of the MoF and the IDB while the CEPD managed the VC industry's funding. Since the policymaking and funding bodies responsible for VC policy have been separate in Taiwan, the creation of VC policies laden with financial support have not been deemed appropriate.[25] Since the 2014 government restructuring, the National Development Council has had this power, so future research is needed to track the evolution of the new distribution of budgetary power on regulative norms informing whether direct or indirect financing is appropriate.

Formal institutions have had a direct impact on the value of the foreign models that have been studied. The tax rate for profits on high-technology investments is zero, as high-technology SMEs are categorized as "strategic industry enterprises" that receive a tax holiday (Wang 1995, 5–6). Only companies "limited by shares" have been qualified to receive these tax exemptions on capital gains in Taiwan (Wang 1995, 10–11). As a result, the use of an LP structure "which would make VC investments eligible for the individual tax rate has not been attractive at all" (author interview, Taipei, 5 January 2012). Silicon Valley's LP structure would actually make tax treatment of venture capital investing less attractive in Taiwan. These aspects of the legal system contributed to the decision to use the paper company structure (as inspired by studying the Japanese VC policy context) rather than deploying a version of Silicon Valley's LP structure.

Normative change occurred in Taiwan, most notably in line with the opposition government's first-ever win, in 2000. Taiwan's democratization began subsequent to the death of its long-time leader, Chiang Kai-shek, in 1975, as political parties were legalized in 1987 along with the end of the martial law era. Major constitutional changes did not occur for another decade, as the populace was only allowed to elect the president in 1996 (Beck et al. 2000). It was in the 2000 election that an opposition party, the Democratic People's Party (DPP), won government; the Kuomintang (KMT) had held power since Taiwan's founding in 1949. The March 2000 election "brought the first transition of executive power from one party to another in Taiwan" (Marshall and Gurr 2012, 1–2).

Taiwan's policymaking process had remained largely intact since the early 1980s. The insular martial law–era process allowed for the quick deployment of industrial policies in line with the regulative norms of top politicians and policymakers. Taiwan's "state corporatism," or "authoritarian-corporatist," political system of 1950 to 1985 simply evolved into a more inclusive model of "social corporatism" by the late 1980s (Wade 2004, 228, 290). Despite political regime changes, the key actors and general framework of the VC policymaking process persisted (Breznitz 2007, 100–125; author interview, Taipei, 6 January 2012). Since the early 1980s, VC policymaking was driven by a "few elite leaders and technocrats" crafting policies (GRIPS 2011, 6). The consistent management of VC policy over time stems from the shared responsibility of this policy by different ministries. This began with K. T. Li, who established VC policy in Taiwan and was not beholden to one specific ministry (as he was "minister without portfolio") when he designed the purposive actions.

Accordingly, Taiwan's VC policies did not change in step with the end of martial law in the late 1980s. The first substantive changes to Taiwan's VC regulations and taxation were only implemented in the early 2000s and as argued here, can best be understood as the result of political platforms driving the normative shift. The year 2000 was the first time Taiwan's challenger political party (the DPP) took office; they had run on a platform that promised to lessen the allocation of state resources to established industries. This political shift manifested into policymakers revising their constitutive and regulative norms in terms of how, and how much, they intervene in markets. Rather than promoters of specific industries, they would be more precise about which industries needed state support: "In 2000 all tax credits were discontinued by the DPP, except for R&D tax credits to really breakthrough technologies. They discontinued tax credits to industries that they deemed to be established and profitable—including the VC market's tax incentive. There are now only 20 percent tax credits for special R&D" (author interview, Taipei, 5 January 2012). The policy changes reflect the normative shock that occurred when the DPP won. Suddenly, the normative environment shifted in line with the DPP campaign—that established industries no longer needed overt support; only biotechnology and new pharmaceutical sectors qualified for government tax credit support. Policymakers came to see themselves as steady-state supporters rather than market builders for the venture capital sector.

In this way, the discontinuation of the VC tax credit should not be conceptualized either as the direct result of democratization nor the result of a political contest (e.g., not merely the fact that DPP won). Rather, the policy change was driven by a normative shift effected by a change in the policy platform of the government (from the KMT to the DPP), which affected policymakers' view of their identities and, accordingly, their appropriate means of intervening. They had a new role; they no longer felt it appropriate to offer tax credits to established industries, including the VC industry. With the DPP's win, the breadth of industries worthy of tax credits was reigned in. Although Taiwanese policymakers had long strived to use tax incentives to drive cutting-edge technological activity, this was the first time that the VC financing to support such activities was conceptualized as truly established. This focus on highly specific sectors has persisted; President Tsai, the second Taiwanese leader from the DPP, continues to preside over tax breaks aimed at specific technologies (Kuo and Han 2017).

Locally Aimed, Taxcentric Policies

Table 5.1 highlights Taiwanese policymakers' use of tax, regulatory, and funding policies in an effort to support local venture capitalists.

TABLE 5.1
Key dates in Taiwan's VC policies

Year	Policy developments
1981	K. T. Li and Li-Te Hsu, former finance ministers, along with a partner at Hambrecht & Quist (H&Q) and a partner at a Taiwanese law firm, took a VC study trip to the United States (Silicon Valley and Boston's Route 128) and Japan
1983	Issuance of Regulations for the Administration of Venture Capital Enterprises and the Project for Promoting Venture Capital Investment Enterprises, which gave a 20 percent tax deduction to first-time VC investors
1985	The Development Fund and Chiao Tung Bank provide NT$50 million and NT$30 million, respectively, to the First VC Investment Program
1991	The Development Fund and Chiao Tung Bank provide NT$ 1billion and NT$60 million, respectively, to the Second VC Investment Program
1998	The Development Fund appoints and funds the administration of the third VC Investment Program to the International Commercial Bank of China
2000	Venture capital investor tax credit discontinued shortly after DPP government elected
2001	Repeal of the Regulations for the Administration of Venture Capital Enterprises and introduction of the Scope and Guidance legislation
2001	Issuance of Regulations on the Scope and Guidance of Venture Capital Enterprises (hereafter referred to as the Scope); the Financial Holding Company Act in 2001 allowed financial holding companies to invest in venture capital

(Continued)

TABLE 5.1
(Continued)

Year	Policy developments
2001	Plans to strengthen the venture capital industry under the National Development Plan to be matched by the establishment of an NT$100 billion VC fund (NT$30 billion public and NT$70 billion private funding)
2004	Amendment of Regulations on the Scope and Guidance of Venture Capital Enterprises to expand funding channels and ease restrictions on investment scope and fund utilization
2004	The Development Fund is placed under direct jurisdiction of the Executive Yuan (Cabinet)
2004	Executive Yuan places venture capital industry guidance and assistance under jurisdiction of MoEA
2005	Scope revisions require venture capital funds with capital commitments from banks, insurance companies, securities firms, financial holding companies, or pension funds to apply to the IDB for approval
2006	Relaxed Scope makes it easier for investors to exit their positions by decreasing the required holding time of company securities and lifting the limit on share sales
2008	Challenge 2008 has the Development Fund investing NT$30 billion alongside NT$70 billion in VC
2012	Bilateral fund of VC funds (Strategic Cooperation on Joint Investments in Venture Capital Funds) formed with the Development Fund and the New Zealand Venture Investment Fund
2013	Launch of From IP to IPO program, running 2013–2017, which includes mentoring on venture capital negotiations by entrepreneurs and venture capitalists in Taiwan and Silicon Valley, to forty selected start-up teams each year
2014	Launch of HeadStart Taiwan, which includes the launch of a new NDF with US$400 million under management, investing in Taiwanese start-ups alongside international VCs (with matching 40 percent provision, as in previous NDF initiatives); Executive Yuan launched the Innovation and Startups Taskforce in December, to coordinate entrepreneurial capabilities across government agencies
2015	As part of the HeadStart program, the National Development Council (NDC) publicizes plans to coinvest alongside other investors in the following four funds: 500 Startups (US$500 million), AppWorks' fund (match 30 percent of LP contributions), Translink Capital III (match 30 percent of LP contributions), and invest US$30 million in a joint venture fund run by the Battelle Memorial Institute's 360ip and Taiwan's Industrial Technology Investment Corporation
2016	Striving to promote Taiwan's innovation and R&D activities and upgrade its start-up and entrepreneurship ecosystem, the NDC announced the launch of the Silicon Valley Asia Development Plan in September

Sources: GIO 1983; 1986; 1992; 1999; 2000; 2001; Yeh 2006; TVCA 2006; MoEA 2012; Executive Yuan Development Fund 2013; MoEA 2014; Horwitz 2015; MoST 2016; National Development Council 2016.

Local, Local, Local

Taiwanese policymakers argued that "every nation must respond to its own social background and economic conditions" (GIO 1983). This is precisely what policymakers did when studying and adapting VC policy. They learned about VC policies as a means of increasing the supply of capital and management expertise for Taiwan's early-stage, high-technology SMEs. VC was not conceptualized as a means of advancing their local financial sector's competitiveness as entrepôt Hong Kong did. Broad competitive pressures—unspecific to the financial sector—stimulated their desire to study ways in which the state could drive the performance of its technology-focused, export-led economy. Economic competitiveness was, after all, essential to the very survival of the (autonomous but politically isolated) Taiwanese state since the 1970s.

Motivated to promote VC to drive competitiveness, Taiwan's highest-ranking industrial policymakers organized a study trip to learn more about ways to support the financing of innovation and high-growth SMEs. Through the knowledge gained on their 1981 trip to the United States and Japan, elite policymakers, particularly K. T. Li, concluded that venture capital markets were needed in Taiwan. VC, they asserted, had been essential to the success of the Silicon Valley cluster and would also be critical to Taiwan's high-technology SMEs' competitiveness. Following their initial studies, policymakers evaluated policies aimed at developing a local, Silicon Valley–like VC market.[26]

However, their cost-benefit analysis did not find either the American or Japanese policies as optimal. Taiwanese VC policymakers felt that a foreign model could not provide a policy blueprint for how to create their local version of Silicon Valley. They valued industrial policy tools that were tried and tested in the local context. Their constitutive norms shaped their identities as being promoters of specific activities, and then from 2000, as supporters of steady-state activity. Policymakers' regulative norms dictated they should support *local* firms through *indirect* funds transfer. These logics of appropriateness resulted in Taiwan's early VC policy efforts adapting the Silicon Valley model toward locally applicable tax credits. The VC paper company structure was designed to fit local investors' preference for having control over investment decisions. The elite-driven policy process—across both the martial law and democratic eras—enabled the persistence of the taxcentric policies that fit policymakers' normatively determined optimality until 2000.

Then, policymakers' norms were updated away from intervening in established markets such as venture capital after the DPP took office. Policymakers no longer saw themselves as driving market development. They were overseeing established industries. In line with this normative shift, their regulative norms no longer deemed it appropriate to extend tax credits to the VC industry. As a result, in 2000 policymakers did away with the 20 percent tax credit for VC investors. Taiwan's VC policy choices through 2000 reflected their norms, particularly their long-held logic of appropriateness that they should promote local firms through the use of tax incentives and locally consistent regulatory structures. The DPP's election win in 2000 served as a critical juncture for the Taiwanese normative environment; policymakers quickly changed their view of their role and of the appropriate ways that they should intervene in the VC market.

If full Bayesian updating occurred, there would have been higher degrees of convergence on the Silicon Valley model. The Silicon Valley policy environment—it was concluded by K. T. Li and his contemporaries—had contributed to the region's success. If they were conventionally rational learners, they should have concluded that replicating the Silicon Valley model of the ERISA reinterpretation, the low capital gains tax rate, and the LP structure was the optimal way of supporting a local Silicon Valley–like market. If boundedly rational, policymakers would have been beholden to reproduce aspects of the American and Japanese models that they found as available and representative. Given the success of the American anchor in advancing the Silicon Valley VC cluster, boundedly rational scholars would have concluded that it would be optimal to design policies to be more United States–like than Japanese. Yet, they did not implement any aspect of the Silicon Valley VC policy model, and they altered what they valued in the Japanese model to better fit their local context. As a result, I argue that the contextual rationality approach best accounts for Taiwan's distinctly local, and tax credit–centric, VC policy formulation.

Singapore

Financier and Director

> You cannot replicate another Silicon Valley; Singapore had to do it our own way.
>
> —K. C. Low, creator and manager of Singapore's Technopreneurship Investment Fund

Singapore is one of the Asian Tigers and considered an economic miracle by many. The small Southeast Asian state transitioned from a "third world country to a first world nation" in one generation (Lee 2000). Gaining independence from Malaysia only in 1965, the Lion City (translation of *Singapura*, its Malay name), under the strong leadership of long-time prime minister Lee Kuan Yew and the People's Action Party (PAP), managed the incredible feat of building infrastructure, institutions, and an economy to a developed country level within fifty years.[1] The private sector, led by multinational corporations' local operations, played a role in this industrialization story, but the omnipresence of the government's supportive tentacles in the economy cannot be overstated. Policymakers picked winning sectors by "imaginatively discerning" which new technologies would be the next big thing (NUS Engineering Faculty 2012). Based on their visions of the future, the Economic Development Board (EDB) actively courted high-technology and financial services firms to establish their regional headquarters in Singapore (King 2006). Through these efforts Singapore became a top semiconductor manufacturer, the busiest port in the world, and a major financial center.[2] Policymakers have long believed this competitiveness is essential to the state's very security and survival (see Han et al. 2011).

As the chapter reveals, VC policy diffusion began in response to rising competitive pressures; venture capital would support local SMEs and further promote Singapore as a regional financial center. VC policies were pursued as part of the policymakers' bid to have vibrant technopreneurship activity and innovation levels (Carney and Zheng 2009). A domestic VC market would help address the "dearth of early stage funding" available to any would-be technopreneurs (author interview, Singapore, 12 September 2012). It was conceptualized as part of national efforts to increase local technology-sector entrepreneurial activity. High-ranking policymakers, such as the former chairman of the EDB (from 1975 to 1981), Ngiam Tong Dow, have said that VC would have a "crucial role to play" for SMEs and innovation to thrive in Singapore (Zhang 2011, 182).

With this catalyst for policy diffusion, this chapter explores how and why Singapore's VC policies mirror the industrial policy strategy its policymakers have pursued since the 1960s: courting international market leaders in order to build domestic expertise in an effort to be a preeminent hub in Asia. It will reveal how constitutive and regulative norms led policymakers to deploy the mammoth US$1 billion Technopreneurship Investment Fund (TIF) in 1999, a fund of VC funds to attract international venture capitalists and a second fund of VC funds, the Early Stage Venture Fund (ESVF), to capitalize Singapore-based VC managers (NRF 2008a). In line with the Singapore normative context, tax incentives were used to attract money from abroad; tax exemptions were given up to ten years as well as credits for investors' losses in start-up investments. Given their enduring aim to attract international capital and talent, policymakers also adopted the Silicon Valley–consistent LP structure and offered nontax incentives for investors in VC funds. One of the most notable nonfinancial incentives is the Global Investor Program (GIP) whereby foreign investors obtain permanent residency (PR) by investing over SGD$2.5 million in approved VC funds (EDB 2012).

Rising Competitive Pressures

Singaporean policymakers have long believed that economic competitiveness, stemming from its position as a manufacturing and financial services entrepôt, is essential to the state's survival. The Southeast Asian nation most acutely experienced rising competitive pressures vis-à-vis Taiwan as a regional technology competitor and Hong Kong as a financial center (author interview, Singapore, 20 September 2012). Policymakers have felt that they need to act in order for Singapore to maintain its manufacturing prowess (Han et al. 2011). Competitiveness is also purported—by policymakers—to depend on its ability to "attract top talent" (King 2006, 145). These pressures motivated policymakers to set out to learn about policies that could advance its technology and financial sector vibrancy (see, for example, ERC 2002; Tan et al. 2004, 1–2).

Policymakers' interest in supporting technology-sector SMEs began in the 1980s (Abeysinghe 2007, 4). The Lion City's reliance on multinational corporations (MNCs) was criticized as "quasi-industrialization" by influential Singaporean economists, such as Lim Chong Yah (Han et al. 2011, 140). In response to this critique, policymakers turned their attention to encouraging MNCs to do business with Singapore's SMEs. Singaporean policymakers said that its entrepreneurial ecosystem was inhibited by its limited talent pool, regulatory environment, insufficient funding, and a weak entrepreneurial culture.[3] To address these weaknesses, agencies such as the National Science and Technology Board (NSTB) and the National Research Foundation (NRF) implemented policies to grow start-up activity in an "if you build it, they will come" manner (author interview, Singapore, 19 September 2012).[4]

Local policymakers held that Singapore "will need a culture that encourages creativity and entrepreneurship, as well as an appetite for change and risk-taking" (Tan 1999, 9). The 1985 recession catalyzed the first widespread acknowledgement that Singapore's reliance on MNCs,[5] rather than promoting MNCs to better develop local SMEs, may have come at a cost (Doh 1996, 350–51; Randhawa and Tan 2009, 31).[6] Following the recession, committees and ministries began expounding on the "strategic" importance of SMEs (see, as an example of the output of such committees, the SME Master Plan in 1989) (Committee on Singapore's Competitiveness 1998, 8) and emphasizing the need for entrepreneurship (Bruton et al. 2002, 200). Policymakers sought to learn about policies that could support innovation, address unemployment issues, and develop a risk-taking culture. It was in this vein that they came to believe that a Silicon Valley–like VC industry would support SMEs by closing the "financing gap" that local SMEs faced (Randhawa and Tan 2009, 34–36).

With this motivation in mind, policymakers set out to learn about aspects of the Israeli, Silicon Valley, and Taiwanese VC policy models. Extensive learning is not unique to the VC policy area; Singaporean policymakers are often cited for their careful research of other countries' best practices. There are numerous examples of Singaporean policymakers studying foreign models: Israel's national military service and government incubator scheme for high-tech start-ups served as templates to learn from (author interview, Singapore, 19 September 2012); the U.S. National Research Council inspired the formation of Singapore's National Research Foundation; and the Singaporean state learned how to measure its policies' performance from Shell Corporation (Han et al. 2011).

In Singapore, policymaking is said to be powered by "a dedication to learning from international best practices and diligent implementation and documentation of plans and outputs" (GRIPS 2010). To facilitate their VC policy learning, policymakers conducted "study trips" and "constructed panels of international experts" for their input (author interview, Singapore, 13 September 2012). One senior policymaker even went so far as to live in Silicon Valley for two years to ensure that he fully grasped the model (author interview, Singapore, 12 September 2012). Their demonstrated ability to meticulously study international best practices helped them adapt VC policy models, such as Israel's Yozma Fund, to the Singaporean context rather than just copy them.[7]

Singaporean VC policymakers have not wanted to be "the first mouse to get the cheese because the first mouse dies, while the second mouse wins" (author interview, Singapore, 20 September 2012). By this, they mean that they do not want to take too great of a risk on a policy that has not already been proven—but by equal measure, they do not want to pursue a policy that is not a fit with the local context. So, they rigorously gather information on effective foreign models and scrutinize how they can "adapt the policies to recreate the same set of circumstances in Singapore" (author interview, Singapore, 12 September 2012). Policymakers ascertain "whether Singapore has the factors that contributed to [the model's] success and how we can replicate them" (author interview, Singapore, 20 September 2012). They acquire information that is valued in light of their regulative norms that hold it appropriate that they supply direct financing to attract (best in class) international firms.

Industrial policymaking in the Lion City has been characterized by its interventionist orientation, its policymakers' high levels of expertise, its concentration of policymaking and budgetary power, and its policymakers' "dogmatic" adherence to core norms (author interview, Singapore, 11 September 2012). Policymakers dance a delicate tango in which they direct resources and activity in nearly all segments of its economy while also simultaneously encouraging the private sector to operate freely. Their constitutive norms inform policymakers' identities as responsible for financing and directing private sector activity, being careful to not replace or crowd out the private sector. They see themselves as essential financiers of activity and are dedicated to meticulously designing the optimal strategies for their distinct local context.

In this light, policymakers studied the Silicon Valley, Israel, and Taiwan policy experiences—the countries with the highest amount of VC per capita at the time. Their interest in the Taiwanese policy model was initiated by high-level conversations between Taiwan's then minister without portfolio, K. T. Li, and Singapore's prime minister, Lee Kuan Yew, about supporting innovation clusters and VC industries (author interview, Taipei, 5 January 2012). Following these high-level discussions, Prime Minister Lee charged his policymakers with closely studying the Taiwanese programs in the early 1980s. Shortly thereafter, they created EDB Investments, essentially a VC fund (an adaptation of Taiwan's National Development Fund), which launched in

1991.[8] EDB Investments invested directly in start-ups—rather than only as matching funds as Taiwan's NDF did—with an aim to promote strategically important pillars in Singapore. Policymakers felt it appropriate to make direct investments, so altered the model accordingly.

Learning How to Build a Local Silicon Valley

By the mid-1990s Singaporean policymakers' overall objective was clear: to build a local version of the Silicon Valley and Taiwanese innovation clusters. Tony Tan set up a Ministerial Committee to conceive of, and oversee, the Technopreneurship 21 initiative (Ho et al. 2002, 336–341).[9] Technopreneurship 21 aimed to replicate the Silicon Valley and Taiwanese models by developing a robust ecosystem for technology-sector start-ups. The committee's explicit aim was precisely "to encourage entrepreneurs to commercialize technology to develop another Silicon Valley or Taiwan" (Tan 1999, 12). After establishing its goal, the Technopreneurship 21 committee members made numerous study trips to countries and clusters deemed to have succeeded in this regard, including the "US (over ten trips to Silicon Valley), Israel, Ireland, Scandinavian countries, Germany, and Switzerland" (author interview, Singapore, 12 September 2012). According to K.C. Low, who was the head of funding programs for the committee, and later the manager of the Techopreneurship Investment Fund (TIF), the aim of these study trips was to "distil the essence of what the countries have done right, and then adapt it to the Singaporean context." Going well beyond what can be learned in a study trip, Low lived in Silicon Valley in 1996 and 1997 to ensure he thoroughly understood the Silicon Valley model.

Low's comments offer a telling illustration of the impact of Singaporean policymakers' interventionist norms on how they study and evaluate a model:

> I spent two years based in Silicon Valley (1996–97) to make sure I really understood how Silicon Valley works. When speaking with members of the Silicon Valley community they repeatedly say that they want the government out, and that Silicon Valley is a product of private effort, not government help. But, Singapore is different, Silicon Valley evolved over a period of thirty to forty years, and the U.S. is a huge market, etc. *I knew that Singapore had to use different, more specific techniques* to advance its VC market. (author interview, Singapore, 12 September 2012, italics added)

As his statement shows, he felt that the drivers of Silicon Valley's VC market success were a confluence of factors over the course of forty years—rather than the product of the enabling LP structure or ERISA reinterpretation (author interview, Singapore, 12 September 2012). As such, the Silicon Valley policy model did not offer him a blueprint that could be replicated in Singapore. This insight reveals that even while learning about the Silicon Valley model with the explicit aim of achieving the same "end" in Singapore, he was thinking about how to adapt it to Singapore's more interventionist context through further studies.

Private sector financing norms led policymakers such as Low to assign high value to the Israeli model; through the provision of direct finance to a cohort of local investors the Israeli Office of Chief Scientist had succeeded in catapulting the rise of a thriving local VC market within five years. This approach was how Singaporean policymakers' felt they should intervene: encourage specific forms of private sector activity through all productive means available, especially through direct funding initiatives (Doh 1996, 348). Already in the 1960s the Singaporean state had become accustomed to directly supporting firms and to opening "its arms to embrace foreign capital to industrialize" (Yeung 2016, 7). The state's financial support—whether originating from domestic coffers or the redirection of international money—was seen as "a necessary catalyst for private investment" (author interview, Singapore, 12 September 2012). These norms are said to be the result of the positive performance of the approach; the state's "financial support for industry has worked thus far," so policymakers "continue to use similar strategies" as they design new industrial policies (author interview, Singapore, 20 September 2012).

Singaporean policymakers first became aware of the Israeli Yozma initiative because a subsidiary of the Singaporean sovereign wealth fund's venture capital arm, Temasek (Vertex Venture Holdings), was one of the original LPs to participate in the Yozma Fund (Avnimelech 2009). The Technopreneurship 21 committee policymakers conducted study trips to Israel to learn more about the Yozma Fund. As a result of these trips, and their subsequent communications with the Israeli Chief Scientist Office, the Technopreneurship Committee "learned from Israel how to bring the private sector in" so that the fund of VC funds initiative (the TIF) was "not just comprised of government money" (author interview, Singapore, 12 September 2012). Policymakers from the EDB and NRF conducted study trips to Israel as frequently as every two months, visiting the Office of the Chief Scientist and the Yozma management team (author interview, Singapore, 18 September 2012; author interview, Tel Aviv, 6 October 2013).

Inspired by what they learned of the Israeli model, the committee, led by Low for financing initiatives, designed Singapore's first fund of VC funds, the Technopreneurship Investment Fund (TIF). The TIF's role was "to develop the VC industry by investing in local and overseas funds, with the intent of accessing deal flows and attracting them and their investee companies to Singapore" (EDB 2002, 50). The aim of attracting foreign investors to the TIF was to "make strategic investments in leading venture capital firms around the world, to promote the formation of indigenous fund management firms, *encourage foreign venture capital firms to set up operations in Singapore,* and in the process catalyze knowledge transfer and network development through overseas portfolio funds" (Koh and Wong 2005, 14, italics added). In this way, "unlike the Israeli Yozma Fund that focused exclusively on supporting domestic VC managers, the larger TIF was designed to attract world class VC managers to Singapore" (author interview, Singapore, 12 September 2012). In line with these regulative norms informing their preference for supplying direct financing to attract international firms, the TIF invested only 25 percent of its resources into local VC managers (Wilkin 2004).[10]

To be sure, it was deemed appropriate to adapt the Yozma model such that the TIF actively courted "top-tier international venture capital firms to locate their regional operations in Singapore" (Koh and Wong 2005, 10). VC policymakers—through the TIF—worked to attract international VC managers to have regional headquarters in Singapore, as the EDB had done with MNCs over previous decades (Kenney et al. 2002, 119). The TIF design was an adaptation away from the Yozma model in line with policymakers' norms that favor the attraction of international firms. As evidence of this, the TIF manager said that "Yozma was different than the TIF as it was narrower in its focus. Yozma explicitly sought to build a domestic Israeli VC industry. The TIF had a broader mandate as it *sought to bring international VC managers into Singapore* and to establish local VC managers as well" (author interview, Singapore, 12 September 2012, italics added). The lion's share (75 percent) of TIF's capital went to international (particularly American) VC managers, due to this norm-derived preference for attracting international firms.

Also in 1999, as part of the Technopreneurship 21 initiative, policymakers deployed an adaptation of Taiwan's tax credit. They did not replicate Taiwan's 20 percent tax credit. Instead, they gave credits for losses incurred on start-up investments (EDB 2000). Policymakers had used industry-specific tax incentives since the 1959 Pioneer Industries Ordinance (Kwong et al. 2001, 27). In the 1998 budget the finance minister confirmed that tax exemptions for VC funds would be extended on a case-by-case basis for up to five years beyond the maximum of ten years (Monetary Authority of Singapore 1998, 21). In addition, Singapore-domiciled VC managers' profits were made eligible for a ten-year tax break (e.g., the tax holiday for pioneer industries) via the Venture Capital Incentive (Section 97) of the Economic Expansion Incentives (Relief from Income Tax) Act (Koh and Wong 2005, 12; Dietrich 2003, 50). The named inclusion of VC managers in the Relief from Income Tax Act came on the heels of an ERC report that outlined the case for VC-specific tax environment improvements. The report proposed the exemption of management fee income from Singaporean tax,[11] a streamline of PE/VC tax incentives into a single package, and the removal of a minimum fund size to qualify for incentives (ERC 2002).

Singaporean policymakers deployed tax incentives to help reduce VC investors' downside risk. The Standards, Productivity, and Innovation Board offered the Enterprise Investment Incentives Scheme for start-up investors, including VC managers. The scheme allowed venture capitalists to deduct up to SGD$3 million in losses incurred against their taxable income (Teng 2011, 35). In addition, the Technopreneurship Investment Incentive Scheme offered an allowance for tax deductions (up to 100 percent of equity invested) on losses from selling qualifying shares or liquidating investments in start-ups (Dietrich 2003, 50; Chia 2005, 27). Singaporean VC investor tax credits, though numerous and generous, do not include a tax credit for investors in the VC asset class as the Taiwanese VC tax policy did. Instead, investor credits are available for losses incurred, not for equity investments in, the VC asset class, as they were in Taiwan.

On the regulatory front, through the 1990s there was no LP structure available in Singapore. Policymakers felt that they already offered private companies, including VC management firms, an attractive regulatory environment via the private company limited structure (which is notated as Pte Ltd) (author interview, Singapore, 12 September 2012). The Pte Ltd is capital gains tax exempt, offers owners a separate entity so that liability for any debts or legal proceedings go in the company's name alone, limits investors' liabilities, and allows the issuance of new shares to new shareholders.[12] The LP structure was not deemed to be needed from an operational point of view, according to Technopreneurship 21 committee members. Their cost-benefit analysis of adopting an LP structure concluded that it was not necessary—it would constitute a significant amount of work to implement, and they felt they already offered a comparable structure.

The Dotcom Crash

The value of various policies was all about to change. Nearly simultaneous to the TIF's launch, the so-called Dotcom Crash kicked-in, and globally, technology companies' valuations spiraled downward. Investors retreated from investing in the high-technology sector, trying to recover from significant losses within a matter of months in the early 2000s. VC firms struggled to raise capital in Silicon Valley, just as in Singapore. Local policymakers urgently evaluated strategies that could help to resuscitate the availability of international capital for Singaporean VC managers.

At the launch of the TIF in 1999, its managers were not primarily focused on the government's financial return, for instance, getting its money back; they would measure performance based on advances in the industry's international stature, size, and professionalism (author interview, Singapore, 12 September 2012). The TIF's rapid distribution of capital conveyed a positive initial message about its potential to deliver on its objective. In 2000, a senior minister made the following comment about the TIF's contribution in its first year of operation: "More VC managers are coming to tap the huge pool of talent in the region. VC managers bring with them not only financial capability, but also management expertise and business network. The [US] $1 Billion Technopreneurship Investment Fund (TIF) launched by NSTB a year ago has greatly increased the presence of VC managers in Singapore" (Heerjee 2000). The 2002 Economic Review Committee (ERC) report echoed similarly positive comments, stating that the TIF achieved early success in attracting VC firms and fostering a technopreneurship community in Singapore (ERC 2002, vi). But as the difficult fundraising and exit environment deepened, and persisted, their assessment of the TIF's performance would sour.

It was in this context, in the initial wake of the Dotcom Crash, that in 2002 Singapore policymakers came to a different conclusion about the value of a structure similar in name, not only function, with the Silicon Valley model. In that year, Singapore adopted the LP structure as an effort to be "obviously familiar to international, especially American investors, by having a VC fund structure that is the same in name and in function" as the LP structure popular in Silicon Valley (author interview, Singapore, 17 September 2012). In the Dotcom Crash lens, the Technopreneurship 21 committee's cost-benefit assessment of the LP structure changed. Now their findings were that the regulatory environment for SME investments could be improved (author interview, Singapore, 12 September 2012) and the ERC report recommended its use (ERC 2002). Previously, the "close enough" legal structure was found to be sufficient. The sharp increase in the need to attract international investment swung the scales such that the same legal structure—by name—was found to be worth it. The LP structure was adopted to help attract international investors by being completely consistent with the Silicon Valley fund structure.

In the early 2000s, the US$1 billion TIF muddled along, as the global technology sector licked its wounds from the crash. The fund deployed its capital as it would, given that it was structured as a ten-year investment vehicle, but the measure by which its performance was viewed began to change. There was new leadership at the NSTB in 2004, which "became intent on financial returns and was less patient in waiting for the long-term development of a VC industry" (author interview, Singapore, 20 September 2012). As a result of the new metrics, the TIF's "first five years of operation were not found to have delivered its new financially-focused key performance indicators, so the TIF was wound down by the EDB" in 2005 (author interview, Singapore, 12 September 2012). The fund's "poor performance" was largely attributed to the timing of its launch on the eve of the Dotcom Crash in 2000 (author interview, Singapore, 20 September 2012). As a result of the poor timing as the key explanation of the disappointing performance, VC policymakers did not update their norms by, for instance, abandoning their preference for direct financing.

As the performance of the TIF was attributed to timing and not policy design, the TIF was not the last fund of VC funds initiative launched by the Singaporean government. NRF policymakers studied the Israeli fund of VC funds model (Yozma) again when conducting research on how to address a more specific gap in equity financing. This research was conducted under the umbrella of the National Innovation and Enterprise Framework for the Next Stage of Economic Growth in 2008. As part of these efforts a delegation led by the NRF chairman, Tony Tan, visited Israel with the intention of learning to better formulate Singapore's second fund of VC funds. Tan shared what the delegation learned about the Israeli Yozma Fund and its impact:

> In the early 1990s, the Office of the [Israeli] Chief Scientist also ensured that start-up companies have a fair chance of receiving venture capital funding at its early stage of growth. This was done by creating a number of early stage venture funds to invest in Israeli start-ups. In addition to providing this much needed source of funding, this program ultimately resulted in the development of a healthy venture capital industry in Israel. Israel's venture capital funds, unlike those in other countries, invest substantially in early stage Israeli start-ups and are now a US$1.4b industry. (NRF 2008b, 2)

Tan's 2008 statement demonstrates the value that he and his fellow NRF policymakers now saw in the Israeli model. He was interested in Yozma's ability to catalyze a VC industry that invested in early-stage companies, as this form of VC investment was lacking in Singapore and could complement Singapore's broader policy environment that encouraged international capital.

Following their studying of the Israeli model (again), in 2008, the NRF launched the Early-Stage Venture Fund (ESVF) to "catalyze the set-up of several early-stage venture capital funds" (NRF 2008b, 1). The ESVF was conceptualized as "a new version of an old idea—a new version of the TIF effectively—that is more focused on the domestic VC firms" (author interview, Singapore, 12 September 2012). Talk of a need for a local focus was evidenced several years before the ESVF's launch. The 2002 Financial Services Working Group Report argued that "the government . . . can do more by *complementing* the current strategy of attracting large international fund management companies with a strategy to develop indigenous start-ups and attracting small and medium-sized fund management companies" (ERC 2002, v). The ESVF was created to address the "lack of funding available to Singaporean start-ups at the Series A and B Rounds" (author interview, Singapore, 13 September 2012). In this way, the initial Early-Stage Venture Fund launch was motivated by policymakers' research on where local start-ups were "missing" access to capital in the early-stage financing landscape (author interview, Singapore, 12 September, 2012).

Even though it was structured to be similar to the Yozma model, the ESVF was deliberately adjusted away from the Israeli model. The Yozma Fund gave its private investors the opportunity to buy out their investment at cost, plus a nominal interest rate and a 7 percent share in future portfolio company profits. The ESVF, instead, offered a straightforward buyout at 1.25 times the NRF's initial investment. Further, in line with the persistent regulative norms informing a preference for attracting international firms, even the domestically designed ESVF money did not only go to local VC managers. While most of the VCs that participated in the first version of the ESVF—Bioveda Capital, Extream Ventures, New Asia Investments, Raffles Venture Partners—were local (Tegos 2015), the first batch of VCs also included a blue-chip international VC manager—Walden International (NRF 2016). The mostly domestic funds were required to invest in local start-ups to ensure impact on the Singaporean start-up ecosystem; they had to have matching private investment commitments of at least SGD$10 million from private investors.[13]

In September 2013 the ESVF terms were changed to encourage MNCs to participate, bringing even this smaller complementary program in line with policymakers' regulative norms that prioritize the soliciting of international firms. They changed the requirements to open participation to international VC managers, as this was "a formula that they were more comfortable with" (author interview, Singapore, 12 September 2012). Policymakers' regulative norms about the appropriateness of attracting international firms led, once again, to a fund of VC funds aiming to bring international firms to invest in local entrepreneurs—as the EDB had done since the early 1960s. The NRF made the change to yet again "attract more investment firms to set up in the country" (Lee 2013). In line with this aim, the participants in the second ESVF include internationally acclaimed VC managers, including Walden International (the American VC firm that was included in ESVF I) and Tembusu ICT fund (a Japanese VC manager).

Only in September 2015, did the ESVF, in its third installment, include local investors with the sole aim of investing in local start-ups. When the ESVF II was announced, deploying SGD$40 million to link large local enterprises with local start-ups through a corporate VC design, it had an explicitly local character (National Research Foundation 2015). It opened a call for Singaporean firms with "corporate venture funds" to "submit proposals on how to grow the local tech ecosystem" (Tegos 2015). The result of the call was the allocation of SGD$10 million each to the following Singaporean firms' corporate venture capital arms: CapitalLand Limited, DeClout Limited, Wilmar International Limited, and YCH Group Pte Ltd (NRF 2016). This iteration of ESVF is the first one that allocates to Singaporean-headquartered MNCs with the mandate of investing in local start-ups. In effect, rather than attracting capital from foreign-headquartered MNCs, the latest edition of the ESVF offers funding to Singaporean MNCs investing locally.

This local-local policy prescription is still conceptualized as part of a broader strategy of maintaining competitiveness as a destination for MNCs. Policymaking bodies, especially the NRF, with Low Teck Seng as CEO, conceptualized the collaborative advance of local firms as part of its broader efforts to attract MNCs in order to maintain international competitiveness. In an interview with *Asian Scientist* in 2016, Low explained that "being ranked highly on international lists helps EDB and NRF attract global technology companies to Singapore, where they will co-create intellectual property and contribute to the economy. [Singapore needs] deeply-rooted locals in leadership positions to complement the many foreign scientists who have come to develop their careers in Singapore" (Chan 2016).

Once again, the ESVF's matching funds for VC investments in local start-ups was conceptualized as a tool for advancing local firms' capability in order to attract MNCs and foreign talent. In a speech in 2016, Low explained that Singaporean firms had to innovate in order to compliment the partnerships with MNCs operating (oftentimes, regional headquarters) in the Lion City (Fai and Kek 2016). The ESVF's role in this effort—in its third iteration as launched in 2016—is to advance the ability of local firms to successfully manage corporate venture capital firms in order to attract MNCs.

A core component of the Silicon Valley regulatory framework, the ERISA reinterpretation, has not been offered in Singapore. Public pension funds, notably the Central Provident Fund in which all citizens must allocate for their retirement (and housing) savings, have not been allowed to invest in VC funds. Pension funds were—as in the other case studies—viewed as a key form of social protection, rather than as capital to be used to support risky asset classes. Instead of leveraging the public pension funding, policymakers deployed regulatory incentives to attract international retail investors to allocate to Singapore-based VC funds, rather than change local regulations that would allow citizens' pension savings to flow to VC investments. This regulatory incentive came in the form of the Monetary Authority of Singapore's Global Investor Program (GIP), launched in 2000 to increase the supply of international investment available for Singaporean VC funds. The GIP offers permanent residency status to foreigners who invest a minimum of SGD$2.5 million in approved Singapore-based VC funds. The GIP helped to raise capital for local VC funds; however, participants in the program are not necessarily good investors for the asset class.[14]

Table 6.1 details the key developments of Singapore's VC policies as discussed in this section, which include funding schemes, tax incentives, and a market-friendly regulatory framework focused on attracting international investment.

Formal Institutions and Norms

Singapore's politically insulated regime, policymaking processes, and concentration of budgetary power reinforced, and expressed, policymakers' constitutive

TABLE 6.1
Key dates in Singapore's VC policies

Year	Policy developments
1991	EDB Investments, a US$100 million government VC fund, was formed to make direct investments in high-growth start-ups
1996	Vertex Venture Holdings (a subsidiary of Temasek, the Singaporean SWF) launches its Vertex International Fund as one of the ten original Israeli Yozma Funds
1999	NSTB, EDB, and TIF Ventures coinvested with angels in the tech sector via the Business Angel Fund
1999	Technopreneurship Investment Fund (TIF), US$1 billion fund of VC funds, launched in April
1999	Technopreneur Investment Incentive Scheme—loss insurance for investors in high-tech start-ups
2002	Scope of the TIF broadened to attract all types of private equity fund managers (e.g., not just early-stage VC managers) to Singapore
2002	Endorsed the recommendation of the Company Legislation and Regulatory Framework Committee, which resulted in Singapore establishing the Silicon Valley-consistent LP structure
2005	TIF was wound down due to scrutiny of its financial performance
2008	The NRF launched the Early Stage Venture Fund (ESVF), by seeding four local VC managers, and one international VC, with SGD$10 million each, matching the private investor monies they raised
2013	ESVF buy-back is opened to international VC managers
2015	The National Framework for Innovation and Enterprise announced the third iteration of the Early-Stage Venture Fund
2016	Four large local enterprises selected as corporate venture capital partners for ESVF III's SGD$10 million each coinvestment in Singaporean start-ups
2017	The Intellectual Property Office of Singapore, along with a private equity firm (Makara Capital) announce launch of SGD$1 billion (US$718 million)

Sources: EDB 2000, 59; ERC 2002, v–vii; Koh and Koh 2002; Goh 2005; Chan 2006; National Research Foundation 2008a; 2008b; 2015; 2016; Califano et al. 2010; Lee 2013; Tegos 2015; Roman 2017.

and regulative norms. The concentration of budgetary power has been a particularly strong enabler of policymakers' norms in favor of financing private sector firms. Singaporean committees, agencies, and ministries responsible for VC policies were able to secure budget and distribute financing to support VC and technopreneurship with ease. Committees and special foundations, such as the Technopreneurship 21 Ministerial Committee and the NRF, were formed and led by high-ranking ministers who were given the authority to plan, fund, and implement VC policies.[15] When high-ranking policymaking champions, such as Tony Tan, were associated with the efforts, policymakers found it especially easy to secure financing (author interview, Singapore, 20 September 2012).

The ease of access to budget for Tan's Technopreneurship 21 committee members informed policymakers' norms when designing the TIF. For them, "concern over securing budget did not factor" into policy decisions (author interview, Singapore, 12 September 2012). They did not consider obtaining budget as a constraining factor in their policymaking process; if a policy initiative was deemed to be worthwhile, budget should be swiftly obtained (author interview, Singapore, 18 September 2012).[16] In light of this ease of budget access, policymakers adapted policy models, like Israel's US$100 million Yozma Fund, into even larger funds of VC funds, as they did with the US$1 billion TIF.

Policymakers have been politically insulated, which has contributed to their finance-laden logics of appropriateness.[17] Policymakers have made VC policy choices unilaterally, although the policymaking process officially included dialogues with the private sector. Government consultation with the private sector was merely a "public relations exercise" (author interview, Singapore, 5 September 2012). The carefully elicited and managed involvement of the private sector in the policymaking process reinforced policymakers' norms that they should "create and implement the policies [they] believe are best" rather than worry about whether or not to finance given activities (author interview, Singapore, 20 September 2012). VC policymakers learned from, but were not beholden to, "industry and academia, including BANSEA, SVCA, and NUS Entrepreneurship Centre" (Wong 2011, 11). The absence of politicization was briefly questioned following the 2011 election, as the PAP only received 60.14 percent of the votes (the lowest share of votes in the country's independence). But the strong 2015 PAP results (69.9 percent of votes, winning them 83 of 89 seats), shored up its strong position, and subsequently, concerns about increased politicization impinging on policymakers' regulative norms waned.

Finance to Attract International Venture Capitalists

Singaporean policymakers' adaptation of the Silicon Valley VC policy model can best be explained by the characteristics of their constitutive and regulative norms. Their constitutive norms envisage an identity in which policymakers provide necessary finance and direction for the market—without crowding out private activity. Following on from that identity, policymakers hold regulative norms that find direct financing and efforts aimed at attracting international firms appropriate. In light of these logics of appropriateness, Singapore launched two funds of VC funds, offered tax relief schemes for VC managers and investors, and adopted the LP structure and extended nonfinancial incentives for international VC investors.

In the face of rising competitive pressures in the 1990s, policymakers initiated efforts to learn about, and adapt, successful VC policy models. They conducted extensive research via study trips, particularly to learn about Israel's

Yozma Fund as well as the policy environments that had driven the success of the Silicon Valley and Taiwan clusters. The Silicon Valley model served as the inspiration; policymakers wanted to foster a cluster of professional venture capitalists. They valued the design of the Yozma Fund for its use of financing to catalyze private investment. While impressed by the effectiveness of the model, their cost-benefit assessment of the model reflected their feeling that the Israeli fund had been too focused on promoting domestic VC managers. Even though international financial institutions were required partners as investors in fledgling Israeli VC funds, policymakers adjusted the model so that the TIF gave 75 percent of its capital to foreign VC managers, whereas Yozma had attracted international capital for fledgling Israeli VC managers. Nearly ten years later, Singapore's second fund of VC funds, the ESVF, was a closer approximation to the Israel model as it focused on domestic venture capitalists—but it was still conceptualized as a complement to their larger international strategy.

Singaporean policymakers adapted everything they studied, to ensure better fit with their normative context. In fact, only the 2002 adoption of the Silicon Valley LP structure was copied intact. The adoption of the LP structure came in line with a spike in pressures to attract capital following the Dotcom Crash; their cost-benefit assessment changed from the late 1990s to the postcrash context of 2002. The LP structure was now conceptualized as worth adopting in order to have the exact same regulatory structure as that of the United States, not just in function (as the Pte Ltd had done) but also in name. In contrast to the level of specificity expectation, the more specific Yozma fund of VC funds and Taiwanese tax credit VC policy models were both adapted.

Bounded rationality would expect that Singaporean policymakers replicate the "anchor" models, which they found to be responsible for the success in the United States, Israel and Taiwan, more or less intact. Conventional rationality, in a similar way, would expect convergence on the policies that demonstrated effectiveness. So again, if we presumed that Singaporean VC policymakers were rational, their beliefs about the optimal policies would have been updated as the result of their meticulous studying, which found that the studied models were responsible for the growth of VC markets in Silicon Valley, Israel, and Taiwan. Instead, the empirical evidence reveals that Singapore's VC policies were adapted away from these models due to policymakers' adherence to their locally rooted norms that favor intervening by directly financing private sector activity, especially supporting international firms (rather than local).

Singapore's formal institutions reinforced its policymakers' norms by concentrating budgetary and policymaking power in their hands. The concentration of budgetary power enabled VC policymakers access to large sums of money, which reinforced their norms regarding financing to promote the constitution and ongoing competitiveness of internationally linked markets. The budget-laden initiatives were facilitated by insulation from public input, except for solicited expert opinions, into VC policymaking. Interviewees noted that if Singapore continues to have a more politicized environment, which briefly occurred in the 2011 election, policymakers' ability to swiftly deploy funding may erode, which could, in turn, lead to norm updating. Yet, the strong election result for the PAP in the 2015 election likely means that we will continue to see finance-intensive efforts to entice the participation of international investors.

7

Analyzing Sources of Adaptation

[A] mistake policymakers make is that they want to just replicate
the model, but they forget that it's a different time and in different
conditions.

—Yigal Elrich, former Israeli chief scientist
and manager of Yozma Group

Silicon Valley–inspired VC policies have diffused to at least forty-five countries. Despite policymakers' shared objective of creating a local Silicon Valley,
there is notable variance in the VC policies implemented across states, both
in terms of difference between the Silicon Valley model and each state's local
approach, and variation across the universe of policy adopters. Core aspects
of the Silicon Valley model were not taken up; none of the states replicated
the ERISA reinterpretation. The nonadoption of ERISA-like efforts comes
even though it is widely acknowledged that the relaxing of the Prudent Man
Rule's interpretation was a core enabler of the growth of Silicon Valley venture capital (Lerner 2009; Lazonick 2009). Rather than competing to offer
institutional investor-friendly regulations, many VC policymakers limit their
participation. They instead offer a myriad of tax credits and funds of VC
funds, which were not present in the source Silicon Valley model (the American policies included broad capital gains tax lowering and SBIC loans for
start-up investors, given as a lever of what they could raise privately). The
findings gleaned in the analytical narratives help explain why these varied
interventionist approaches—rather than convergence on the acclaimed
model—characterize the global VC policy diffusion trend. To aid this effort, this chapter analyzes how an understanding of learning as contextually

rational can best account for the decisions to implement adaptations of VC policies in Hong Kong, Taiwan, and Singapore.

The VC policies that have been implemented internationally are not copies of the U.S. policies. True, elements of the Silicon Valley VC policy model, namely, the limited partnership (LP) fund structure, diffused more or less intact to several states. However, the transmission of the limited partnership structure is one of the only VC policy elements deployed internationally that does resemble the Silicon Valley model. Numerous states restrict VC fundraising and exit options rather than embrace ERISA-like regulations that allow pension funds to invest in the VC asset class. For example, in Taiwan there are limits on the amount of money that insurance companies can contribute to a venture capital fund (in proportion to other investors), and regulations stipulate that investors have to receive specific consent in order to be eligible to invest in venture capital. Internationally, there have been indirect restrictions on VC activity through caps on foreign ownership of domestic firms, rules on when companies are eligible to list on a public exchange (e.g., five years of continuous profitability or a minimum market capitalization), and the sectors in which private companies can operate.

This chapter unpacks the implications of the findings presented in the analytical narratives of Hong Kong, Taiwan, and Singapore. It examines findings in light of the contextual rationality approach's expectations for how constitutive and regulative norms shape policy diffusion and policymaking. I will discuss state-of-the-art expectations, particularly their ability to account for the form and extent of variation. Diffusion scholarship's expectations are that the diffusion mechanisms and the studying of multiple models of varying levels of specificity can propel adaptation, and as a consequence, variation across adopting countries. I also compare the case findings in light of the expectations following from the bounded and conventional conceptualizations of rationality. I conclude that policymakers' norms—not the strength of the policy model's performance—are the compasses that point to the optimal route for each state's yellow brick road to Oz, which in this case, are policies aimed at building local Silicon Valley–like venture capital markets that propel entrepreneurship and innovation.

East Asian VC Policy Choices

Globally, and in East Asia in particular, there has not been a duplication of the Silicon Valley VC policy environment. The case studies reveal that the pattern of diversity amid convergence is primarily the result of the persistence of local norms informing VC policymaking. Policymakers implement policies that are locally appropriate in an effort to optimize their cost-benefit assessments. Table 7.1 highlights the VC policies undertaken by each state, illustrating the variety of policy paths taken within this cluster of similar states.

TABLE 7.1
Comparing VC policies

VC policies	Hong Kong	Taiwan	Singapore
Fund of VC funds	ARF II gave four private VC managers approximately US$100 million to invest in 1998	No national fund of VC funds; a bilateral fund of VC funds was launched with New Zealand in 2012[1]	US$1 billion fund of VC funds launched in 1999 to invest in foreign VCs, and a domestically focused US$100 million fund, giving matching funds for local investment
Tax	VC subject to general low corporate tax rate of 15 percent until an offshore fund tax exemption in 2005	20 percent tax credit initiated in 1983; extended to corporations in 1991; discontinued in 2000	0 percent tax for pioneer industries; in 2002, VC-specific tax exemptions and tax credit for start-up investment losses
Regulation: legal structure	Use of established LP structure; China enacted VC regulations in 2005	Paper company structure, rather than the LP structure	Private company limited (Pte Ltd) used until the LP structure was adopted in 2002
Regulation: incentives and restrictions	Pension funds are not allowed to invest in nonpublicly traded assets, including VC	Investor type maximums; variety of institutional investors not allowed to invest in VC	GIP offers Singaporean permanent residency for foreigners investing in VC; pension funds not allowed to invest in VC

[1] Beginning in 1985, the National Development Fund began investing via matching funds. Then in the 2000s the Development Fund also started offering coinvestments alongside VC managers.

The following paragraphs explore the sources of the VC policies summarized in table 7.1 on a "row by row" basis. They detail the drivers of adaptation according to each policy arena—that is, explaining outcomes across funding, taxation, and regulation.

Funding

Each of the three cases pursued some form of a fund of VC funds, but for different reasons and in different forms. Hong Kong was the first state to launch a fund of VC funds in 1998. Shortly thereafter, but in a fundamentally distinct form, Singaporean policymakers deployed their Technopreneurship Investment Fund in 1999. Taiwan only much later (in 2012), and as part of a bilateral trade initiative, was party to a fund of VC funds structure that offered matching funds alongside private investment capital. Why did each state deploy a fund of VC funds, and why in such different forms? Instructive to the broader narrative, each state's policymakers found that their form of giving capital to private VC managers was an "appropriate" way of advancing the local VC market. But their constitutive and regulative norms are quite different, and as a result, their funds of VC funds took varied forms. The following paragraphs explore the distinct normative contexts that shaped these varied fund of funds' efforts.

Hong Kong, the first state to launch a fund of VC funds, followed its constitutive and regulative norms, which valued indirect financing. Constitutive norms informed the identity of Hong Kong policymakers as protectors of the positive nonintervention approach, and then regulative norms held that it was optimal to provide indirect financing to international firms. Their poor experience managing the ARF—in which they directly invested a small amount of money—reinforced their normative position that it was not appropriate for the state to make direct investments in firms. In light of their regulative norms that they should not finance firms directly, policymakers found it optimal to entrust private, professional investors with the responsibility of choosing which firms were worthy of VC investment. Based on this determination, Hong Kong's ITC policymakers designed the ARF II so that it endowed four international VC managers with an attractive management fee in exchange for investing US$100 million in local start-ups. They viewed the fund of funds structure as a way of *not* investing directly in start-ups; it was consistent with norms that held that policymakers should enable market activity through the indirect allocation of funding to international firms.

The next fund of VC funds launch was Singapore's TIF. Singaporean policymakers' norms, in contrast to those in Hong Kong, held that direct government funding to leading international firms was the appropriate means for supporting the private sector. They strove, with the initiation of TIF, to bring a world-class VC cohort to Singapore by acting as an anchor investor. The constitutive norm of the financier and director identity encouraged their central role in driving market activity. In effect, once VC policy was on the agenda, they wanted to act decisively. How they would do that was determined by their regulative norms, which long held that it was appropriate to directly provide funding to entice international firms to set up local operations. The TIF succeeded in bringing VC managers to Singapore but was considered a financial failure by 2004. The financial failure of the TIF was not blamed on the design of the direct financing initiative; instead, the poor performance was blamed on its timing on the eve of the Dotcom Crash.

Singaporean policymakers, still holding norms that financing is appropriate, studied how to design another fund to act as a domestic complement to the broader international strategy. With these considerations, the ESVF was designed to plug holes in the availability of early-stage risk capital. But a domestic fund of VC funds did not fit with policymakers' norms that they should solicit international firms, and so an international VC was included in its first iteration. By its second iteration, the ESVF structure again reflected entrenched regulative norms: it solicited international VCs to invest in local start-ups. Even in the third wave of investment, the ESVF was articulated as an effort to promote large local enterprises investing into local start-ups with the express aim of making Singapore more attractive to international firms.

Taiwan was the last case study to launch a fund of VC funds. Taiwanese policymakers, true to their private sector financing norm, did not invoke direct financing to promote the VC market. They only came to be party in a fund of VC funds in 2012 through the provision of matching funds in a bilateral fund of VC funds with New Zealand. Policymakers' norms held that they should avoid the direct allocation of funding to private firms; if they were to provide funding, since the mid-1980s, it was deemed optimal that it is done when firms demonstrate that they can raise private money. In providing matching funds, they have felt they are reinforcing private investment decisions, rather than making investment decisions themselves. What's more, the bilateral fund of VC funds has been conceptualized as a tool for promoting trade across New Zealand and Taiwan, not in propping up a specific cohort of venture capitalists. In this way, it is another avenue for supporting local start-ups with private investors taking the lead.

As the foregoing paragraphs illustrate, the East Asian funds of VC funds proved to be a "means" by which policymakers strive to reach different "ends." The fund of VC funds tool was deemed the appropriate path in order to attract an international cohort of venture capitalists in Singapore, to reduce the state's onus in "picking winners" in Hong Kong, and to drive bilateral activity through the provision of matching funds in Taiwan. In line with the varied objectives, the fund of VC funds structures—the means—took markedly varied forms. Fund sizes ranged from US$100 million to US$1 billion. The first fund was launched in 1998 in Hong Kong, the second in 1999 in Singapore, and the last country to act was Taiwan in 2012. The funds of VC funds differed in their eligibility requirements. Eligible participants ranged from fledgling domestic venture capitalists (Singapore's ESVF); to established venture capitalists (Taiwan's bilateral fund with New Zealand); to marquee, international VC firms (Hong Kong's ARF II and Singapore's TIF). Funds also varied the incentive structures offered to participating VC managers, ranging from modest to high management fees, and differences on whether the participating venture capitalists could buy out the government's position. Variations in size, time of launch, eligibility of participants, and incentive structures are only some of the differences, but they alone demonstrate the variety of means pursued within this one VC policy instrument. These differences align with each state's distinct normative context, which guided policymakers' cost-benefit analyses.

Tax

Table 7.1's second row, VC tax policies, reflects variance across the timing (ranging from 1983 to 2005 for first VC-specific tax policy action) and means (e.g., tax credit or lower tax rate). They also vary in terms of their intended end. Tax policies were valued for their purported ability to improve the risk profile for local investors (Taiwan) or to compete against other localities by offering ever-attractive tax rates (Hong Kong and Singapore). Taiwan acted in 1983 by offering a tax credit that policymakers contended was the optimal means for increasing local venture capitalists' participation. For them, the appropriate way to improve private actors' profitability and lower their risk was to deploy a 20 percent tax credit, as they had previously, and effectively, done for the ICT sector. It was not until two decades later that Hong Kong and Singapore came to deem the use of tax policy levers as a valuable tool for promoting venture capital. In their evaluation of policy tools, policymakers in both Singapore and Hong Kong concluded that it was optimal to use a different means than Taiwan's tax credit. They valued tax policies that would help them attract international investors, not improve the risk-reward considerations of local investors. Acting in line with the regulative norms that valued international firm support, in 2002 and 2005, Singapore and Hong Kong, respectively, implemented tax exemptions for venture capitalists, in order to improve the attractiveness of their locality to international VC managers.

This points to the finding that differences in tax policy design primarily stem from differences in regulative norms informing the international versus domestic firm support. *Taiwanese* policymakers held that it is appropriate to design tax advantages for *local* investors, while *Hong Kong* and *Singaporean* policymakers' norms value efforts to attract *international* capital. In line with their prioritization of reducing local investors' risk, Taiwanese policymakers designed a tax credit that limited the exposure that local investors took—not only improving the profit margin as the Hong Kong and Singaporean tax approaches did. As a result of their international firm orientation, policymakers in Hong Kong and Singapore offered discounted tax rates to attract capital. For Hong Kong policymakers, tax exemptions fit their aversion to financing private sector activity directly, but represented a compromise in light of their broad tradition of horizontally low tax rates. They only came to find a tax exemption valuable in the face of strong competitive pressures vis-à-vis Singapore and China in the early 2000s. Singaporean policymakers conceptualized the tax exemption means as another appropriate way to promote Singapore as a destination for international venture capitalists, in addition to their funding initiatives and regulatory incentives. It was another tool to compete with the offerings of other locales, not instead of the financing they would continue to provide.

Regulation

The LP structure—the legal structure that is extensively used by Silicon Valley venture capitalists—is available in two out of the three cases: Hong Kong and Singapore. While the fact that two out of three of the case studies used the LP structure may suggest widespread adoption, the LP structure was only adopted as part of VC policy efforts in one state: Singapore. Hong Kong was a longstanding holder of the LP structure given its British colonial roots (the Limited Partnership Act of 1907); policymakers did not adopt the LP structure as part of state efforts to promote VC. For Singapore, the LP structure was adopted expressly as means of mirroring the Silicon Valley VC model. Singapore's local legal structure (the private company limited) offered the same apparatus, operationally, for investors. In the 1990s, policymakers felt they did not need to adopt the LP simply in order to have a structure that had the same name. But, following a dearth of VC activity in the wake of the Dotcom Crash, cost-benefit calculations placed a higher premium on efforts to attract international capital. In this context, the costs of adopting the LP structure—an exact replica, in name and operation—were now outweighed by the potential benefit of attracting international investors (especially American investors).

Decidedly inward-looking (in terms of capital raising) Taiwanese policymakers did not, as one would expect, adopt the LP structure. Instead, they felt it appropriate to design a legal environment that pleased local investors, by addressing concerns about control and risk. They designed the paper company structure because it suppressed the managerial power of venture capitalists in investment decision-making processes. Taiwanese policymakers' regulative norms held that they should reduce the risks faced by domestic sources of capital in order to promote local venture capitalists. As local investors were skittish about investing in the high-risk asset class, policymakers viewed the paper company as the ideal legal structure, as the holder of capital—not the investment manager—retained power over investment decisions. As an interviewee explained, Taiwanese policymakers learned about the LP structure but reversed the positions of LPs and general partners in order to adapt venture capital in a way they deemed optimal for the local context.

Finally, case studies varied in the regulatory incentives and restrictions offered and imposed. In the Singaporean case, policymakers valued policy tools that would attract international investment. As a means of increasing the number of investors, they designed the Global Investor Program (GIP), which offered Permanent Residency status for foreign, high-net-worth individuals who invested more than US$ 1 million in Singaporean venture capital funds. The GIP was designed in line with policymakers' regulative norms that suppose it appropriate for the state to attract money from abroad.

Policymakers in each case maintained restrictions on the domestic sources of funding for the venture capital market. The 1979 change to the ERISA interpretation by the U.S. Department of Labor—which changed the definition of "prudent" to enable pension fund managers to invest in venture capital—enabled a transformational flow of pension fund assets into the Silicon Valley venture capital market. Though East Asian policymakers were aware of the significant impact the ERISA reinterpretation had in availing private money for venture capital, similar regulations were not implemented in any of the cases. Policymakers in each context shirked from changes that would funnel public pension monies toward venture capital. They formulated means by which the state provided capital (e.g., Singapore's hefty fund of VC funds), attracted international money (Hong Kong and Singapore's tax and regulatory efforts) or derisked venture capital investments for local, private companies (e.g., Taiwan's tax credit).

The reluctance of East Asian policymakers to allow pension funds to invest in the VC market stems from the strict social protection purpose of these funds. Pension funds are seen as a key instrument of life savings, rather than conceptualized as a critical source of capital for investment (Pai 2006). The paternalistic role of the state—think of Singapore's Central Provident Fund—in ensuring that citizens have retirement funds precluded the use of life savings as a source of funding for propping up the VC asset class. Such public pension funds give citizens a fixed return; their funds are not exposed to high-risk asset classes or employed for economic objectives (Asher 1999). Instead of leveraging pension fund assets, policymakers contended that it was appropriate that (such high-risk) capital come from private companies' profits (this was true in Taiwan from the 1980s and was recently adopted in the third iteration of the ESVF in Singapore) or foreigners (either foreign VC managers and their LPs in Hong Kong and Singapore's funds of VC funds, or foreign high-net-worth investors via Singapore's GIP).

Contextually Rational, Rather than Boundedly or Conventionally Rational, Learning

Scholarship in which rationality is conceptualized as bounded expects that learning leads to convergence, as policymakers only deviate superficially from the policy models (of leaders and peers) that they study. Advocates of conventionally rational learning similarly expect convergence on an optimal version of the studied policy model. The contextual depiction of rationality, as developed in this book, expects diffusion to result in the deployment of policies that are distinct from the model and from one another; rigorous studying is based in a normative context, so determinations of policy value are context specific.

The contextual rationality framework contends that the value of a model's evidence is not viewed in some acontextual or objective realm; it is essential to know the normative environment within which policy information is evaluated in order to know the value assigned to it. Policymakers did not replicate the anchors of the leaders or peers whose policies they studied. Nor did they pursue optimal policies according to some acontextual or ahistorical evaluation. Policymakers in each state designed policies that were distinct, and optimal, according to their own constitutive and regulative norms.

Their constitutive norms informed how they valued models in light of the extent of state intervention. Regulative norms informed rational processes of valuing the form of intervention. This informed policy design such that an acceptable means of financing (direct or indirect) of (foreign or domestic) firms was deployed to promote a Silicon Valley–like end. By investigating normative context, the contextual rationality approach expected norms to lead policymakers to pursue VC policy strategies distinct from one another and from Silicon Valley. The centrality of context-specific norms in steering VC policy diffusion processes supports the sociological underpinnings of this approach, and concomitantly, supports the pleas of scholars such as Lenschow et al. (2005) and Yeo and Painter (2011) that domestic-level analysis is needed in diffusion research.

The study revealed that policymakers' access to information is full; they do not merely access superficial information. The Singaporean case serves as a particularly poignant example. A key VC policymaker (the creator and manager of Singapore's US$1 billion fund of VC funds, the TIF) wanted to ensure that he fully understood the Silicon Valley VC policy environment. He lived in Silicon Valley for two years (1996–97) to make certain he did. He concluded, as a result of his extensive studies, that the Silicon Valley environment left too much to market forces. This, he explained, would not work in Singapore—the government needed to play a more prominent role as U.S. policies worked for the U.S. context but would need to be adapted to fit Singapore.[1] His accessing of information is best understood as "full" or complete: he acquired knowledge on the design, interworkings, and performance of the policy model. But he then concluded that the highly regarded model was not optimal for his local context.

Policymakers' view of the U.S. model as neoliberal—despite intimate familiarity with the various regulatory, tax, and funding components—speaks to the strength of the narrative that Silicon Valley VC is the result of market forces. Even those policymakers who understood that purposive action contributed to the industry's rise concluded that it was ultimately market forces, not the overt policy levers to attract capital (via the ERISA reinterpretation) and promote greater profitability (through the capital gains tax rate change and the launch of NASDAQ), that explain its success. Their conclusion that Silicon Valley's ephemeral success is the result of market forces supports the argumentation of recent scholarship that the United States succeeds in projecting a neoliberal persona while delivering strategic thrust (see, for example, Wade 2016 and Block 2008).

The Role of Norms in Policy Diffusion

The first norm investigated—the interventionist orientation identity, a constitutive norm—had a large influence on acquiring and valuing information in the VC policy learning process. Interventionist orientations determined which VC policies were studied subsequent to the Silicon Valley model. For example, when Singaporean policymakers learned about the Silicon Valley VC policy model they set out to study policy models closer to their identity as policymakers that play a central role in driving private activity. This led them to learn about Yozma, the Israeli fund of VC funds, which was attractive given their norms that it is best to direct public funding as a means of promoting foreign firms to set up operations locally. In a similar way, Taiwanese policymakers, led by their constitutive norms that favored policies in which they promoted local investment activity, studied Japan's regulatory structure as an alternative to the strong manager role that the LP structure inferred. Hong Kong policymakers' constitutive norms posited that they are meant to intervene to support innovation activities. But as they saw themselves practicing positive nonintervention they set out to learn about policy tools that encouraged, but did not direct, activity. This depiction of a sequence of choices in a rational learning process—rather than the "all alternatives are evaluated before a choice is made"—is consistent with the behavioral model of rational choice (Simon 1955, 110).

Private sector financing norms—one of policymakers' regulative norms examined in the study—shaped how policymakers valued policies that directed financing to firms. The cases reflect a low to high spectrum in terms of the extent to which private sector financing norms deem direct funding of private sector activity appropriate: Hong Kong exhibits a propensity to utilize indirect financing, Taiwan indirect, and Singapore direct. Hong Kong and Singapore serve as extreme examples of the phenomenon. Feeling the limits of laissez-faire in supporting innovation, Hong Kong policymakers tried to manage a modest amount of VC money themselves via the ARF. However, after a few years of feeling uncomfortable with managing the investments themselves, they considered alternative strategies that they would find more appropriate. It was in this context that ITC policymakers, in 1998, evaluated a structure that put the investment decision making in the hands of private investors. This calculation prompted them to hire four established, international VC managers to invest the ARF II money on their behalf. Hong Kong's fund of VC funds (the ARF II) was conceptualized as an appropriate means for reducing the extent to which the government had to directly finance firms, rather than policymakers' attempt to choose fledgling VC managers to form an initial VC cohort.

When funds of VC funds have been deployed, typically the government's investment in the fund of VC funds, not the lucrative management fee, was the reward. In contrast to this practice, Hong Kong policymakers' norm-based valuation of the fund led to their decision to have the ARF II pay a 3 to 4 percent management fee to the VC managers as well as a share of the profits. Their policy evaluation concluded that it was optimal to pay a premium for professional investment management to ensure that they were not choosing investments directly. The Singaporean funds paid industry-standard management fees, and in light of their design to incentivize performance, offered attractive performance fees and the option for the venture capitalists to buy out the government stake. In the TIF and ESVF, policymakers specifically choose the VC firms they thought would best succeed on building out Singapore's venture capital market and designed incentive structures to match. They were not paying a fee to outsource investment decisions; they were investing in the VC managers with the greatest potential of achieving outstanding performance.

Only one of the case studies—Singapore—had regulative norms pointing toward the use of direct funding, but all three case studies deployed funds of VC funds. Funds of VC funds were even pursued in the two cases—Hong Kong and Taiwan—where private sector financing norms did not favor direct financing. This outcome was driven by how the funds were conceptualized as achieving distinct ends by policymakers. As mentioned above, for Hong Kong, the fund of VC funds' structure represented a means whereby policymakers no longer had to choose which start-ups to invest in. By creating a fund of VC funds, rather than continue with the direct management of the ARF VC fund, they outsourced the "picking winners" responsibility to the hired VC fund managers. In the Taiwanese case, the funding scheme came onto the policy agenda as a means of supporting trade, not as a driver of a venture capital market in Taiwan. It was designed to fit the matching funds approach that they were comfortable with since (at least) 1985. In sum, while indirect or direct financing norms did not inform a binary "yes or no" decision of whether or not to deploy a fund of VC funds, the norm was instructive in shaping the form that the fund took.

Then, policymakers' regulative norms informing whether they support local or international firms had a significant impact on the design of VC policies. Their inclination toward supporting local, or attracting international, firms affected the design of VC regulations, nonfinancial incentives, tax treatments, and funds of VC fund designs. As an illustration, Hong Kong's international firm-inclined norms motivated its policymakers to ensure an internationally consistent tax environment. They valued policy tools that brought consistency with international investor practices, including a competitive tax regime. In stark contrast, in Taiwan, policymakers' focus on local firms led to their valuing policies that promoted local investment in VC. This motivated their use of a heterodox paper company structure and tax credit only relevant to local investors. In Singapore, policymakers were clear that it was most appropriate to design policies that would attract international venture capital money and talent. This translated into their first adaptation of the Yozma model (the TIF) such that it allocated 75 percent of its funding to international VC managers who set up operations in Singapore (whereas the Israeli model channeled money from international investors to local venture capitalists). In addition, Singaporean policymakers created the GIP (which offered permanent residency in exchange for VC investment) to attract international VC investors, adopted the internationally attractive LP structure, and adjusted the terms of their second fund of VC funds (the ESVF, which was originally designed to support local VC managers) to encourage international investment.

In the two cases where policymakers' regulative norms prioritized the support of international firms (Hong Kong and Singapore), each VC policy strategy fostered international participation across regulatory, tax, and funding elements. Locally focused Taiwanese policymakers deployed policies that explicitly promoted local venture capitalists through locally appropriate tax credits and regulatory tools. Taiwanese policymakers deployed regulations and tax credits so that local, successful high-technology firms (e.g., Acer and TSMC) could finance the growth of local high-technology SMEs. Unlike Hong Kong and Singapore, in Taiwan the VC industry was seen as a means to support its local high-technology SMEs, not as a means of attracting international capital or broadening its competitive position as a financial hub. As a result of regulative norms prioritizing domestic over international firms, it is unsurprising that the Taiwan's regulatory environment for VC (the paper company structure and restrictions on investors) is the most inconsistent with the Silicon Valley VC policy model (the LP structure and ERISA reinterpretation to broaden the investor base).

Norm Continuity and Change

Normative shifts primarily occurred in response to particular moments of heightened competition or in major political shifts, which acted as critical junctures, leading policymakers to question their existing conceptualization of self in terms of their intervention in market building and the appropriate ways in which they intervene. The most marked constitutive shift was not a radical one; it was one whereby Hong Kong policymakers who once felt that the words *industrial policy* would make their stomachs "curl up inside," as famously declared by the last governor of Hong Kong, came to see themselves as active supporters—but not directors—of innovation activities. Rising competitive pressures and the East Asian financial crisis weakened the cohesiveness of their normative context. Positive nonintervention was still their aim, but it was increasingly understood to include more overt intervention in the name of supporting innovation.

This constitutive norm shift was only accompanied by a modest update to regulative norms. Policymakers had long had to ask for LegCo approval—but that was the equivalent of getting a rubber stamp before the 1997 handover. From 1997, policymakers met significant scrutiny when presenting their budget requests to the LegCo. The acute political scrutiny involved in budgetary requests reaffirmed their regulative norms that indirect finance was appropriate. Though policymakers updated their constitutive norms so that they saw themselves as supporters of innovation, their regulative norms still placed a preference on indirect financing and international firms. They did not want to be the object of public critiques—and so minimized the extent to which they had to seek LegCo approval by continuing to ask for little funding. The role of the state to which they identified was, after all, just one of supporting innovation through positive nonintervention, still not directly investing in firms.

In Taiwan, the election of the long-time opposition party, the DPP in 2000, resulted in movement toward a new identity for policymakers; rather than being developmental state supporters of new markets, policymakers began seeing themselves as supporters of steady-state markets. Regulative norms still held indirect financing to be appropriate, but even the tax credits that had been construed as the optimal form of indirect financing all of a sudden seemed too overt. From 2000, sector-specific tax credits became "too much" for established sectors, including venture capital. Even though Taiwan's martial law ended in 1987, policymakers only underwent a normative shift away from intervening in markets when the first non-KMT political party took power. Only when the DPP took power did policymakers come to increasingly see themselves as having a less hands-on role in supporting established markets. This normative position crystalized quickly; policymakers would only support nascent sectors, not those already functioning. As a result, policymakers implemented the discontinuation of the VC industry tax credit by 2000.

Questions remain as to what would happen in Singapore if the PAP loses its stronghold on political leadership. Increased public scrutiny can inhibit policymakers' norms with respect to the appropriateness of private sector financing activity. It is, of course, difficult and problematic to try to predict the future. Instead, this book relays the sentiment that several interviewees expressed: that further advances in political accountability—construed as the PAP losing its dominant share of votes—could result in a normative shift away from the use of government funding. Singapore's political environment appears to have stabilized, with the PAP having a strong result in the 2015 election. Norms may not be updated as much as interviewees expected in the run-up to the election. In the case of stable political environments, I do not expect downward pressure on interventionist norms unless the performance of the economy falters. As long as economic performance seems to justify the finance-laden, international firm-prioritizing approach, and the PAP maintains a firm grasp on power, policymakers will retain their identities as financier and director. This follows as many of the forty-five states that have launched funds of VC funds are democratic. Steady-state democracy and funds of VC funds are clearly not incompatible. A sudden change to budgetary power or policy approval, or significant political leadership shift, can act as a critical juncture, creating a window for a change in policymakers' norms, but regime change and changes in party leadership do not themselves necessarily catalyze norm contestation.

The ease with which policymakers could secure sign-off, and budget, for policies had a particularly strong impact on reinforcing direct financing norms. In cases where policymaking processes endowed budgetary authority to the policymaking bodies, as in the case of Singapore, the policymaking process enabled the ease of budgetary discretion directly to firms. Policymakers in the Singaporean context did not have to wait for an external party to decide how or when they could deploy money, which reinforced their normative position that it is appropriate to allocate funding directly to private firms. They effectively only had to ask their manager if they could get budget for a project. As a result, when the Technopreneurship 21 committee decided to create a fund of VC funds in 1999, and the NRF chose to introduce a second fund of VC funds in 2008, policymakers launched these (sizeable) funds with ease. In contrast, in cases where policymakers had to seek external approval for funding—as in Hong Kong—norms reflected a preference for indirect financing.

What State-of-the-Art Diffusion Scholarship Expected, and What Actually Happened

This section thematically analyzes the case study findings in light of what state-of-the-art diffusion scholarship expects. It evaluates the ways in which the existence of multiple VC policy models (e.g., more than just the Silicon Valley model), and models of varying levels of specificity (e.g., Silicon Valley's broad policy environment versus Israel's highly-specific fund of VC funds model), impacted VC policy choices. In doing so, it offers an assessment of the extent to which diffusion mechanism expectations can account for patterns of diversity amidst convergence. The overall conclusion is that expectations that focus on properties of the diffusion model (e.g., specificity and the number of models) and the mechanisms (e.g., competition) are too blunt of an instrument for explaining the complex reality of policy diffusion. These expectations overlook the domestic arena within which policy information is valued, and as a result, struggle to account for the form and extent of variation.

Diffusion Models

The Silicon Valley venture capital policy model is the source model. It was held as the policy model to learn from and also held as policymakers' ultimate aim. Policymakers also studied the experiences of other countries, including Taiwan, Israel, and Japan. They were empowered to choose and adapt elements of the multiple successful policy models, knowing that there was not only one specific formula that works. Thus they concluded it appropriate to combine and adapt their own versions of the aspects they valued in the Silicon Valley model, as well as elements from Japan, Israel, and Taiwan. This led to a cherry-picking mentality, where policymakers chose to deploy adaptations of various means from the models they studied. They did not feel compelled to re-create one model in its entirety. This finding dovetails with Falkner and Gupta's (2009) argument that only limited degrees of convergence are likely when multiple policy models exist. In effect, given their normatively rooted cost-benefit analyses, policymakers chose the most appropriate aspects from the policies they studied. This two-part adaptation drove divergence across the cluster as different elements were selected as appropriate by each state—and even those most relevant elements were adapted differently. As an illustration, Taiwanese policymakers were empowered to use a heterodox paper company structure because of their simultaneous studying of the American and Japanese VC legal structures. The multiple model thesis does not, however, explain why Taiwanese policymakers then went on to make investor-friendly modifications to the Japanese corporate structure model in order to make their own.

Another expectation emanating from state-of-the-art diffusion literature is that more or less convergence occurs when policy models are more or less specific, respectively (Weyland 2006). Policy models that are more specific, for instance, a blueprint, are expected to lead to higher degrees of convergence. In contrast, vague policy models should lead to lower degrees of convergence. In applying this to VC policy diffusion, the Israeli VC policy innovation (the Yozma Fund) and Taiwanese tax credit—both specific policies—should result in more convergence because they offer blueprints that do not require interpretation. On the other hand, the vague Silicon Valley policy environment (that constituted a mix of regulatory and tax conditions, as well as leverage financing via the SBIC program) should propel less convergence. Policymakers should, according to the policy-specificity logic, interpret the Silicon Valley model to include different aspects, and as a result, come to different conclusions about how to design their local policies.

The policy models' various levels of specificity did not have such a straightforward impact. The highly specific policies were not transmitted intact into any of the East Asian environments. When the specific fund of VC funds and tax credit policy models were transmitted into policy action, only the core designs of those models were kept. When the Israeli fund of VC funds was studied (in Singapore), policymakers deployed a fund of VC funds. However, they made substantial adaptations to the size, mix of participants, and funding terms. Singaporean VC policymakers, exceedingly well versed on the Yozma model, did not copy the Israeli blueprint that they acknowledged as being the catalyst for the Israeli VC market's growth. Instead of their interpretation of the model driving their adaptation, they changed the intentions of the fund away from investing in promising domestic VC managers toward soliciting top international VC managers. Policymakers knew that the Israeli fund invested in fledgling local VCs, but they felt it would be optimal for their local version to attract foreign managers. As such, the TIF allocated 75 percent of the funds to foreign VC managers. The skeleton of the Yozma fund of VC funds was reproduced, but the meat of the model (e.g., the size, terms, and participant mix) was significantly altered. If the transmission of the Yozma Fund were the equivalent of a *Star Trek* "beaming up" of Captain Kirk, it would be as if a man were in fact transported, but Kirk's physique, facial features, and voice had changed. Thus, the highly specific Yozma model was not immune to adaptation in the diffusion process simply because it was specific.

The less specific Silicon Valley VC policy environment—as expected—did not stay intact as it diffused. Core components of the Silicon Valley policy model (capital gains tax treatment, the LP fund structure, the SBIC program, and the ERISA regulation) saw little local uptake: capital gains tax rates were not universally lowered, the LP structure was only purposely adopted in one case, and the ERISA-like legislation was not adopted in any of the cases. These regulatory tools were not transmitted into local policies as East Asian policymakers came to one (or more) of three conclusions in their evaluation of the model. Their different interpretations of what the vague model constitutes was not the primary driver.

First, Silicon Valley VC was the result of a historically unique confluence of factors. Because of the role of contingency, policymakers who studied the Silicon Valley model felt that they needed to explore how other states did it. Interviewees commented that if the Silicon Valley VC policy model had been more of a blueprint, they would not have studied the other policies as much. But, as it was, they felt compelled to study the role of policy in other contexts. They conceded that simply replicating the regulatory context and tax treatment that contributed to the phenomenon would not be a sufficient means of achieving their goal of reaching the same end point: a vibrant VC cluster. The Silicon Valley model had also been affected by the U.S. national security complex, immigration, and other factors over a number of years. Israel's Yozma fund, in contrast, was a specific policy tool that catapulted the growth of the local VC industry, on top of favorable trends such as an influx of Russian immigrants with engineering talent and a series of Israeli companies listing on NASDAQ, among other factors.[2]

The second conclusion was that the Silicon Valley regulatory and tax environment, even if it was responsible for the success, was too different from their normative context. Though scholars have acknowledged the Silicon Valley model as interventionist, the perception of the American policymaking context remained one of a hands-off state, and Silicon Valley VC the product of market forces rather than punctuated policy efforts. Policymakers consistently concluded that the U.S. policies were implemented in the name of neoliberalism, and as such, normatively distanced from their local values. This led to their desire to seek out information on alternative policy models that were more interventionist in name and intent. Again, it was not the value nature of the model that drove adaptation, but, in this case, lack of normative value assigned to the market-led path.

A third conclusion was that formal institutional contexts were too different for the American policies to work as mere transplants. Formal institutions in East Asia, particularly legal structures and tax regimes based in colonial Japanese heritage in the case of Taiwan, contrasted with Anglo-American contexts. The LP structure did not provide the same advantages in all markets as it did for American investors. In Taiwan, the capital gains tax rate would have been higher than what the corporate tax rate, and related subsidies, offered early-stage investors in high-technology SMEs. Thus, the LP structure, a core component of the Silicon Valley model, was not advantageous given the formal institutional environment in Taiwan. This mismatch was extenuated by the differing position of Taiwanese policymakers' constitutive and regulative norms vis-à-vis that of the American environment.

Diffusion Mechanisms

Scholarship on the impact of diffusion mechanisms generated the following expectations: emulation, coercion, and competition would lead to high degrees of convergence on the internationally revered Silicon Valley VC policy environment, whereas learning—when conceptualized as conventionally or boundedly rational—would lead to only modest changes to the most proven policy model. The study did not find evidence of coercion and emulation mechanisms. The absence of emulation is particularly interesting in light of policymakers' rhetoric about wanting to replicate the Silicon Valley VC cluster. The absence of emulation supports the case for fully informed learning; policymakers conduct rigorous studies based on their local normative context, rather than pursue knee-jerk imitation. Coercion did not occur, as VC policy elements were not required by an international organization or strong state. Policymakers in each state chose to study potential VC policy tools on their own volition, not at the behest of any external party. Given the absence of copycat policymaking, and pressure from other states or institutions, this section does not further discuss the coercion and emulation mechanisms.

Evidence of the competition mechanism was found to be a motivator of VC policy diffusion in all three cases. Competition pressures were especially strong for policymakers in the context of the global ICT sector (especially for Taiwan) and in maintaining world trading post and financial center positions (particularly Hong Kong and Singapore). In contrast to its expected consequences, competition did not drive convergence on neoliberal policy choices. Instead of propelling the Silicon Valley policy environment, competitive pressures motivated policymakers to consider alternative policy options. This led to their study of the Japanese, Taiwanese, and Israeli policy models, which offered blueprints of other interventionist approaches, and for them to evaluate local policy experiences as instructive for VC policymaking.

As an illustration, Taiwan's policymakers learned about VC policy in response to competitive pressures to attract international capital (quite urgently in light of the pressures stemming from their U.N. derecognition). It was in this context that Taiwan's VC policy diffusion began in 1981, by way of a study trip to the Silicon Valley, Boston's Route 128, and Japan. By studying foreign policy models, policymakers in all three states created veritable menus of policy options that they could consider and adapt for their local context. From the outset of their VC policy efforts, and then in subsequent years, they designed policies that were inspired by various models, domestic experience, and judged to be locally appropriate. As a result, they choose to concede tax revenue (Taiwan) or invest public funds across VC funds (Hong Kong and Singapore) in varying ways. Competition catalyzed learning that produced marked adaptation in all three cases; policymakers, as a result of their contextually rational learning, went well beyond cosmetic changes to the Silicon Valley model.

The expectation that competition would drive convergence on the highly successful American model stems from the globalization thesis. The volume and velocity of capital flows, according to the globalization thesis, corner policymakers into offering similar, low-tax, regulatory-friendly environments. In the VC policy arena, competition should handcuff policymakers into opting for VC policies that closely resemble the Silicon Valley's enabling regulatory and horizontally low-tax environment, not the use of funding (à la SBIC-types of programs). In contrast to these expectations, competition, even in the case of neoliberal Hong Kong, did not result in replicas of the Silicon Valley policy environment, let alone in the pursuit of neoliberal strategies.

Rather, competition drove even Hong Kong's self-proclaimed neoliberal policymakers to learn about more overt VC policy strategies, such as VC-specific tax exemptions. In Singapore's case, its policymakers repeatedly commented that they felt increasing competition vis-à-vis Hong Kong and China in their bid to be the premier financial center in East Asia. Acting in response to these pressures, and in line with policymakers' norms, Singaporean policymakers learned about VC policy options by studying Silicon Valley primarily, but also Israel and Taiwan. They studied the Israeli Yozma Fund as a model for how to use public funding to attract foreign venture capital managers. Across the three cases, competitive pressures motivated and justified the studying of additional policy models, rather than propelling policymakers to respond by replicating only the market-enabling components of the Silicon Valley model. Competition was the catalyst for learning how to intervene, not a propeller of convergence on a supposed orthodoxy.

The competition mechanism expects convergence in one particular policy area: taxes. The expectation is that there would be a similar reduction in tax rates. Instead of merely lowering the tax rate on VC profits (as the original U.S. model did), numerous VC policymakers (including those in Taiwan and Singapore) chose to give sector-specific tax credits to VC investors or to exempt tax payments for the VC sector (as Hong Kong did). Taken together, VC policymakers chose different tax rates for VC managers' profits—zero, capital gains tax level, or corporate tax rates—and various tax credits. The use of VC-specific tax exemptions and credits is not consistent with the American reduction of the capital gains tax rate. Through a tax incentive tailored for VC investments, the state promotes sector-specific activity. The capital gains tax rate applies to the profits earned by any type of investor when they sell an asset, whether it be a house, stock, or company that they have held for more than one year. Thus, one of the core elements of the Silicon Valley model that the globalization thesis expected to drive convergence was adapted differently in each case. This finding undermines the explanatory power of the globalization thesis. It suggests, instead, the persistence of policymakers' abilities to choose distinct policy paths.

States' pursuit of distinct, interventionist strategies coincided with heightened global competitive pressures in the 1990s. This is heralded as a time of globalization, a supposed "retreat of the state" (Strange 1996), a supposed "decline of the developmental state" in East Asia (Yeung 2016; Hundt 2014; Fields 2012) and the advance of the "golden straitjacket" (Friedman 1999). It is characterized as an era in which neoliberalism, as promulgated by the Washington Consensus, was at its zenith (Williamson 2004). In effect, market forces and policy consensus seemed to align against a role of the state in the economy. In this very context, interventionist VC policy choices proliferated. The desire to foster venture capital, a quintessentially neoliberal construct, led to the proliferation of more, and different, purposive actions. In a Polanyian way, the strict adherence to the market model coincided with expanding intervention by the state in the market. Vogel (1998) similarly found in the realm of liberalization, in a bid to support free markets, there was more state action. The state enabled the *international growth* of the venture capital market in order to compete in the increasingly interconnected and high-technology global economy, and above all, to be more innovative. The globalization pressures that policymakers felt fueled different forms of the "competition state" (Cerny 2007) rather than a retreat of the state, or turn to a mere "regulative" or "neoliberal" state. The venture capital state is a form of the competition state, as the state has an enhanced role as an economic actor—one that directly finances winners and constitute markets—rather than getting out of the way of market forces. Policymakers, in this bid to promote innovation-centric activities, retained their "room to move" (phrase borrowed from Layna Mosley's 2000 article) in venture capital in an age of globalization.

Policymakers' ability to choose distinct forms of VC tax policy should not be construed as a clear triumph of state power over markets. VC tax policies—be it tax credits, lower rates, or exemptions—all represent different forms of policymakers' reduced taxation of the VC industry. Although they retain their ability to choose a distinct form, policymakers are choosing among various ways to concede their tax proceeds. They either reduce tax rates for a broad category of investment or give tax credits to VC investors. In this sense, VC policymakers respond to competitive pressures by studying different ways in which they can minimize, rather than increase, their tax revenue from VC activity.

Only in one case—Taiwan—did policymakers implement what was effectively an increased tax on the VC sector. When the 20 percent credit for investments in Taiwanese high-technology start-ups was repealed in 2000, venture capitalists' tax liabilities increased. Even in this instance, the tax rate was not ratcheted up—policymakers simply took away a credit. This suggests that VC policymakers can choose to discontinue sector-specific tax incentives. In the context of globalization pressures in restricting policy choice, this one instance of discontinuation occurred in the case in which policymakers' norms confer a preference on local firms, not in attracting international capital. Taiwanese policymakers are not designing VC tax policy in order to please international investors. This suggests that globalization pressures bore a greater impact on states that prioritized the attracting of international firms. In this way, norms affect the extent to which competitive pressures restrict policy choices.

State-of-the-Art Diffusion Scholarship's Functionalist Accounts for Diversity

Some diffusion scholars expect that differences in relevant economic structures or levels of development can explain diffusion outcomes (see, for example, Swank 2008; Lenschow et al. 2005). As a result of the mutual dependence that technology start-ups and venture capitalists have on each other, in the VC policy area the functionalist economic structure expectation would be that the number of high-growth ICT start-ups constitutes the demand for VC markets (Avnimelech and Teubal 2006). Technology start-ups are a favored area for VC investors, since technology-focused firms are capable of delivering disruptive products and services, and in so doing, building high-growth, high-value companies (Klingler-Vidra et al. 2016). Similarly, technology start-ups rely on VC managers for early-stage funding. Without positive cash flows or collateral, banks do not give credit, and other types of investors lack the operational expertise and networks to help high-technology start-ups grow (OECD 2007; Lerner et al. 2014). So, levels of ICT start-up activity—and changes in those levels—could be expected to affect policymakers' interest in learning about VC policies.

The results of this study find that economic structures, specifically high-technology SME activity levels, did not affect policy directly, nor did it appear to impact policymakers' norms. Technology start-up activity levels, and the ability of local start-ups to access financing, did not prompt policymakers to initiate venture capital policy diffusion. Policymakers instead viewed venture capital as a catalyst for high-technology SME activity; they studied VC as a means of driving competitiveness in financial and technology sectors. VC policy diffusion first occurred in the state with high initial SME activity levels (Taiwan), as a vibrant local VC market was construed as the solution to local firms' funding needs. In states with low initial SME activity levels, however, it was not a rise of SME activity levels that instigated VC policy diffusion. Rather, policymakers in these states (Hong Kong and Singapore) became interested in VC markets in light of broader competitive pressures. They held that VC would help promote innovative SME activity, which would foster further economic development and diversification away from financial services.

Also in contrast to domestic functionalist explanations of VC policy diffusion, the financial sector's relative balance of bank and capital market activity did not affect policy diffusion. This nonevent reflects venture capital's ability to transcend conceptualization as only a bank or capital market component (see Klingler-Vidra 2016 on venture capital as "patient capital"). It also stems from the increasingly comprehensive nature of East Asia's financial sectors (Rethel 2010; Walter and Zhang 2012).[3] In Hong Kong and Singapore, bank and capital market activities have been vibrant, with the two sectors even being close to parity (in terms of asset and equity values). In these entrepôt states, the VC industry is positioned as another financial services offering, rather than exclusively bank- or capital-market related. As a result, norms did not dictate they should support only equity or credit financing for private sector firms. For example, in Taiwan, though banks dominated the financial sector's provision of financing to SMEs through the 1990s, the bank dominance did not diminish regulative norms that it was appropriate to support equity-based financing of private sector firms through tax credits. Instead, the lack of bank financing for SMEs was so bleak that policymakers were compelled to support equity-based venture capital markets as an alternative solution for local SME funding.

Explanatory Power of Contextual Rationality and State-of-the-Art Diffusion Scholarship

This chapter examined the findings of the book's analytical narratives on East Asian VC policy diffusion. State-of-the-art diffusion scholarship's expectations were examined in light of the case study findings. Broadly, diffusion's existing analytical tools fell short in their ability to account for the extent and form of variety characterizing VC policy diffusion. In contrast to the expectation that the competition mechanism would drive convergence, competitive pressures prompted vigorous studying, which resulted in adaptation and variety away from the Silicon Valley VC policy model. The existence of multiple policy models affected policy choices. The existence of multiple policy models did contribute to the limited degrees of convergence on the Silicon Valley VC policy model. But the multiple models do not account for the forms of adaptation at the onset of each country's VC policy efforts. What's more, policy diffusion is often not a single event; initial policy information diffuses, and policy action is taken, but it does not stop there as the local government then revisits the source for more, and updated, information, and iterates varying versions of policies over time. There is presumed to be a "dynamic adjustment over a sequence of choices" rather than a onetime policy decision (Simon 1955, 112).

Diffusion scholarship offers explanations that fall short in their ability to account for the form and extent of diversity that characterizes VC policy diffusion. There is some evidence that the existence of multiple VC policy models contributed to varied adaptions of VC policy instruments. Policymakers were empowered to pursue a "cherry-picking" strategy of selecting aspects of various countries' VC policy strategies. The specificity of the different models, particularly the vague nature of the Silicon Valley VC policy environment and the highly specific nature of the other models, did not produce the expected effects. The specific models (e.g., Israel's Yozma Fund) were altered in each case, while the only policy element that was translated intact was one aspect of the vague Silicon Valley VC environment (the LP structure in Singapore). Taken together, the model's specificity does not necessarily determine the extent to which more or less convergence occurs. Specificity of the models is not able to account for *how* models are adapted differently.

The diffusion mechanism expectations produced a similar result. Competitive pressures acted as a catalyst for learning rather than a downward pressure toward convergence on an orthodox, for instance, Silicon Valley–like, approach. Learning processes then drove policymakers to study additional models, and then adapt those models as the result of cost-benefit analysis in line with their norms. Overall, the diffusion scholarship expectations offer a meat clever rather than a scalpel for investigating precisely how policy diffusion takes shape in adopting states. The expectations help explain the existence of variety in some ways, but not the form of variety. They place too much emphasis on what is being diffused, and not enough analytical space for accounting for the environments in which information diffuses.

Policy information does not simply diffuse into a receiving space or a "black box"; rather, policymakers' normative contexts inform the acquisition of policy information and the value it is assigned. The restrictive pressure that market forces are said to have over policymakers' choice sets—in pushing them toward "orthodox" approaches, thereby reducing the role of the state—did not feature in VC policy diffusion. As Polanyi rightly asserted, the free market is embedded in the social system of the modern bureaucratic state, even in the avowedly neoliberal states such as Hong Kong and the United States. Competitive pressures empower norm-guided learning; they do not override policymakers' norms about how they should act to achieve the desire policy aim.

Conventional rationality and bounded rationality both expected convergence on the "anchor" Silicon Valley model, for the reasons identified above. For conventional rationality, an assessment of the optimal strategy would lead to the updating of beliefs, such that policymakers would copy the highly effective Silicon Valley model. The bounded rationality approach, on the other hand, would expect imitations of leader and peer policies as cognitive biases limit policymakers' ability to adapt the anchor policy model. Both of these varieties of rationality miss the cause of variety. They can account for which policies are studied, but are less adept at accounting for the particular forms of policies designed as the result of policy diffusion.

The process by which policymakers study a successful external model is neither conventionally rational nor boundedly rational. Policymakers do not conduct detached cost-benefit analyses of a large number of policy models, in which the preferred policy is the one that is "objectively" most efficient. They neither evaluate models nor design policy in line with a utility-maximizing assessment that is devoid of normative context. Similarly, policymakers are not boundedly rational; they are not beholden to cognitive shortcuts that anchor them to closely replicate the means pursued by leaders or peers.

This book's contextual rationality approach offers an alternative. It stipulates that constitutive norms underlie policymakers' identities. According to their identities, policymakers hold context-specific logics of appropriateness, or regulative norms. These regulative norms inform cost-benefit analyses such that policymakers come to different valuations, even of highly effective models; the highest valuations go to policies that are deemed appropriate for their local context, not those that seem to best replicate what was successfully implemented elsewhere. As a result of this norm-driven evaluation, policymakers subsequent design of adaptations reflects their locale-specific preferences; they are, in effect, "anchored" by their local logics of appropriateness, not the promise of a foreign model because of the strength or consistency of its performance. Thus, only by examining the role of policymakers' norms in the international diffusion process can we understand why states necessarily choose to pursue different yellow brick roads in order to reach the same Oz.

The Future of Venture Capital States

Distinct Interventions to Build Markets

Partners at most VC firms invest in businesses they think will become viable, or at least worthy of an acquisition, in the shortest time possible. . . . That doesn't leave much appetite among VCs for start-ups working on ambitious, long-shot projects.
—Christopher Mims, "Humanity's Last Great Hope: Venture Capitalists"

Governments can pick the VC management firms that are capable of forming an initial cohort of venture capitalists. Rather than wait for would-be venture capitalists to avail themselves, states have helped to constitute markets by choosing and supporting initial market participants. In fact, more than being capable, this book argues that government intervention has been essential to the development of venture capital clusters internationally. Even the supposedly neoliberal genesis of the VC market in Silicon Valley was the result of VC policymakers going beyond the offering of an enabling regulatory and tax structure. In the American policy landscape, in which Silicon Valley VC activity flourished, government investment and direction instigated private market activity. The road to creating and sustaining Silicon Valley venture capital activity is paved with interventionist tools in the name of supporting free market innovation and entrepreneurship. As VC diffuses internationally, states design distinct purposive actions.

This is not the first political economy study to find that state involvement underlies the facilitation of free markets. At multiple points this book has evoked the work of Karl Polanyi, who famously asserted that intervention enabled the existence, and persistence, of the market. For Polanyi (2001, 147) "the introduction of free markets, far from doing away with the need for control, regulation, and intervention, enormously increased their range." Steven Vogel (1998) found that deregulation in Britain and Japan in the 1980s and 1990s was underscored by more rules. As the title of Vogel's book aptly captured, with "freer markets" came "more rules." Especially pertinent to this study's focus on venture capital, Weiss (2014) revealed that American policymakers were behind "America Inc." in the high-technology sector, in the name of national security. Doug Fuller and contributors to his edited volume (2010) on "the limits of laissez-faire" explained how the desire to support innovation motivated policymakers in Hong Kong, the world's "most free economy," to step up their intervention. In this book's exploration of venture capital policy diffusion, the same themes are at play: more state involvement, not less, has propelled the global spread of a supposedly archetypal manifestation of laissez-faire: venture capital.

The overarching aim of VC policy diffusion is the fostering of local hubs of innovation-centric entrepreneurial activity along the lines of the Silicon Valley high-technology cluster. Innovation and entrepreneurship, which have become synonymous with Silicon Valley, are hoped to propel economic competitiveness and job creation. Public strategies for promoting innovation-rich entrepreneurship range from headline-grabbing programs, such as StartUp Chile,[1] to long-term investments in educational systems, including the British government's introduction of computer programming into the national curriculum in 2014 for seven-year-old pupils. As a result of numerous locales trying their hand at promoting Schumpeterian versions of innovation-rich entrepreneurial activity, there exists a veritable public venture policy menu. The menu consists of instruments across eight categories: (1) instituting regulatory changes and incentives, (2) offering tax credits, (3) appropriating government funding (including funding for R&D, grants, equity investments), (4) constructing infrastructure investments (e.g., Korea's super-high-speed broadband), (5) building clusters, networks, and institutes (e.g., Taiwan's Hsinchu Park), (6) attracting talent and investment, (7) extending stock market access for start-up, and (8) improving the education and training environment (e.g., national curriculum changes or the creation of high-technology universities, such as ShanghaiTech) (Klingler-Vidra 2014b). Venture capital policy, the focus of this book, constitutes a subset of this menu: policies (regulations, tax, or funding) deployed with the explicit aim of increasing local venture capital markets, both in terms of personnel and financial resources.

States across a remarkable range of geography, culture, regime type, and size have implemented variations and combinations of venture capital-focused policies. In fact, all forty-five countries studied here—all OECD, G-20, and Asian Tiger countries—deployed their own version of VC policy. This book revealed why, in contrast to the transcendent exuberance about being more Silicon Valley–like, policymakers do not replicate the policy environment within which Silicon Valley VC emerged. It uncovered why even states of similar population and economic sizes, that are geographically and culturally proximate and at comparable levels of industrialization, implement VC policies that are different from one another and distinct from the Silicon Valley model. As has been argued here, learning is driven by policymakers' normative setting, and this leads to these individual, and overt, adaptations of the model. Policymakers intervene in distinct ways in the name of promoting the innovation and entrepreneurship activities that the free market is meant to bring through its own internal mechanisms.

The Visible Hand of the Venture Capital State

Governments' notorious inability to pick winning companies was, for a long time, an unquestioned truism.[2] However, there is an increasing awareness that states can support firms and sectors effectively. Weiss (2014) reveals that it is the U.S. national security state behind the American technology sector's prowess. Mazzucato (2013) demonstrates that many of the technologies that we hold to be the product of private risk-taking and ingenuity, such as the iPhone, are actually the result of public selection and investment. Rather than the mantra that "governments can't pick winners," governments are increasingly seen as—and in many ways, are expected to be—facilitators of local (high-tech) entrepreneurial activity. The expected role of governments around the world is, over time, increasingly more akin to the developmental state role as epitomized by the Japanese MITI and less like the laissez-faire approach (historically) associated with the United States.

Policymakers now sit at the intersection of two opposing realities: that they shouldn't be too heavy-handed in promoting private activity, and that they must act to support local innovation and entrepreneurship. Embracing this new reality, in 2013 the UK government's Tech City initiative launched the Future Fifty program, which selects the country's fifty most promising "growth-stage UK-based digital companies" and helps to accelerate their growth (Tech City UK 2015). Going a step further, the British Business Bank was created by the UK government in 2014, with the remit of investing £1 billion into local SMEs. The "hidden developmental state," as Fred Block (2008) labeled U.S. efforts, appears to be more and more publicly visible in countries around the world.

While governments are joining the innovation and entrepreneurship support bandwagon, there is evidence to suggest that, in fact, governments cannot effectively support winning aspects of entrepreneurial ecosystems. Recent research suggests that there is a negative relationship between public subsidy and entrepreneurship, as public investments in entrepreneurship stifle precisely the same activities that they aim to encourage (Islam 2015). Public entrepreneur funding schemes have mixed records; some are said to "crowd-in" private investment, while others have the unintended effect of crowding-out private investors (Afonso and St. Aubyn 2008). Venture policy efforts often fail to produce the desired results due to issues of "poor design decisions" and "top-down" approaches (Lerner 2009, 135).

VC policies, in particular, fail as they do not fit with the way local ICT firms access finance and with the capital needs of the ICT sector (Klingler-Vidra et al. 2016). Policy design issues include failure to fit programs with legal contexts (e.g., Malaysia and New Zealand); inadvertently fostering dependence on continuing subsidies (e.g., Finland); funds being too large or too small (e.g., American state VC funds are too small and Canada's Labor Fund Program in the 1990s was too big); insufficient flexibility (e.g., initial stipulations of the American SBIR program); and not listening to the private sector (Lerner 2009, 80–92). Insufficient understanding of the needs of venture capitalists and start-ups has led to a waste of government money and attention on venture capital in numerous states. Yet policy failure analyses point to improper design, rather than too much state involvement.

Despite this checkered policy performance, this book argues that successful VC market development has, more often than not, been the product of overt policy action. VC industries—including that in the United States—have flourished *because* the state has been hands-on in directing funding and giving specific incentives to venture capitalists. In contrast to the truism that governments can't pick winners, policymakers have been essential to establishing initial cohorts of venture capital managers in each of the most vibrant clusters of VC activity. Though under the guise of neoliberalism and national security, U.S. regulatory, tax, and funding efforts are acknowledged as ways that the state intervened to establish and help grow the supposed neoliberal triumph of Silicon Valley VC (see Lazonick 2009).

In the global cases of VC industry success, venture capital clusters grew precipitously because policymakers did more than respond to market failures: they identified a new market to create and invested, through funding, tax relief, and regulatory changes, to jumpstart local venture capital activity. Taiwan's VC industry—which was a world leader in per capita VC activity up to 2000—is claimed to be the world's most successfully engineered VC market (Gulinello 2005). China's early advances in venture capital activity stemmed entirely from government investment (Liu 2015), and public funding proved essential for establishing venture capital in the Baltics (Sabaliauskas 2015). Perhaps most remarkably, Israel created the world's largest VC market, on a per capita basis, through public investment in and coordination of an initial cohort of venture capitalists (Avnimelech and Teubal 2008).

The visible hand of the state in venture capital has manifested in a variety of forms of public funding, tax breaks, and regulatory solutions. A reliance on public rather than private coffers was particularly visible in two aspects of Silicon Valley VC policy diffusion: the absence of ERISA-like regulations (which allowed pension funds to invest in the high-risk asset class) and the proliferation of government funds of VC funds. International policymakers have not revised VC investment regulations so that all investor types, especially public pension funds, can allocate to venture capital as the 1979 ERISA reinterpretation did for American venture capitalists. Instead of adopting regulations that enable private investment, states have often acted as LPs themselves, launching funds of VC funds. The United Kingdom serves as a good example of this two-pronged trend. In spring 2017 the UK Treasury initiated a review of patient capital for innovative, high-growth SMEs (following the Kay Report and government publications on the "valley of death" in funding in 2013). There is suggestion that UK pension funds could be a greater source of patient capital if the government lifted the limit up from £5 million (*The Economist* 2017). As it stands, UK pension funds are not able to provide the same anchor investor role that they have in the United States. At the same time, the British Business Bank, which manages public money, is deploying £1 billion in capital for SMEs. In pursuing this strategy, policymakers serve as economic actors who invest in specific firms that may become winners instead of changing regulations such that private investors could act in this capacity.

The employment of visible public efforts to constitute VC markets resonates with Polanyi's assertion that the road to the free market was opened, and kept open, through centrally coordinated interventions. As Polanyi foresaw, the absence of the state is not a viable means for local Silicon Valley–like VC markets to be constituted. The visible hand of the state is necessary in constituting even quintessentially neoliberal markets such as venture capital. More than a night watchman, policymakers have acted as financiers, educators, and cheerleaders for VC markets ranging from Saudi Arabia to Israel to Singapore. They intervene in locally rooted, and decidedly interventionist, ways. In response to competitive pressures and in the name of supporting entrepreneurship and innovation, they design locally appropriate means for prompting venture capital activity rather than waiting for VC managers to spontaneously spring up from favorable bedrock.

The Contextual Rationality Approach

Diffusion research has presumed that learning—whether construed as conventionally rational or boundedly rational—drives convergence. While top-line convergence has occurred in a number of empirical areas, rarely is the convergence "complete" or "perfect" (Solingen 2012). Rather than only explaining broad trends—as quantitative diffusion research would—the contextual rationality approach developed in this book offers tools for analyzing what happens beneath the veneer of convergence. Its fundamental premise is that policymakers' norms lead them to hold context-distinct policy preferences, and therefore their learning leads them to arrive at *different* conclusions about the optimal means. Thus, policymakers who are contextually rational arrive at different valuations of how policy models can best be adapted locally. Their *different* cost-benefit analyses propel them to design *different* policies aimed at achieving the same end as the policy model they study. As a result, the contextual rationality framework's orientation is to expect diffusion to result in variation rather than convergence.

By employing the contextual rationality framework to analyze policy diffusion, the book reveals why policymakers are not limited to reproducing the most consistently successful policies. It also explains why they are not beholden to have their prior beliefs replaced in full Bayesian updating processes, as a conventionally rational conception of learning would suggest. When learning about new policy realms (or policy innovations), policymakers' norms do not change to match the normative environment underscoring the successfully implemented model. Their rational learning processes—though rigorous and based on cost-benefit analyses—rely on local norms; valuation of policy optimality is derived from norms that inform which policy form is appropriate. Policymakers do not become "technical, rational and therefore culture-neutral" (Finnemore 1996, 328). They are simultaneously technical, and rational, and guided by nationally derived norms in their analysis of policy information. Rather than policy evaluations leading them to conclude that the optimal policy means is the one that has been most consistently, and effectively, deployed elsewhere, they conclude that the locally appropriate policy means is optimal.

Norms empower policymakers to alter, combine, and dismiss elements of even high-performing policy models employed by leading or peer states. The role of norms in the learning process accounts for why and how policymakers conclude that they need to pursue an end and, at the same time, find it optimal that they pursue different means than what they studied. New policy information does not supplant existing norms informing expectations about appropriate policy paths; it does not anchor them into replicating what they study. Appropriateness, rather, determines the value of potential policy choices. Rather than norms being updated by studying—as beliefs are in Bayesian conceptions of rational learning—norms are primarily updated through changes in local environments. The experience of critical junctures—formal institutional changes, shifts in socioeconomic conditions, and adverse policy experiences—can trigger norm updating. In this study on VC policy diffusion, as an example, regulative norms informing whether direct private sector financing was an appropriate policy tool were updated by competitive pressures and political shifts.

The centrality of domestic normative contexts in molding international policy diffusion outcomes suggests that a one-level framework—that examines only international or domestic factors—or an approach landing squarely in either side of the "rationalist versus constructivist" or "descriptive or prescriptive" debates—could not account for the complexity of how information is valued and acted on in international learning processes. Diffusion frameworks investigate properties of the diffusion model and process to account for degrees of convergence, whereas domestic analyses point to institutional differences to explain incomplete convergence. As a result of their orientations, diffusion theories expect convergence while domestic approaches expect variety. But neither approach possesses the tools to account for the reverberations between the two realms. This manifests into insufficient analytical muscle for explaining the empirically common phenomenon of temporally clustered policy actions with similar aims that take markedly different forms. By fusing the domestic arena into the international diffusion process, and contextualism into rationality, the contextual rationality approach offers a new analytical approach for investigating the reality of diverse policy choices within diffusion trends.

The contextual rationality approach offers an alternative conceptualization of rationality than conventional and bounded rationalities. Like conventional rationality, it assumes that policymakers are fully informed and that they operate according to cost-benefit analyses that strive to maximize utility. In contextual rationality, however, policymakers, rather than being full Bayesian learners, are seen as actors whose norms are not updated in light of foreign policy information. Even after rigorous policy studies, resulting in an understanding that policy drove success elsewhere, their cost-benefit analyses still value policies in light of their appropriateness for the local context.

The conceptualization of rationality as contextual does not assume policymakers to be limited in their pursuit of information or to be less than exhaustive in their analysis of policy costs and benefits. In this way, the approach operates according to a fundamentally different presumption than bounded rationality. Bounded rationality expects that policymakers rely on cognitive biases to short cut their learning process. Using cognitive heuristics, boundedly rational policymakers study policies implemented by the states they deem to be leaders or peers. These models then serve as "anchors" from which policymakers cannot deviate when they devise policy for local use. This book's contextually rational approach presumes that policymakers study the policies of leaders or peers, among others. But, they then adapt what they learned in light of what they deem to be appropriate for their local context. In fact, even when policymakers are explicitly interested in replicating specific models, they are not "anchored" into only modest adaptations. Instead, constitutive and regulative norms anchor their set of appropriate choices.

Thus, unlike both conventional and bounded rationality, the contextual rationality framework expects policymakers' learning and evaluation processes to conclude that distinct adaptations are optimal for their local use. Contextual rationality, as a result, serves as an analytical tool for investigating diversity amid convergent trends, whereas conventional and bounded conceptions of rational learning, for different reasons, expect convergence.

The contextual rationality approach also offers an analytical explanation for why state-of-the-art diffusion literature is not fully able to account for the form of variation in diffusion trends. State-of-the-art diffusion scholarship holds that more specific models are more likely to be copied whereas vague policy principles leave room for interpretation. The vagueness of models should lead to variety across adopters. The contextual rationality approach argues that further nuance and delineation of causal mechanisms is needed; policy specificity alone does not have such a direct impact on diffusion. Even when policymakers learn about highly specific policy models, they still adapt blueprints for local use. As an illustration, Singaporean policymakers studied the highly specific Israeli Yozma Fund with gusto. Meticulous study of an effective, specific model should lead, according to diffusion scholarship, to replication. Yet, in light of their cost-benefit analysis, they changed nearly every term in order to fit the fund of VC funds model with their norms that prioritized the allocation of funding as a means of attracting international firms. Vague models, on the other end of the spectrum, do not, in and of themselves, contribute to variance across adopters simply because they leave room for interpretation. Whether models are characterized by high or low specificity, policymakers study, evaluate, and design local VC policies in line with their norms, not due to their ability to interpret a model. This means that state-of-the-art diffusion scholarship is missing a step in its causal logic: policymakers' norms, not the degree of specificity or the number of models, determine how policy models are morphed to fit the local context.

The contextual rationality framework helps to analytically account for why competitive pressures and the learning process do not unilaterally force convergence on neoliberal strategies. Scores of studies in diffusion literature have articulated why competition reduces policymakers' choice set, such that they have to converge on similar, neoliberal approaches (Elkins and Simmons 2005; Simmons et al. 2008; Swank 2008; Levi-Faur 2005a). This book revealed that competition does not foster convergence, and does not even handcuff policymakers into pursuing neoliberal approaches. Instead, the interrelated nature of competition and learning mechanisms empowers policymakers to decide how to react to competition. This builds on the work of scholars such as Kogut and Macpherson (2008) and Meseguer (2009), in identifying mechanisms that act in concert rather than as standalone forces in processes of diffusion.

Competition to attract international investment does not itself produce policy action. Instead of triggering a race to the bottom, or convergence on either successful or neoliberal approaches, competition catalyzes learning and evaluation. To be sure, competitive forces bring new policy areas onto the policymaking agenda and then policymakers study available options and formulate how to localize their own policy efforts. Even in the face of competition, domestically informed learning processes mold the diffusion process, rather than a knee-jerk policy response devoid of (local) consideration. This is why political economy scholars need analytical tools that do more than focus on properties of the diffusion model (e.g., the specificity) and process (e.g., the mechanism). We need approaches that evaluate the characteristics at the point of adoption for how policymakers evaluate and adapt models in normative context. This is where this book's contextual rationality framework strives to add value.

The contextual rationality approach goes beyond arguing that norms foster diversity in the face of policy learning. The approach enables analytically guided narratives, employing constitutive and regulative norms as the key empirical concepts in order to delineate expectations for the varied policy choices pursued by a group of adopting states. In this way, the contextual rationality framework does not just expect variation; it expects particular adaptations based on each case's constitutive and regulative norms, as demonstrated in this study of VC policy diffusion to Hong Kong, Taiwan, and Singapore.

Future research can extend this approach to explore the empirical reality of diffusion driving variety amid convergence in other empirical areas. To do so, similar methodologies should be pursued: scholars first need to distinguish the norms relevant to the particular empirical area. They would then investigate how these norms impact the learning and policymaking processes in the cases explored. The norms articulated here—the constitutive norm of policymakers' interventionist orientation and the regulative norms informing preferences for private sector financing and local versus international firm support—are likely to be relevant to a multitude of industrial policy areas, but it would be a stretch to apply these norms to entire national policymaking contexts. Different and more specific articulations of norms may be beneficial, though there is always the trade-off between comprehensiveness and parsimony in which each study tries to strike the Goldilocks balance of getting it "just right."

Venture Capital as a Panacea for Entrepreneurship and Innovation

Venture capital holds an enviable position, in terms of its public perception, among alternative asset classes. Hedge fund and sovereign wealth fund managers are often depicted as predatory, opaque, and profiting at the expense of the real economy. In these finance sectors, policy centers on promoting transparency and patience, through tools such as the Alternative Investment Fund Managers Directive and the proposed Financial Transaction Tax. The venture capital industry, in contrast, is upheld as a panacea for economic growth, innovation, and high-quality job creation. Rather than reign in market activity, as policymakers strive to do in hedge fund regulations, they eagerly deploy public resources in order to expand the volume, sectoral, and geographic reach of venture capital.

There are several characteristics of the VC model that contribute to its distinctly positive connotation. First, venture capitalists invest in companies for years, whereas many other investor types are motivated by short-term profitability and hold investment positions for days, minutes, or even seconds (as in algorithmic trading). Beyond their provision of long-term capital, venture capitalists are revered for the extensive relationships they develop with early-stage, high-risk portfolio companies. Their industry expertise and networks are purported to help start-up companies grow. This sets VC apart, as venture capitalists are conceptualized as more than financiers; they are also skilled, networked, and patient operating partners. For these reasons, venture capital has been dubbed "humanity's last great hope" for its unique ability to fund technological research (see Mims 2014), attesting to its position as a necessary, rather than untrusted, segment of the financial sector. But is this rosy picture of venture capital—as smart money that is essential to entrepreneurship and innovation—warranted? More precisely for the purposes of this book, should states be deploying scarce resources in an effort to build local venture capital markets? If so, how can they do so with the greatest positive societal impact?

In the fallout of the global financial crisis and among fears of the social impacts of the increase of the breadth and speed of automation, populations expect more government support for entrepreneurs, innovation activity, and early-stage finance. Policymakers must act. So they invest in, provide tax breaks to, and improve the regulatory environment related to innovation and entrepreneurship. Supporting venture capital is a politically low-risk strategy in this realm as policymakers can quantify the output of their support and because of the exceptionally positive perception of venture capital. VC policy is, as a result, a popular policy arena for policymakers looking to promote innovation and entrepreneurship. This helps fuel new VC policy efforts across the globe—or, new venture capital states.

Yet there remain questions about how venture capital should be supported in the contemporary era. In many ways, the advance of the venture capital state does not tally with contemporary trends in early-stage financing. Today's high-technology entrepreneurs require less money to start a business than they did even ten years ago. Even prominent venture capitalists argue that less investment capital is needed for today's start-ups given that they now have less up-front capital expenditure (see, for example, Kupor 2014; Suster 2014). Capital needs are decreasing as technology start-ups are able to access open-source software and cloud computing services, which require much less money than software development and servers did in the early 2000s (Blank 2013). The lower capital requirements mean that the equity gap is not as vast or as detrimental as it once was for fledgling technology firms.

Furthermore, the smaller funding requirements are being met by a proliferation of new forms of entrepreneurial finance; there has been a marked growth of angel investment syndicates, peer-to-peer, and crowdfunding platforms. In this vein, VC states assess whether there is a dearth of seed capital and if venture capital is the best solution. There has been a move whereby government support of venture capital is given in an attempt to increase

VC in the very early stages, such as preseed and seed stages. Seed funding grew as a proportion of overall venture capital deal volume, from the run-up to the global financial crisis through 2014, partly due to these demands for smaller amounts of capital and due to other political economy drivers (Klingler-Vidra 2016). In 2015 and 2016, there was a trend toward "preseed" as ever-smaller investments are made in start-ups that have achieved initial milestones (Beisel 2016; Yuen 2016).

At the same time, especially since the global financial crisis, firms are staying private for longer. As a result, they are seeking increasingly large sums of investment capital at later stages (Bullock 2016). For example, Uber, already worth more than US$68 billion as of June 2016, raised US$3.5 billion from the Saudi Arabia sovereign wealth fund rather than go public by listing on NASDAQ (MacMillan 2016). Together, funding trends are bifurcating such that start-ups need less money at the critical "valley of death" stage—where they used to encounter the equity gap—but more money for their longer tenures as privately held companies. To support the reality of private company financing today, government support of venture capital should increasingly encourage the provision of small amounts of capital to entrepreneurs with only an idea (preseed or seed funding) or large allocations for companies with established revenue streams in need of capital to expand their product offering or geographic presence (growth capital).

Socially, there is a question for national policymakers: Is investment in local venture capital markets beneficial for the local political economy? Venture capital often enables local companies to "go global" and either move headquarters to the United States, or get acquired by an American company. As a result, there is an inherent tension in supporting local innovation and entrepreneurship when so much of the start-ups in the technology sector are "born global" (Almor and Sperling 2008). Start-ups aim for international markets, and in many respects, strive to build their business globally and in particular, in the Silicon Valley. Thus local VC markets, which can act as a provider of small amounts of early-stage VC money, facilitate local entrepreneurs to then go on to fundraise from American venture capitalists. Even in the successful case of Israel, local venture capitalists provide the earliest rounds of funding, and then international—and particularly American—VCs take larger positions in later rounds. Then the VC-backed companies, in many cases, move the management team to the United States in order to be closer to their investors and their biggest market. The successful entrepreneurs often stay in the United States, either further building their business, selling to an American behemoth (e.g., Google or Facebook), or going public on NASDAQ. In each case, there is an effective brain drain from the local market, as the successful entrepreneurs often stay abroad, and future financial gains on the government's investment (of tax payer money) are captured by foreign firms and foreign tax authorities.

Aside from local investments for international growth, there is a fundamental critique of venture capital as a solution to promoting innovation. It stems from scholars who question whether investment in venture capital has ever been an effective way of supporting entrepreneurship and innovation. Lazonick (2009), Golomb (2014), and Mazzucato (2013) are some of the most vocal critics of the notion that private investors, such as venture capitalists, drive *real* innovation.[3] They instead argue that the state has been the real risk-taker responsible for producing today's transformative technologies. In a presentation in London in 2014, Israel's chief scientist (who is himself a former venture capitalist), Avi Hasson, made this point exactly, saying "governments are more tolerant of real risk than venture capitalists can be" (Hasson 2014). Venture capitalists are not investing in basic, or blue-sky, research, nor are they supporting radical innovation (see Hall and Soskice 2001; Taylor 2004 for critical discussion of radical versus incremental innovation).

Rather than blue-sky technologies, they invest in the start-ups that commercialize existing technologies. They invest in the start-ups that make only incremental advances on top of existing innovations. Google serves as an illustrative example. The technology on which Google was based was the result of basic R&D that was funded by the U.S. government (Weiss 2014). Google's founders did an exceptional job of *commercializing* basic research, but they were not responsible for financing or developing the underlying technology. In contrast to the argument that VC is singularly able to promote humanity's critical blue-sky research, critics assert that venture capitalists cannot (or do not want to) afford to invest in truly risky endeavors, nor technologies that are years, let alone decades, away from commercial use. Venture capitalists profit privately from the investment risk that the public sector shoulders.

Another critique of venture capital's benefit to society points to the narrow range of companies in which it invests. Wiens and Bell-Masterson (2015) revealed that even among the five thousand fastest growing companies in the United States in 2014, only 6.5 percent received venture capital. Venture capitalists only consider investing in start-ups that have the potential to disrupt an existing business and serve a giant market (e.g., Google, Facebook, etc.). Reflecting this focus on technology start-ups, in the first quarter of 2015, more than 85 percent of VC deals were in technology sector firms, across the Internet, software and related fields, telecoms, other IT, clean technology, and semiconductors, and electronics categories (Preqin 2015b, 110). Venture capital is allocated to a very particular type of company; one that is capable of producing exceptional financial returns based on the prowess of the management team or the usability and novelty of the technology. This again runs counter to the exuberance expressed by the *Wall Street Journal* about venture capital as "humanity's last great hope." Venture capitalists invest in a narrow type of company rather than endure the true risk associated with investing in the development of blue-sky research into a broad range of applications.

There is another growing critique of venture capital's societal value, which focuses on its patience for long investment tenures—one of the attributes that lends to venture capital's desirability. The critique is that venture capitalists are not investors who are dedicated to building world-changing businesses over the long-term. Their investment mandates force them to propel portfolio companies to achieve sizeable exits within a set number of years—typically ten years as that is the lifespan of the LP-structured fund. In the United States and Europe, investment durations—as IPO markets have been soft—have been six to ten years (Ernst & Young 2012, 12; Doidge et al. 2011). In venture capital terms, ten years is a long time, as this is the legal maximum that funds have before having to return the capital (plus returns) to their investors. But, ten years is not long enough time for deep innovations, such as the twenty or more years required for advances in life sciences (Sivan and Klingler-Vidra 2016). Blue-sky, basic science breakthroughs can take decades, rather than months or years, which underscores the inevitability that venture capitalists are necessarily investing in applied research, products, and services that need commercialization, rather than "basic research" or "deep innovation."

Increasingly, venture capitalists' patience for a ten-year investment is dissipating. They express their impatience by investing in companies that are likely to exit quickly, by investing in late-stage companies, and through the sale of equity stakes on private markets (such as the NASDAQ Private Market). Venture capitalists are fixated on investing in the next Uber, in the hopes that the start-up could achieve a multibillion-dollar valuation in less than five years in operation. Oculus Rift and Snapchat, founded in 2012 and 2011, respectively, reached US$1 billion valuations in less than eighteen months; even Google, founded in 1998, did not become a unicorn—a private company with a valuation in excess of US$1 billion—for eight years. In line with these extraordinarily fast and steep valuation trajectories, venture capitalists increasingly seek to invest in start-ups they hope are capable of achieving similar outcomes. The evidence suggests that as the focus on start-ups turns toward those with the greatest growth potential, more venture capitalists invest in unicorns. By 2014, more than 161 VC firms had invested in unicorns, up from 104 the year before (CB Insights 2015).

In Asia, venture capitalists express their impatience and low-risk tolerance by investing in later-stage companies. By investing in companies at the growth or mezzanine stages, they commit to a shorter intended investment period and the investment has a lower chance of going to zero (Kenney et al. 2002). In China and India, for example, investments in later-stage "more mature, revenue-generating or profitable" companies have resulted in VC funds' average holding times in these markets being between two-and-a-half and four years as of 2011 (compared to six- and ten-year tenures in the United States and Europe) (Ernst & Young 2012, 12–13). Rather than invest in start-ups developing prototypes, Asian venture capitalists invest in (later-stage) firms that need capital for lower-risk activities, such as international expansion or further product development. VC money is allocated to established companies looking to expand their product or geographic offering, rather than early-stage start-ups developing their technology or business. Thus, venture capital in Asia does not play the high-risk financier role that it is acclaimed for playing in Silicon Valley.

In addition, venture capitalists do not shield start-ups from short-term performance pressures as VC's positive perception portends. Start-up management teams, to varying extents, make operational decisions based on the expectations of their investors. Venture capitalists apply pressure on start-up management teams to deliver short-term performance, particularly in user growth, product launches, and market growth strategies. Hirschman (1970) terms this using their "voice." Their voice is used to influence specific decisions, including the salary, bonus, and equity options offered to new members of a firm's senior management. The phenomenon whereby company management teams act to please their major shareholders has been advanced as a guiding principle of corporate behavior for nonfinancial companies (Hall and Soskice 2001, 60) and has been widely covered in the financialization[4] literature (see van der Zwan 2014; Lavapitsas 2009; Aglietta 2000). Though typically associated with publicly traded companies, "shareholder value" can also be used to pressure companies who receive private equity investment (Deeg 2009, 568); private equity investors "apply high profit expectations to firms and plan on selling their participation within a fixed period."

Ultimately venture capitalists exercise their shareholder power by choosing whether to commit to future rounds of funding. The investment model is such that those who invest at early stages are needed as investors in multiple rounds as the start-up matures, in order to signal an advance in quality and accomplishment (Gompers and Lerner 1999). When a venture capital manager does not participate in a "follow-on investment," it sends the market a negative signal; it suggests, especially to other venture capitalists considering investment, that the start-up is not promising. In many ways, the decision to not participate in future funding is a means of "exit," which lends power to their voice (see Klingler-Vidra 2016 for more on "venture capital as patient capital").

Such a message could diminish the valuation of the start-up in its next funding round. Worse yet, it could undermine the start-up's ability to raise funding from other reputable venture capitalists. VC-backed companies encounter a "funnel" whereby fewer and fewer start-ups are able to raise subsequent funding rounds. In examining the 2009 "vintage" (e.g., investment year), analysts found that 75 percent of companies that raised seed capital were orphaned or died, and only 54 percent of companies that raised seed funding were able to raise a second funding round (CB Insights 2014, 12–13). Thus, the threat of withholding participation in future funding rounds, especially by venture capital funds that led a start-up's seed, or A round, heightens a start-up team's awareness of its need to perform in the short-run in order to please its VC shareholders. Rather than venture capital's concentrated ownership "blunting short-term market pressures on company managers" (Culpepper 2005, 175), venture capitalists constitute investors with concentrated ownership blocks who are *imposing* short-term imperatives on entrepreneurs. This "exit" pressure motivates regular product releases rather than big gambles; inhibiting founders' aim of achieving major innovations.

In addition to short-term pressure from VC block-holders, cycles in VC funding are associated with turns to increased leverage. As start-up valuations increase, many firms struggle to successfully raise subsequent funding at favorable terms, and worse yet, as the cycle cools down, start-ups face difficult decisions: do they raise their next round at a lower valuation than the previous one, or do they exit at a lower equity valuation (Tom 2017)? In these "overheated" segments of the cycle, start-up founders turn to alternative sources of financing—notably debt—rather than realize a lower valuation.[5] Increased debt obligations have different pressures than equity ownership; loans need to be serviced in timely manners, so if a start-up stumbles, it still owes loan payments to its creditors. Pressure to pay debt obligations can force high-growth firms to prioritize activities that produce short-term cash over long-term product value. The pressure to repay debt, for fledgling firms that may not have steady revenue streams can even force firms into premature exits. Altogether, the cyclical nature of the VC industry, in which valuations rise and fall systemically, can drive high-growth firms toward debt financing that applies even-greater pressure toward short-term decisions.

There is increasing awareness in the public psyche that the use of state resources to promote innovation incurs social costs. The development of Hong Kong and Shenzhen's Lok Ma Chau Loop proves a salient illustration; the Hong Kong and Shenzhen governments agreed to develop eighty-seven hectares of land as the Hong Kong/Shenzhen Innovation and Technology Park (*South China Morning Post* 2017).[6] The use of eighty-seven hectares of land for yet another science park in high-density, land-starved Hong Kong comes, to some, as the wrong use of a precious resource, and one that chiefly benefits property developers (Van Der Kamp 2017). These critics say the Lok Ma Chau Loop could offer relief for a long-established and, according to some, untenable, housing crisis.

More broadly, the allocation of millions, or even billions, of dollars to innovative firms and venture capitalists has a distributional cost. Innovation-centric, high-risk entrepreneurship is most available to those who are most able, financially, to take the risk and those endowed with a specific skill set (university-educated, and often computer science–focused, youth with strong social networks) (Zhang and Dodgson 2014). Small segments of the population benefit directly from the growing pot of government resources for innovative start-ups. This can further the inequity of societies as those who are left behind (the low-skilled workers and the ageing population) face tenuous job prospects and may have less direct funding available for their social protection.

Venture capitalists are trending toward investing in start-ups that promise to propel efficiency through the automation of tasks and services. In 2016 alone, start-ups with artificial intelligence as part of their core product offering (excluding robotics and augmented and virtual reality) raised $5B in funding; further these start-ups accounted for a fourfold increase from 160 deals in artificial intelligence companies in 2012 to 658 in 2016 (CB Insights 2017). Artificial intelligence promises to offer exceptional returns to investors, but will disrupt existing sectors and ways of doing things, and contribute to particularly rampant job destruction. In Barak Obama's farewell address in 2017, after sharing White House–led research that the majority (83 percent) of jobs paying less than twenty dollars an hour in the United States would be eliminated through automation by 2030 (Executive Office of the [U.S.] President 2016), he reiterated his sentiment that the relentless pace of innovation-driven automation is causing job losses. Automation—that venture capital enables—is not limited to the United States, or even developed country contexts. In Dongguan China, for example, the local government has invested in an official automation support program to help local factories eliminate jobs (*The Economist* 2017), and a report by the International Labor Organization raised the possibility that 90 percent of garment and footwear workers in Cambodia and Vietnam could be lost to "sewbots" (Hoskins 2016). There is a growing tension in this interplay between government and high-tech investment, as government support for venture capital—which facilitates the establishment and growth of companies capable of delivering such disruptive innovation—has never been greater, just as widespread demands for social protection from automation proliferate.

The Future of Venture Capital States

As many states have established venture capital markets, the aim and scope of the VC policies—that strived to constitute initial venture capital markets—necessarily changes. Rather than enabling the new market—as K. T. Li did in Taiwan in the early 1980s—the role of the venture capital state centers on addressing specific market failures. States become more precise surgeons addressing specific deficiencies in venture capital markets. This shift is already under way in many countries, including the East Asian states examined in this study. As an illustration, Singaporean policymakers' launch of the 2008 ESVF, their second fund of VC funds, had the specific objective of plugging a particular gap in Singapore's early-stage funding environment, not in attempting to build a local venture capital market. Another illustration is the United Kingdom's Seed Enterprise Investment Scheme that offers tax relief on investments in seed stage companies, as this earliest stage was specifically identified as lacking market participants.

The venture capital state's more targeted nature does not mean that the state's role is decreasing. In Polanyi's terms, the road to the market is not only opened by interventionism—it is interventionism that keeps the road open. East Asian venture capital markets, though established, professional, and internationally linked, will continue to see explicit state involvement. The competition among East Asian states to attract regional venture capital money continues to rise as China has already become a giant in the global VC industry—the world's second largest VC market since 2015 (Liu 2015). As the Chinese regulatory environment improves, Shanghai, Beijing, and Shenzhen grow as preferred locations for VC managers investing in mainland China (rather than Hong Kong or Singapore as domiciles). Concomitantly, the renminbi has overtaken the U.S. dollar as the preferred fund currency denomination in China and is increasingly an internationally used currency for venture capital investments (Fuhrman 2016). Rather than leave the further growth of its VC industry to market forces, Chinese policymakers continue to step up their support. On January 15, 2015, the national government announced that the Government Guidance Fund, a fund of VC funds program, received an additional RMB40 billion to further attract private money into the Chinese venture capital market (Liu 2015, 121). The overall size of the China VC pie grows as companies like Alibaba achieve extremely successful IPOs; but the competition to participate in China's VC sector advances at an equal—if not greater—rate.

Countries that compete regionally as the would-be location for where VC funds may be domiciled strive to offer attractive environments for RMB-denominated VC funds investing in mainland China. Singapore launched an RMB clearing platform to advance its position as a destination for trading in, and around, Chinese mainland assets and currency. It is not alone; by the second quarter of 2016 there were already eight international RMB clearing hubs (Lockett and Hughes 2016). In light of growing competition, East Asian policymakers will continue their concerted efforts to employ new renminbi-friendly legal structures, tax incentives, and funding instruments. They will consider new and different options that make their locale an attractive destination for entrepreneurial and investment activities. As they do, policymakers will study and evaluate different policy options in line with their logics of appropriateness and will, as a consequence, pursue their own strategies. Rather than harmonization, East Asian VC policies will formulate policies that optimize local cost-benefit analyses in order to address local competitiveness and funding gaps relevant to local, mainland, and Western markets. They will continue to be diverse, just as they have been since the Silicon Valley VC policy model first began to diffuse.

Regionalization will continue to affect the shape of venture capital states in East Asia. It manifests as the design of regionally, rather than nationally, defined investment mandates. Hong Kong and Taiwan are increasingly part of "Greater China" investment strategies. Since 2011, mainland-based investors have been able to invest in Taiwanese ICT firms (Kwong 2011). Rather than set up venture capital funds specific to Taiwan, especially in light of its heterodox regulatory environment, investors establish Greater China funds that allow them to opportunistically invest in Taiwanese ICT firms as part of their portfolio. Hong Kong poses ever-greater opportunity and challenge as the "dragon's head" of the Pearl River Delta.

In Europe, there is a bifurcation of pressures. The so-called Capital Markets Union would allow for the use of a passport for VC managers, so that they could seamlessly operate across Europe (as the Banking Union allows) (EU Business 2016). At the same time, there is threat of profound splintering, as Brexit will see the United Kingdom negotiate the terms on which it will separate from the European Union by March 2019. Funds in the United Kingdom receive a large share of their money from investors from continental European, such as the European Investment Fund. It alone provided approximately £2 billion to 144 British venture capital funds between 2011 and 2015; and, worryingly to UK-based funds, in May 2017 there was talk of the European Investment Fund freezing future investment in UK funds (Ghosh 2017).

The second aspect of regionalization stems from the institutionalization of knowledge-sharing across national venture capital associations. While Europe and Latin America have had regional VC associations since the 1990s, the movement toward a regional VC association is relatively new to East Asia. The Asian Venture Capital and Private Equity Council (AVCPEC), spearheaded by the HKVCA in 2012, aims to improve information sharing on venture capital performance and regulation across the region (author interview, Hong Kong, 3 January 2012). AVCPEC, with nine regional associations as founding members, has an explicit objective of harmonizing regulatory environments.[7] It "seeks to promote professional standards and a suitable regulatory framework for investment across the Asia Pacific" (HKVCA 2015). As the entity matures it may contribute to policymakers' considering it appropriate for their regulatory, tax treatments, and funding efforts to be similar to other AVCPEC members.

There are reasons to believe, however, that VC association lobbying will not drive harmonization. In Taiwan, for example, the TVCA has been lobbying for changes to the regulatory environment for more than two decades but has still not achieved its objectives. In Europe, though the European Venture Capital Association publishes extensively on best VC policy practices for its European constituents, we have not seen convergence in national approaches. The forty-five-country dataset compiled in this study found that there was variation across the funding, taxation, and regulatory arenas within Europe, just as there was within and across Asia and the Americas. Regional VC associations may impact the dissemination of VC policy information, but this will not necessarily affect which policies are valued as appropriate, let alone determine how contextually rational policymakers design their local policies.

Aside from regional considerations, venture capital states are increasingly mindful of their role in promoting sustainable investments. In the United States, the Securities and Exchange Commission is considering a proposal for a Long-term Stock Exchange. The Long-Term Stock Exchange—proposed by Silicon Valley investors and entrepreneurs—strives to align investors' incentives with long-term economic value rather than short-term profits. In so doing, they aim to promote patience in VC investment practices. As Kay (2012) so poignantly highlighted, financial markets are increasingly characterized by their frequent trading and arms' length relationships, rather than close partnerships focused on long-term activities. This is motivating the UK treasury's research into further allowing pension funds to provide greater amounts of patient capital to venture capital funds (*The Economist* 2017). However, should venture capital prove to not be patient—by not delivering long-term investment horizons, by exiting rather than using their "voice" and by failing to demonstrate loyalty—the allure of the asset class could be tarnished among policymakers.

Beyond the forty-five states explored in this study, there will be an increasing number of venture capital states. Future venture capital states include countries outside of the OECD, and not necessarily competitors in the global ICT sector. Developing countries aspiring to leapfrog their development through the promotion of entrepreneurship and innovation are implementing VC policy. Vietnamese policymakers studied the Silicon Valley VC policy model, and concluded that they, too, wanted to build a local Silicon Valley. Rather than copy the Silicon Valley model, they adapted the model to further their local context by making it credit, rather than equity, based (Klingler-Vidra 2014a). Taking their support further, the Vietnamese state launched a VC fund and implemented changes to the regulatory context to promote more investment activity (Vietnam Breaking News 2016). Jamaican policymakers, in partnership with the World Bank and private investors, launched "Start-Up Jamaica" in 2014, an accelerator program inspired by, but adapted from, Start-Up Chile, not least with its Bob Marley-inspired tag line "get up, start up." Shortly after its launch, the Jamaican government announced plans to "partner with private fund managers to launch the first venture capital firms on the island" (McGinnis 2015). Most recently, Saudi Arabia's Public Investment Fund caught headlines in June 2016 for its US$3.5 billion investment in Uber—effectively making Saudi Arabia the largest venture capital state (MacMillan 2016). These new venture capital states are pursuing efforts to constitute markets, rather than fine-tune competitive positioning or filling specific funding gaps, as mature venture capital states are doing.

Vietnam, Jamaica, Saudi Arabia, and North Korea—the book opened with the vignette of the North Koreans' 2011 Silicon Valley trip—are just a few of the (perhaps least likely) examples of future venture capital states.

Like their predecessors, in order to constitute Silicon Valley–like VC markets, they are adapting the models they study in line with their normative contexts. The adaptations do not merely reflect different regulatory structures and varied capital gains tax treatments. Rather than keeping the core of the Silicon Valley model intact, efforts to constitute the next wave of venture capital markets are again proving to be as varied as those policy paths pursued thus far. Their efforts are consistent with the Polanyi assessment that it has always been, and will be, the visible hand of the state that builds and maintains the road to the free market. Again in the name of instigating the innovation and entrepreneurial activities that should spring spontaneously from unfettered capitalism, this study concludes that future venture capital states will pave their own yellow brick roads to reach Oz, just as venture capital states have done since the 1950s.

Notes

1. The Venture Capital State

1. The Republic of China (ROC), also known as Chinese Taipei, is referred to as Taiwan throughout this book.

2. As will be quickly revealed, this book is sympathetic with accounts of the essential role of the state in establishing Silicon Valley's VC market through the allocation of significant funding beginning in the 1950s, and facilitating its growth through an overhaul of the tax and regulatory environment, as well as ensuring viable exit paths via the launch of NASDAQ in the 1970s (see, for example, Lazonick 2009; Block 2008; Weiss 2014).

3. Diffusion in social sciences research is defined as "any process in which the prior adoption of a trait or practice alters the probability of adoption for remaining non-adopters" (Strang 1991, 335). In this study, the term *diffusion* is understood in a manner similar to the works of DiMaggio and Powell 1983; Dolowitz and Marsh 2000; Dolowitz and Sharman 2009; and Simmons et al. 2008. See Klingler-Vidra and Schleifer 2014 for distinction between diffusion, convergence, and institutional isomorphism; Bennett 1991 for seminal work on policy convergence; and Haas 1992 for epistemic communities and policy coordination.

4. Finnemore and Sikkink (1998, 901) discuss the potential for states to be "critical" and therefore not adopt a norm. And, as will be discussed, Acharya (2009) conceptualizes the localization of foreign norms in Southeast Asia's normative context.

5. With that said, several diffusion research projects investigate a small number of cases (e.g., Weyland 2006) or pair quantitative examinations with case study research (e.g., Meseguer 2009's Costa Rican case study).

6. The term *conventional rationality* is used to refer to "full," "calculated," "complete," and "instrumental" rationality, though the author acknowledges differences between these terms, particularly that instrumental rationality has a focus on cost. See March 1978 for delineation of "alternative rationalities", Barros 2010 for conceptualizations of rationalities attributed to Simon's broad category of "bounded rationality" (including global rationality and procedural rationality), and Townley 2008 for an exploration of the treatment of several forms of rationality in organization studies. The "contextual rationality" framework developed here has congruence and difference with several of these brief depictions, including contextual, adaptive, and selected rationality.

7. See Jepperson et al. 1996, 59, for further discussion on state identity.

8. Even in the Israeli case, policies that did not fit the local context, such as the Ministry of Finance's Inbal Fund that attempted to tie VC activity to the local stock market, failed (see Avnimelech and Teubal 2008).

9. Taylor (2016) argues that the performance of countries—in terms of innovation output—is explained by *why* they are innovating (security concerns inform national motivation) and *how* (the politics, institutions, and networks that affect innovation policy and activity).

10. Note that many of these policies have also failed to achieve their objectives (Lerner 2009; Klingler-Vidra et al. 2016).

11. Alternative case selection methods include choosing comparative states according to size (e.g., Katzenstein 1985) or economic competitiveness (e.g., Evans 1995; Breznitz 2007).

12. The Heritage Foundation and the Cato Institute rank Hong Kong at the top of their economic freedom rankings for 15+ and 35+ years, respectively.

2. Contextual Rationality

1. The term *contextual rationality* has been used elsewhere; March (1978) designated a set of ecology, sociology, and organizational behavior scholarship as developing "ideas of contextual rationality," and Browne and Patterson (1999) invoked the term contextual rationality to describe how the nominating behavior in Japanese district elections was maximized according to local contexts. In her 2008 book, *Reason's Neglect*, Barbara Townley spends a chapter on the treatment of contextual rationality in organization studies.

2. The "policy transfer" scholarship (see Rose 1991) does not suffer this limitation as the policy transfer focus is on the local contexts between which policies spread.

3. This includes Varieties of Capitalism, comparative institutional, national systems of innovations and comparative business systems research programs (this includes the works of Whitley 1992; 2007; Walter and Zhang 2012; Witt and Redding 2013; Deeg and Jackson 2007; Edquist 1997; and others). Comparative programs offer expectations as to the roles of institutional settings as drivers of market structures and performance (Crouch 2009).

4. Crouch (2009, 85) discusses the debate about whether the Varieties of Capitalism approach has, and can, account for economic policy choices. He notes that Iversen and Soskice (2006) responded to this critique by exploring how economic arrangements affect policy choices.

5. Lenschow et al. (2005, 802) define institutions quite similarly: "organizational structures, formal and informal rules, and policymaking procedures."

6. There are other ways of articulating the differences between simple and complex learning. For Fearon and Wendt (2002, 63), complex learning involves preference formation whereas simple learning is about an external environment.

7. This book focuses on risk, rather than uncertainty, given rational choice theory's use of probability distributions (Simon 1979). The presumption, in rational choice theory, that probabilities can be modeled suggests an understanding of the operation of risk, not a reflection of uncertainty. For engagement with the important distinction between risk (known unknowable to which probabilities can be assigned) and Knightian uncertainty (in which the unknowns are unknowable) see Nelson and Katzenstein 2014; King 2016; Steiner 1983; and Knight 1921.

8. In Rational Choice theory, the basis of preference formation is societal utility of potential outcome (e.g., income, reputation) rather than the policymakers' self-interest.

9. This follows Nelson and Katzenstein (2014, 368), who do not distinguish between "social conventions" and "norms."

10. Elizabeth Thurbon (2016, 4–6) uses the terms *mindset, worldview, ideas, consensus* and *orientation*. In this book, the constitutive norm being investigated—policymakers' interventionist orientation—speaks to their self-identity, rather than ideas more generally. The term *mindset* is not as well conceptualized in the political economy literature; constitutive norms allows for greater precision in terms of self-identification and the formulation of interests.

11. Organization as a conceptual category—the last of North's three categories of institutions—refers to "groups of individuals bound by some common purpose to achieve objectives" (North 1990, 5). Organizations are not ahistorical or contextual; rather, March and Olsen (1998, 947) assert that the creation of organizations stems from the "desires of political actors." This understanding of organization as an entity points to political bodies such as state agencies, firms, and departments. Organizations, in the case of VC policy diffusion, include

Hong Kong's Innovation and Technology Commission (ITC), Taiwan's Council for Economic Planning and Development (CEPD), and Singapore's Economic Development Board (EDB).

12. The theory of contestation holds that norms are susceptible to contestation at the constituting stage, the social recognition stage, and in its cultural validity, which is determined—and redetermined—upon implementation (Wiener 2014, 29–31). The focus of this book is less on the original validity of the norms; there is some discussion of the history of constitutive and regulative norms in each case study so that the reader sees sources of the normative context within which VC policy learning occurred. But the bulk of the study looks at VC policymaking in a longitudinal sense, meaning that it is more interested in the third stage: the ongoing cultural validity of policymaking norms.

13. Legitimacy refers to a "collective audience's shared belief" that "the actions of an entity are desirable, proper, or appropriate within some socially constructed system of norms, values, beliefs, and definitions" (Suchman 1995, 574, as cited in Bernstein 2011, 24).

14. One could argue that "normative complementarities" are another form of complementarities, and as of yet, has not been investigated in VoC scholarship.

15. In many respects, the contextual rationality approach developed in this book draws on economic sociology explanatory underpinnings. The aim of the contextual rationality approach is to analyze the role of social structures and institutions in shaping policy choices. Such analytical frames underpin a substantial body of work in the political economy field (see Smelser and Swedberg 2005; Stark and Balasz 2012). Granovetter (1992, 4) explains that a foundational assumption of economic sociology is that "economic action (like all action) is socially situated, and cannot be explained by individual motives alone." The challenge, according to Granovetter and other economic sociologists, is for researchers to both acknowledge and investigate the social structure in which actors are embedded and to allow for contingency.

3. Venture Capital and VC Policy

1. Dan Breznitz's works on *Innovation and the State* (2007) and *Run of the Red Queen* (2011), which examine venture capital activities as part of innovation systems, and Robyn Klingler-Vidra's work on the variety of venture capital policies (2014a; 2015), serve as notable exceptions.

2. The venture capital asset class typically has about US$100 billion of investment per annum, whereas larger alternative asset classes, such as bond markets, private equity, and hedge funds, account for trillions of invested capital. An apex was reached in 2014, as venture capital investments in start-ups in the United States alone reached US$51.12 billion—the highest level since 2000 (Fitzpatrick 2015), and Q2 and Q3 in Europe produced the highest quarterly venture capital investments since 2001 (Dow Jones VentureSource 2014, 2).

3. The due diligence process, particularly for the more institutionalized VC firms, also includes legal and finance teams within VC firms; these teams raise a number of concerns with the start-up based on their reviews of documentation, including legal teams reviewing the start-ups' contracts and finance teams assessing the capital structure.

4. Venture capitalists are not always experienced entrepreneurs or technically trained. Their background is more often in finance (e.g., former bankers) in markets such as Japan and Hong Kong, as opposed to the profile of the experienced entrepreneur in the United States and United Kingdom. (Kenney et al. 2002). Consistent with their banking backgrounds, venture capitalists in Hong Kong view investments as "pure play, late-stage financial transactions" as opposed to long-term financial and operational partnerships with early stage start-ups (Klingler-Vidra 2015). This informs the treatment of VC investments as financial transactions rather than operationally focused relationships.

5. Seed deal volume was smaller in 2015 and the first half of 2016 as venture capital activity retreated after its historic peak in 2014. The decline has come as part of an overall slowdown in VC activity, though fundraising levels continued to reach new peaks through Q2 2016 (see Pitchbook 2016).

6. Figure 1.1 indicates that VC policy was first initiated in the United Kingdom in 2000, not 1945, as 3i was deployed as a vehicle for financing SMEs, not as a tool for supporting a nascent VC industry. As explained in this chapter, in order for policy measures to be considered

"venture capital policy" they have to aim at building or supporting venture capital, not only as a tool for supplying capital to start-ups.

7. Business angels are private, individual investors who invest in start-up companies. The amount of money that angels provide to start-ups is typically less than VC managers, and typically at an earlier stage of investment.

8. As discussed by Avnimelech and Teubal (2006; 2008), VC policies are part of a three-phase innovation and technology policy life cycle in which business sector R&D and innovation support is necessary prior to VC policy. They argue that business sector support is Phase 1 and VC policy is Phase 3. Others examine the preconditions for venture capital; Gilson and Black 1999, for example, explore the extent to which venture capital markets depend on the existence of a (vibrant) stock market.

9. The shortage of VC funds, and therefore the existence of an equity gap, is debated. Several studies give evidence to the contrary, such as the European Central Bank's January 2005 working paper (#430).

10. Broader contextual contributors include American R&D spending, the presence of top universities, the colocation of large technology firms and start-ups, a positive regulatory environment, and access to exits via stock market IPOs (Avnimelech and Teubal 2004).

11. The capital gains tax rate in the United States has fallen further; the long-term capital gains tax rate as of 2016 is 17 percent for most taxpayers and 20 percent for the highest tax bracket. However, at the time of writing there is increasing discussion about venture capital profits (e.g., carry) being taxed at corporate income tax rates, rather than long-term capital gains tax rates, in the United States

12. As of summer 2017, the Trump administration is widely expected to remove the low capital gains tax rate that venture capitalists have enjoyed since the 1970s. The administration has publicly committed to making the U.S. tax system simpler, removing loopholes (including a majority of standard tax deductions) and lowering posted rates.

13. On the national level, the funding program that aided the success of the Silicon Valley VC market was the U.S. Small Business Administration's 1958 Small Business Investment Company (SBIC) program. The SBIC program (which provided loans to venture capital funds) and the Small Business Innovation Research (SBIR) program (which invested in SMEs directly, by prioritizing SMEs as recipients of government procurement) were deployed to support innovative American SMEs. Though the Silicon Valley VC market was not the specific target of SBIC funding, it was the overwhelming recipient. These funds proved essential to the market's early growth; SBICs "provided the major source of VC funding" through the 1960s and 1970s (Weiss 2014, 57). SBIC continues to provide billions of capital, annually, to the American VC industry. The Small Business Administration, on its website, proclaimed that SBIC provided $6 billion in funding (in the form of leverage) in the fiscal year to 30 September 2016.

14. For more on Gestalt psychology in political economy, see De Vecchi 2003 on the impact of Gestalt on Hayek's thinking.

15. The relative decline in external security concerns relative to domestic tensions, according to Taylor (2016), can explain the fall of a nation's innovation performance, or said another way, why countries succumb to "Cardwell's Law" over time (in inability to produce at the technology frontier over a historically long period of time).

16. Hong Kong's Applied Research Fund II and Singapore's Technopreneurship Investment Fund were the victims of poor timing, in addition to design issues. Both funds were launched just before the Dotcom Crash in 2000, which had a detrimental impact on their performance (Author interviews, Hong Kong, 20 December 2011 and Singapore, 21 September 2012). Despite the similarly poor timing, Singapore's fund did succeed in attracting international blue chip investors, which was a clear preference of Singaporean policymakers (before it was wound down).

4. Hong Kong

1. At Chris Patten's Public Event at the London School of Economics and Political Science on July 11, 2017, entitled "First Confession: A Sort of Memoir," I asked if he still felt this way. He explained that, for him, Hong Kong's approach was to "do no harm," unlike Singapore, whose involvement was akin to "social engineering."

2. Hong Kong ranks as the world's fourth leading financial center (Yeandle and Mainelli 2016).

3. Hong Kong is the forty-fourth largest economy according to the World Bank rankings of GDP in Purchasing Power Parity terms for 2015.

4. Some blame Hong Kong's weak positioning as a technology center in Asia on the government's neoliberal approach, and therefore its lack of industry-specific industrial policies during the 1980s (Lall 2004, 17; Fuller 2010, 1–5).

5. Funding for the first ARF came from the Finance Committee of the Legislative Council, as it approved HK$200 million from the Capital Investment Fund in December 1991 (GIO 1994, 87).

6. An Industry and Trade Bureau review "pointed out [that] the need to protect the seed capital and the requirement for a 5 percent return have created a hampering effect on the ARC in providing equity injection to approved projects because the return in the form of dividend is less certain. Consequently, most of the approved projects have been given loans with rather stringent conditions" (Hong Kong Trade and Industry Bureau 1998, 2).

7. The ARF II's structure was not motivated by studying the Israeli model. Only in May 2000 did Hong Kong's financial secretary, Donald Tsang, visit Israel "to gain first-hand knowledge on the country's success in the development of innovation and technology" (ISD 2000, 361). His trip was organized by Israel's OCS (the Israeli government office responsible for the Yozma Fund and other VC policy measures) and had been designed to help Hong Kong policymakers "learn about how the Israeli Government provides assistance and support" (*People's Daily* 2000). Hong Kong policymakers, however, did not learn about the specifics of the Israeli policy model through direct encounters with the Yozma team (author interview, Tel Aviv, 6 October 2013).

8. As of May 31, 2011, the valuation of the twenty-four investments made by the fund managers was 50 percent of the corresponding total investment costs (Hong Kong Legislative Council Panel on Commerce and Industry 2011).

9. The ARF assets have been in liquidation ever since. As at the "end May 2011, twenty projects were exited while four are still active" (Hong Kong Legislative Council Panel on Commerce and Industry 2011, 2).

10. Articles 107 and 108 of the Basic Law lay out the objective of Hong Kong's low-tax policy.

11. The Hong Kong tax regime consists of low tax rates across four types: profits tax (for corporations), salaries tax (individual tax), property tax, and estates tax (Tang 1996, 40).

12. As chapters 5 and 6 will reveal, Taiwan offered a 20 percent tax deduction for venture capital investors beginning in the 1980s, and Singapore ensured that the VC asset class was tax-free early on. It was not until this legislation in 2005 that Hong Kong policymakers enacted a VC-specific tax exemption.

13. Though the Hong Kong SAR regime did not deploy VC-specific regulations, the PRC has. The PRC's VC regulations matter to Hong Kong since they need to be consistent with PRC government legislation, given Hong Kong's one country, two systems arrangement with mainland China since 1997 (Stillman 2002). So, Hong Kong's venture capital regulations, if there were any, would need to be consistent with Chinese VC regulations. Chinese VC legislation came via the PRC's Provisional Measures for the Administration of Venture Capital Enterprises. The Provisional Measures detail registration requirements for domestic and foreign VC managers operating in China, as a means for the PRC government to promote the development of venture capital, to "standardize their investment activities and to encourage them to invest" in high-technology SMEs (Wang & Co 2006). The PRC's Provisional Measures have named the regulatory authority, reporting requirements, structures available (e.g., the limited liability company), and the scope of business activities considered to be venture capital activity in China.

14. The creation of the ITB followed three years of vigorous debate, particularly the push-back by the LegCo (as the ITB was proposed in 2012). The case for the ITB as a bureau-level entity was that the ITC was overwhelmed with its responsibilities in tactically managing the Science Park and Cyberport, so a larger, better resources entity with better access to the chief executive was needed to strategically drive Hong Kong's promotion of innovative activities. In effect, the ITB could, more than the ITC was able to, coordinate innovation policy efforts through its access to the chief executive and its larger institutional structure.

15. Cheng (2013, 224) notes that most analysts describe Hong Kong's executive-led system as a "hybrid regime type with varying levels of democracy in various political institutions."

He states that fifteen years after Hong Kong's transition began (in 1997), there "has been no significant progress in democracy" (Cheng 2013, 226). A major protest for democracy took place in the autumn of 2014, with protestors expressing their "dissatisfaction with the pace of democratization" and, specifically, their desire to directly elect the chief executive (Yung 2014, 1). In line with calls for advancing democracy, the Chinese government promised that the Hong Kong populace can elect their chief executive in the 2017 election, and elect all seats in the Legislative Council in the 2020 election (Cheng 2013, 242).

16. During the British colonial period the LegCo members were largely the governor's appointments of prominent businessman and other elite members of society. The Hong Kong legislature's positioning vis-à-vis civil servants grew as a result of the introduction of direct elections of thirty seats (Koehn 2001, 107). Civil servants, no longer guaranteed legislative approval of policy, had to start lobbying the LegCo to gain sign-off in the Hong Kong SAR government. The LegCo, since the 1990s, questions officials via "value-for-money" audits or in asking for oral or written answers in response to their questions about operations (GIS 1995, 27).

5. Taiwan

1. The CEPD ceased to exist, in a stand-alone form, as of January 22, 2014. It was merged with the Research, Development, and Evaluation Commission to form the National Development Council (NDC). The policy efforts of the NDC are covered in this book since its creation in 2014 (notably, HeadStart).

2. The ROC's official diplomatic relationship with the United States ceased in the years following UN derecognition, as the United States severed relations in December 1978 and closed its U.S. Embassy in Taipei in 1979 (GIO 1983, 346). American public and private exchange continued to flourish with Taiwan despite the unofficial relationship status (CEPD 2010).

3. Note that the venture capital policies did not reflect this sentiment as virtually no efforts were made to attract foreign investment. In recent years, competitive pressures to attract money for the Taiwanese VC industry has peaked interest in adopting the LP structure. As Taiwan's VC activity levels declined, particularly since 2000, local VC managers have lobbied their industry association to push for the adoption of the LP structure. The general secretary of the TVCA commented that "if local VC managers want American money they need the LP," and "the LP structure would be for foreign investors" (author interview, Taipei, 5 January 2012). Though the TVCA has lobbied CEPD, MoF, and MoEA policymakers for an LP structure, it has not yet materialized.

4. The prominent role of SMEs in the Taiwanese economy has been the result of policies that did not support national champions, choosing instead to focus on domestic SMEs producing computer components (Fuller 2002, 19; Breznitz 2007). It should be noted that SME centrality to the economy is not specific to Taiwan; SMEs account for 60 to 70 percent of employment, on average, across the OECD.

5. The rigid financial structure through the 1980s was said to be politically motivated, so the state could monitor and direct financing as a means of limiting competing centers of private sector power vis-à-vis large companies (Breznitz 2007, 103–11).

6. Taiwan's limiting of foreign investors' access persists even today. In fact, Taiwan was being considered for inclusion in the Morgan Stanley Capital International (MSCI) World basket of countries (along with Korea), which would endow it with developed country status. MSCI ended its considerations in June 2014, however, due to the "absence of any significant improvements" in foreign investors' access to financial markets (Hong and Hunter 2014).

7. The three men were the minister of finance, a partner of a major law firm in Taiwan, and a partner from Hambrecht & Quist (author interview, Taipei, 5 January 2012).

8. K. T. Li was a senior, influential member of the KMT from the 1960s; Li was the minister of economic affairs from 1965 to 1969, minister of finance 1969 to 1976, and minister without portfolio from 1976 to 1988 (GIO 2001, 71). K. T. Li is called the "father of the economic miracle" in Taiwan, for his vision in building Taiwan's technology industry. A partner at H&Q "came to Taiwan and introduced the idea of venture capital to K. T. Li. He listened to the H&Q executive and then supporting VC became K. T.'s idea" (author interview, Taipei, 6 January 2012).

9. The term *Silicon Valley—Hsinchu Connection* was coined by AnnaLee Saxenian and refers to the movement and interactions of people and capital between Silicon Valley and Taiwan's local science park, Hsinchu, as well as the broader collaboration between these two high-technology clusters. This connection was formed in the 1950s when top Taiwanese students began moving to the United States to study (primarily Ph.D.s in engineering) by way of American-Taiwanese funding programs, such as U.S. Agency for International Development (Greene 2008, 55). In the early 1980s, Taiwanese policymakers began to conceptualize this brain drain as a "brain bank" and solicited the return of talent by fostering local high-technology sector opportunities (Wade 2004, 191; GIO 1983, 196). These local technology opportunities centered around Hsinchu Park, K. T. Li's creation, which was established in 1979 as an effort to build a Taiwanese version of Silicon Valley and to attract overseas Chinese back to Taiwan (Lee 2000, 562). Through these efforts, by the late 1980s, 180,000 Taiwanese engineers had returned, many from Silicon Valley (Fuller 2002, 16).

10. Dr. Ta-Lin Hsu is the founder and chairman of H&Q Asia Pacific, one of the first VC firms to enter Taiwan. H&Q Asia Pacific was a founding member of the Technology Review Board, which advised the Executive Yuan on technology matters.

11. Morris Chang was born in China, moved to Hong Kong in 1948, and then to the United States to complete his BSc and MSc at MIT. He then worked for Texas Instruments for twenty-five years and also got a Ph.D. from Stanford University. Texas Instruments had sponsored his doctoral studies in the 1960s and he had become group vice president there. He left Texas Instruments in 1983 to become president of General Instrument Corporation (1984–85) and was then recruited to Taiwan by K. T. Li to be the head of ITRI. In 1987 he founded Taiwan Semiconductor Manufacturing Company Ltd. at the behest of K. T. Li (author interview, Taipei, 6 January 2012; GIO 2001, 13).

12. Stan Shih has maintained relationships with senior policymakers; he was appointed as a technology advisor to Presidents Lee and Chen, beginning in 1996 (Kirby 2002; GIO 2001, 98) and has also been a managing director of the public research institute—the Industrial Technology Research Institute.

13. Policymakers design of Hsinchu Science Park in the late 1970s was part of their efforts to create a local Silicon Valley (Wang 1995, 2).

14. Japan's VC regulations (until 2002) had forbidden pension funds from investing in VC, prevented VC managers from undertaking their monitoring and control functions, and forced VC investors to accept "unlimited" liability (Kenney et al. 2002, 70–79). Moreover, Japan's historically bank-dominated, domestic and credit-based VC industry, unlike the pension fund and institutional investor mix that is common in Western VC markets, is dominated by banks and insurance companies (31 percent) and corporate VC managers (19 percent), while pension funds and endowments account for less than 5 percent of investments in Japanese VC funds (Walter and Zhang 2012, 140–41). The Japanese VC industry became more equity-friendly from the 1990s, but it is important to note here that at the time the Taiwanese policymakers studied the Japanese VC industry environment, it operated without an LP structure, forbade pension fund investments in the asset class, and had a high level of corporate VC managers participating in the market, relative to markets like the United States.

15. Taiwan's adaptation away from Japanese legal legacies is not only true of the VC industry. Taiwan's financial sector laws and regulations have been adapted away from the Japanese model by the KMT's leadership and its desire to suppress major business conglomerates (Aviles 2009, 23). For example, in Taiwan "banks are prohibited by law from taking shares in the companies to which they lend or from having representatives on the board of directors, in sharp contrast with Japan" (Campos et al. 1996, 110).

16. Since at least 2006, the TVCA has lobbied the CEPD for local adoption of the LP structure (author interview, Taipei, 5 January 2012). The TVCA was founded in 1992 by twenty-two VC fund managers in Taipei and maintains its independence from the government.

17. Taiwanese VC managers accept the restrictive regulatory environment as it affords tax exemption (as long as they invest in high-technology SMEs) as well as the "prestige and credibility that comes with the special approval of the government" (Wang 1995, 21).

18. These restrictions were partially relaxed in 2004 when the MoEA drafted a relaxation of the Scope, as the limit on bank and insurance company investment amounts in venture capital was eased (Yeh 2006, 8). Nevertheless, pension funds do not have access to the venture capital asset class in Taiwan.

19. Their reluctance toward financing private sector firms led policymakers to choose to support computer components production as a strategically important sector as it did not require deep pockets. The industry was also attractive as semiconductors were, and have been, one of the world's fastest growing consumer product markets. The semiconductor market has had high annual industry growth rates (over 30 percent) and yearly sales upward of US$300 billion.

20. The CEPD was an advisory body to the Executive Yuan cabinet and was outside the "ordinary machinery" of the Taiwanese government (Wade 2004, 196–98). The CEPD fit into the policymaking process by setting the broad policy plan, the IDB crafted industrial policies and then implemented them (GRIPS 2011, 2; Wade 2004, 201), and the ITRI, III, and other research institutes and think tanks helped set industry strategies based on research in their respective industries (Breznitz 2007, 100–135; GIO 1986, 288). As part of a large government restructuring in 2014, the CEPD was merged with another agency; the resulting entity is the National Development Council.

21. As discussed in this chapter, the decision to discontinue the tax incentive reflected a normative change in how the state should affect industrial strategy, said to be driven by the March 2000 election of the opposition party, the DPP.

22. Taiwanese corporate venture capitalists seek to buy companies for reasons other than strictly their financial return. These reasons include using the SME's technology, acquiring a talented team, or heading off potential competition.

23. The bilateral New Zealand—Taiwan fund of VC funds was constructed based on the NZVIF rather than through Taiwanese policymakers directly learning about Yozma (author interview, Tel Aviv, 6 October 2013). This transmission through the New Zealanders, who underwent a "formal process of learning from the Yozma program" (Avnimelech 2009, 22), is clear when examining the bilateral fund of VC funds' structure (MoEA 2012). Notably, like Yozma, the bilateral fund of VC funds requires private sector matching of funding (to the tune of 40 percent).

24. In fact, some say that the MoEA and IDB do so much consulting of private experts that the IDB "outsources" policymaking to semigovernmental think tanks such as the TIER and CIER (GRIPS 2011, 4).

25. The distribution of policymaking power also undermines the ability of private actors to lobby for VC policy change. The TVCA director commented that he did not "have a supervisory body to communicate with directly" (author interview, Taipei, 5 January 2012). The TVCA has been lobbying to make the CEPD the supervisory authority for the venture capital industry since they already manage the Development Fund.

26. These policymakers acted as "institutional carriers" (Scott 2003) in terms of diffusion scholarship, as they brought the new institutional form of venture capital, and its relevant policy options, onto the policymaking agenda.

6. Singapore

1. Singapore is classified as a developed country (or advanced economy) according to the International Monetary Fund and World Bank. It is also included in the MSCI World basket of developed countries, instead of the MSCI Emerging Markets group, which many of its neighbors are classified as. In Asia, only Singapore, Hong Kong, Japan, and Australia are included in the developed economies basket.

2. Singapore has ranked, at least since the mid-2000s, as the fourth most important financial enter in the world (Yeandle and Mainelli 2016).

3. The four pillars for economic strategies identified by the Technopreneurship 21 Ministerial Committee were: education, facilities, regulations, and finance (Ho et al. 2002, 336).

4. Singapore's NRF was named and modeled after the U.S. National Research Council (author interview, Singapore, 19 September 2012).

5. A caveat is in order here as Singaporean policymakers' first foray into financing SMEs came nearly ten years before the 1985 recession, via the extension of credit (loans up to SGD1 million) through the EDB and Development Bank of Singapore's Small Industries Finance Scheme, beginning in 1976 (EDB 1982, 34).

6. The recession showed that Singaporean employment, for example, was highly susceptible to MNCs' personnel decisions (Economic Committee 1986; 1991). This overreliance on

MNCs for manufacturing employment was further demonstrated by a 1985 National Productivity Board report that found that the employment-share of SMEs in manufacturing had declined from 61 percent to 32 percent between 1986 and 1983 (Luk 1985).

7. Singaporean VC policymakers actively shared details of their SME and innovation policy successes with fellow members of regional forums, such as the APEC SME Working Group (author interview, Singapore, 24 September 2012), and their industrial expertise is said to be well known even by their critics (Han et al. 2011).

8. EDB Investments Ltd invests in high-growth companies, domestically and abroad, and invests across the VC, PE, and corporate ventures channels. The EDBI comanaged VC funds include Cluster Development Fund, ED Ventures Pte Ltd, EDB Ventures 2, Pte Ltd, PLE Investments Pte Ltd, Mobile Commerce Venture Fund, BioMedical Sciences Investment Fund, Pharmbio Growth Fund Pte Ltd, Life Sciences Investment Pte Ltd, Singapore Bio-Innovations Pte Ltd, and the TIF (Wang 2002, 13).

9. Dr. Tony Tan is a high-profile civil servant and politician. He was elected president in 2011 and previously held senior positions across government entities, including chairman of the Government of Singapore Investment Corporation (the Singaporean SWF), chairman of Singapore Press Holdings, and the creator and head of the Technopreneurship 21 Committee and the NRF.

10. The US$1 billion TIF was divided into three subfunds: US$500 million went into a broad based fund, US$250 million for a strategic fund, and US$250 million for an early stage fund (Dietrich 2003, 51). The TIF had several government affiliations to achieve these aims. It was comanaged by the National Science and Technology Board (NSTB) and the Government of Singapore Investment Corporation (Chia 2005, 27) and was owned by EDB Investments Ltd.

11. Performance fees were already exempt as they are capital gains (the VC managers' share of profits from portfolio company exits). Management fees are the revenues VC managers make for running their funds, regardless of performance. Because management fees are not capital gains, they had not previously been tax exempt.

12. The seven advantages of the Pte Ltd structure are as follows: (1) separate legal entity with its own legal identity, (2) limited liability entity, (3) perpetual succession—the company's persistence does not depend on the involvement of any of its members, (4) ease of raising capital—able to issue shares to new shareholders, (5) credible image, (6) easier transfer of ownership, and (7) tax benefits and incentives including a low corporate tax rate (less than 9 percent for profits up to SGD 300,000 and up to 17 percent for profits over SGD 300,000), a capital gains tax exemption, and dividends can be distributed to shareholders tax free (no double taxation at the entity and shareholder levels) (GuideMeSingapore 2013).

13. Despite this domestic intention, Walden International, a well-established international VC manager, has received ESVF money for its Seed Ventures IV Pte Ltd (S4). The NRF selection of Walden's fund was positioned as giving money to a successful Singaporean VC (Walden's founder, Lip-Bu Tan grew up in Singapore and attended Nanyang University) who had "pioneered many venture capital concepts in Asia" (NRF 2008a, 6).

14. In interviews Singaporean venture capitalists expressed sentiment that GIP program participants are "risk-averse and uninterested in the underlying VC investments" and have "just wanted their capital back in five years' time" (author interviews, Singapore, 12 and 13 September 2012).

15. As background on the Technopreneurship 21 Ministerial Committee, in 1994, Tony Tan was tasked with designing policies to further Singapore's knowledge-based economy. The culmination of his team's five years of research and deliberations was the creation of the 1999 Technopreneurship 21 initiative, in which the NSTB (and then the EDB) pledged to provide financial support, tax incentives, and regulatory reforms for the VC industry (EDB 2000, author interview, Singapore, 12 September 2012). The second VC policymaking committee, the NRF, was established in 2006 as a department under the Prime Minister's Office. The NRF was tasked with supporting research, innovation, and enterprise by setting a national innovation strategy and by allocating funds.

16. In light of the 2006 and 2011 election results (the worst in PAP history as it only obtained just over 66 percent and 60 percent of the vote, respectively) (Kennedy 2011), there was discussion of greater scrutiny of government spending and a need to ensure that initiatives now reach more stakeholders.

17. Since 1965, Singapore's People's Action Party PAP has achieved a remarkable proportion of votes at each election. Its worst-ever election result came in 2011, when the PAP only won

approximately 60 percent of the popular vote, and won only 81 of the 87 parliament seats (Gopalakrishnan and Lim 2011, 51). Interviews revealed that the 2006 and 2011 elections increased sentiment that the PAP may need to seek greater policy input from the electorate.

7. Analyzing Sources of Adaptation

1. With the view that the American model was too neoliberal to be appropriate for his local context, the Singaporean policymaker set out to learn about more overt and funding-centric means of supporting VC markets. The policy levers—ERISA, tax advantages, and SBIC—were construed as neoliberal support. Along with his colleagues, he then set out to acquire information on the Yozma Fund via study trips, as well as ongoing dialogues with counterparts in the Israeli Office of Chief Scientist.

2. For more on the success of the Israeli *Start-up Nation*, see the account given by Senor and Singer 2009 in the book by the same title.

3. Equity markets have grown across East Asia, in absolute terms as well as a percentage of financial transactions, driven by market forces and by through industrial policies to support capital markets (Rethel 2010, 493–94).

8. The Future of Venture Capital States

1. Startup Chile is a government initiative, launched in 2010, with the expressed aim of placing Santiago on the global start-up map by offering tax rebates, networking, and mentorship to entrepreneurs who spend money setting up their business—and physically living in—Chile for one year.

2. A truism fervently criticized by Polanyi and others (see Block 2001, xxxvi).

3. Another critique of venture capital's contribution to societally impactful innovation stems from questions of the social value that "apps" such as SnapChat provide. Many, even within the VC industry, are critical of the ability of such products and services to advance society's way of life.

4. Financialization refers to the web of interrelated processes—economic, political, social, technological, cultural—through which finance has extended its influence into other realms of social life (van der Zwan 2014).

5. Perhaps manifest of such pressures, PitchBook data (Tom 2017) revealed that the debt component of venture financing deals increased from $4.3 billion in 2013 to nearly $14 billion in 2016.

6. This collaboration coming, of course, within the broader efforts facilitated by the Mainland and Hong Kong Closer Economic Partnership Agreement, which was signed in 2003, and more recently as part of the conceptualizing of the region as the China Greater Bay Area economy rather than mainland, Macau, and Hong Kong as separate entities (Zhou 2017). In Taiwan, cross-border innovation activities have been supported by the wider Economic Cooperation Framework Agreement, which reduced tariffs and barriers on several sectors, including banking, since 2010.

7. The nine founding members of AVCPEC are the Australian Venture Capital Association Limited, HKVCA, Japan Venture Capital Association, New Zealand Private Equity and Venture Capital Association, Taiwan M&A and Private Equity Council, China Association of Private Equity, India Venture Capital Association, Korea Venture Capital Association, SVCA and the Malaysia Venture Capital & Private Equity Association.

List of Interviews

6 January 2011, Israeli minister of commercial affairs in the United Kingdom, London, UK

19 January 2011, founder of a Singapore-based early-stage investment management firm, videoconference

18 March 2011, director, European Venture Capital Association, Brussels, Belgium

22 June 2011, manager of Finland's fund of VC funds, Helsinki, Finland

20 December 2011, head of Hong Kong Science and Technology Parks, Hong Kong

20 December 2011, head of data for the Asian Venture Capital Journal, Hong Kong

21 December 2011, senior manager for the Hong Kong Innovation and Technology Commission Technopreneur Funding Schemes, Hong Kong

3 January 2012, executive director, HK Venture Capital and Private Equity Association, Hong Kong

5 January 2012, general secretary of the Taiwan Venture Capital Association, Taipei City, Taiwan

5 January 2012, manager, Committee of Communications Industry Development Office of MoEA's Institute for Information Industry, Taipei City, Taiwan

5 January 2012, planner at Institute for Information Industry and curator of Start-up Digest, Taipei City, Taiwan

6 January 2012, angel fund investor, Taipei City, Taiwan

6 January 2012, chairman of the KT Li Institute for Digital Information (and colleague of K. T. Li), Taipei City, Taiwan

6 January 2012, senior specialist, CEPD Department of Economic Research, Taipei City, Taiwan

5 September 2012, head of policy Southeast Asia for a technology MNC, Singapore

11 September 2012, associate professor, National University of Singapore, Singapore

12 September 2012, former manager of the TIF from 1999 until 2005, and member of the Technopreneurship 21 Ministerial Committee, Singapore

12 September 2012, Singapore Venture Capital Association member, Singapore

13 September 2012, country policy head for technology MNC, Singapore

13 September 2012, Singapore-based entrepreneur and former civil servant, Singapore

16 September 2012, founder of incubator and private sector contributor to National Research Foundation, Singapore

17 September 2012, VC manager and member of SVCA leadership, Singapore

18 September 2012, founder of Singaporean incubator supported by government funding, Singapore

18 September 2012, journalist focused on reporting entrepreneurship and VC news and manager of a government-sponsored incubator, Singapore

18 September 2012, director of Singaporean university enterprise support center, Singapore

19 September 2012, confidential government ministerial ICT policy panel meeting, Singapore

20 September 2012, VC manager and former civil servant, Singapore

20 September 2012, head of entrepreneurship promotion, SPRING, Singapore

20 September 2012, head of SME healthcare and biomedical programs, SPRING, Singapore

24 September 2012, APEC Small & Medium Enterprise Working Group director, Singapore

25 September 2012, Agency for Science, Technology and Research (A*STAR) deputy director of planning and policy, Singapore

25 September 2012, A*STAR head of planning and policy, Singapore

25 September 2012, CEO of Singapore-incorporated media start-up company, Singapore

6 October 2013, founder and manager of the Yozma Group, Tel Aviv

6 February 2015, general partner at venture capital firm, London

References

Abeysinghe, Tilak. 2007. "Singapore: Economy." *NUS Course Outline.* September.

Acharya, Amitav. 2004. "How Ideas Spread: Whose Norms Matter? Norm Localization and Institutional Change in Asian Regionalism." *International Organization* 58(2): 239–75.

———. 2009. *The Making of Southeast Asia: International Relations of a Region.* Ithaca, NY: Cornell University Press.

Adam Smith Institute. 2009. *The Effect of Capital Gains Tax Rises on Revenues.* London: Adam Smith Institute.

Afonso, Antonio, and Miguel St. Aubyn. 2008. "Macroeconomic Rates of Return of Public and Private Investment: Crowding-In and Crowding-Out Effects." European Central Bank Working Paper Series No. 864. February.

Aglietta, Michel. 2000. "Shareholder Value and Corporate Governance: Some Tricky Questions." *Economy and Society* 29(1): 146–59.

Almond, Gabriel A. and Stephen J. Genco. 1977. "Clouds, Clocks, and the Study of Politics." *World Politics* 29(4): 489–522.

Almor, Tamar, and Gilad Sperling. 2008. "Israeli Born Global, Knowledge-Intensive Firms: An Empirical Inquiry." In *Handbook of Research on European Business and Entrepreneurship: Towards a Theory of Internationalization,* edited by L. Dana, M. Han, M. Ratten, and V. Welpe. Cheltenham, UK: Edward Elgar, 316–36.

Amable, Bruno. 2003. *The Diversity of Modern Capitalism.* Oxford: Oxford University Press.

Amsden, Alice. 1979. "Taiwan's Economic History: A Case of Etatisme and a Challenge to Dependency Theory." *Modern China* 5(3): 341–79.

———. 2001. *The Rise of "The Rest": Challenges to the West from Late-Industrializing Economies.* Oxford: Oxford University Press.

Aoki, Masahiko, Gregory Jackson, and Hideaki Miyajima, eds. 2007. *Corporate Governance in Japan: Institutional Change and Organizational Diversity.* Oxford: Oxford University Press.

Arrington, Michael. 2010. "Accel Sold Big Chunk of Facebook Stock at $35 Billion Valuation." *TechCrunch.* November 19.

Asher, Mukul G. 1999. "The Pension System in Singapore." World Bank Social Protection Discussion Paper Series No. 9919. Washington, DC: World Bank.

Asian Venture Capital Journal (AVCJ). 2005. *Asian Private Equity 300 Guide*. Hong Kong: AVCJ.

Au, Kevin, and Steven White. 2009. "Hong Kong's Venture Capital System and the Commercialization of New Technology." Hong Kong Innovation Project Report No. 5. Hong Kong: HKIP.

Aviles, Andres. 2009. "Impacts of Japanese Colonialism on State and Economic Development in Korea and Taiwan, and its Implications for Democracy." Manuscript, Naval Postgraduate School. June.

Avnimelech, Gil 2009. "VC Policy: Yozma Program 15-Years Perspective." DRUID Summer Conference, Copenhagen Business School.

Avnimelech, Gil, and Morris Teubal. 2004. "Strength of Market Forces and the Successful Emergence of Israel's Venture Capital Industry: Insights from a Policy-led Case of Structural Change." *Revue Economique* 55(6): 1265–1300.

——. 2006. "Creating Venture Capital Industries That Co-Evolve with High Tech Clusters: Insights from an Extended Industry Life Cycle Perspective of the Israeli Experience." *Research Policy* 35(10): 1477–98.

——. 2008. "From Direct Support Of Business Sector R&D/Innovation To Targeting Venture Capital/Private Equity: A Catching-Up Innovation And Technology Policy Life Cycle Perspective." *Economics of Innovation and New Technology* 17(1–2): 153–72.

Axelrod, Robert. 1986. "An Evolutionary Approach to Norms." *American Political Science Review* 80(4): 1095–1111.

Aylward, Anthony. 1998. "Trends in Venture Capital Finance in Developing Countries." International Finance Corporation Discussion Paper No. 36. July. Washington, DC: IFC.

Barros, Gustavo. 2010. "Herbert A. Simon and the Concept of Rationality: Boundaries and Procedures." *Brazilian Journal of Political Economy* 30(3): 455–72.

Bates, Robert H., Avner Greif, Margaret Levi, and Jean-Laurent Rosenthal. 1998. *Analytical Narratives*. Princeton: Princeton University Press.

Baygan, Günseli. 2003. "Venture Capital Policies in Israel." OECD STI Working Paper 2003/3, Industry Issues. Paris: OECD.

Beisel, David. 2016. "Atomization of Seed Rounds Part I: An Explanation." *Genuine VC*. June 14.

Bell, Stephen. 2005. "How Tight Are the Policy Constraints? The Convergence Thesis, Institutionally Situated Actors and Expansionary Monetary Policy in Australia." *New Political Economy* 10(1): 65–89.

Bennett, Colin J. 1991. "What Is Policy Convergence and What Causes It?" *British Journal of Political Science* 21(2): 215–33.

Berger, Suzanne, and Richard K. Lester. 1997. *Made by Hong Kong*. Hong Kong: Oxford University Press.

Berger, Thomas U. 1996. "Norms, Identity, and National Security in Germany and Japan." In *The Culture of National Security: Norms and Identity in World Politics*, edited by Peter J. Katzenstein. New York: Columbia University Press, 317–56.

Bernstein, Steven. 2011. "Legitimacy in Intergovernmental and Non-state Global Governance." *Review of International Political Economy* 18(1): 17–51.

Berry, William D., and Brady Baybeck. 2005. "Using Geographic Information Systems to Study Interstate Competition." *American Political Science Review* 99(4): 505–19.

Blank, Steve. 2013. "Why the Lean Start-up Changes Everything." *Harvard Business Review*. May.

Block, Fred. 2001. "Introduction." In Karl Polanyi, *The Great Transformation: The Political and Economic Origins of Our Time*. Boston: Beacon Press.

———. 2008. "Swimming against the Current: The Rise of a Hidden Developmental State in the United States." *Politics and Society* 36(2): 169–206.

Braun, Dietmar, and Fabrizio Gilardi. 2006. "Taking 'Galton's Problem' Seriously: Towards a Theory of Policy Diffusion." *Journal of Theoretical Politics* 18(3): 298–322.

Breznitz, Dan. 2007. *Innovation and the State: Political Choices and Strategies for Growth in Israel, Taiwan, and Ireland*, New Haven: Yale University Press.

Breznitz, Dan, and Michael Murphree. 2011. *Run of the Red Queen*. New Haven: Yale University Press.

Browne, Eric C., and Dennis Patterson. 1999. "An Empirical Theory of Rational Nominating Behavior Applied to Japanese District Elections." *British Journal of Political Science* 29(2): 259–89.

Bruton, Gary D., David Ahlstrom, and Kulwant Singh. 2002. "The Impact of the Institutional Environment on the Venture Capital Industry in Singapore." *Venture Capital: An International Journal of Entrepreneurial Finance* 4(3): 197–218.

Buchanan, James M., Robert D. Tollison, and Gordon Tullock, eds. 1980. *Toward a Theory of the Rent-Seeking Society*. College Station: Texas A&M University Press.

Bullock, Nicole. 2016. "Technology 'Unicorns' Staying Shy of IPOs." *Financial Times*. February 9.

Busch, Per-olof, and Helge Jörgens. 2005. "The International Sources of Policy Convergence: Explaining the Spread of Environmental Policy Innovations." *Journal of European Public Policy* 12(5): 860–84.

Califano, Howard, Arkajit Roy Barman, and Daniel Lubrich. 2010. "The Singapore Venture Report." *NanoCore*. Singapore. August.

Campos, Jose E., and Hilton L. Root. 1996. *The Key to the Asian Miracle: Making Shared Growth Credible*. Washington, DC: Brookings Institution.

Capoccia, Giovanni. 2015. "Critical Junctures and Institutional Change." In *Advances in Comparative Historical Analysis*, edited by James Mahoney and Kathleen Thelen. Cambridge: Cambridge University Press, 147–79.

Carlsnaes, Walter, Thomas Risse, and Beth A. Simmons. 2012. *Handbook of International Relations*. London: Sage.

Carney, Richard W., and Loh Yi Zheng. 2009. "Institutional (Dis)incentives to Innovate: An Explanation for Singapore's Innovation Gap." *Journal of East Asian Studies* 9(2): 291–319.

Casper, Steven, Mark Lehrer, and David Soskice. 2009. "Can High-Technology Industries Prosper in Germany? Institutional Frameworks and the Evolution of the German Software and Biotechnology Industries." In *Debating Varieties of Capitalism*, edited by B. Hancké. Oxford: Oxford University Press, 200–220.

CB Insights. 2014. "The Top Venture Capital Investors by Exit Activity—Which Firms See the Highest Share of IPOs?" New York, NY.

———. 2017. "The 2016 AI Recap: Startups See Record High In Deals And Funding." January 19. New York, NY.

Cerny, Philip G. 2007. "Paradoxes of the Competition State: The Dynamics of Political Globalization." *Government and Opposition* 32(2): 251–74.

Chan, Juliana. 2016. "The Builder: Professor Low Teck Seng." *Asian Scientist.* February 24. http://www.asianscientist.com/2016/02/features/sg50-pioneer-teck-seng-builder/.

Chan, Kevin. 2006. "Speech by Mr. S. Iswaran, Minister of State for Trade and Industry, at Singapore Venture Capital and Private Equity Association Annual Dinner." *SVCA* 27 September.

Checkel, Jeffrey T. 1999. "Norms, Institutions, and National Identity in Contemporary Europe." *International Studies Quarterly* 43(1): 83–114.

Cheng, Joseph Y. S. 2013. "Democratization in Hong Kong: A Theoretical Explanation." In *Democracy in Eastern Asia: Issues, Problems and Challenges in a Region of Diversity*, edited by Edmund S.K. Fung and Steven Drakely. Routledge: New York, 224–45.

Cheung, Anthony B. L. 2004. "Strong Executive, Weak Policy Capacity: The Changing Environment of Policy-making in Hong Kong." *Asian Journal of Political Science* 12(1): 1–30.

Cheung, Peter T. Y. 2011. "Civil Engagement in the Policy Process in Hong Kong: Change and Continuity." *Public Administration and Development* 31: 113–21.

Chia, Siow Yue. 2005. "The Singapore Model of Industrial Policy: Past Evolution and Current Thinking." *ADBI: Second LAEBA Annual Conference.* Buenos Aires.

Choi, Alex Hang-Keung. 1994. "Beyond Market and State: A Study of Hong Kong's Industrial Transformation." *Studies in Political Economy* 45: 28–64.

Council for Economic Planning and Development (CEPD) Executive Yuan, ROC (Taiwan). 2010. *Economic Development ROC (Taiwan).* Taipei City: CEPD.

Crouch, Colin. 2009. "Typologies of Capitalism." In *Debating Varieties of Capitalism*, edited by B. Hancké. Oxford: Oxford University Press, 75–94.

Culpepper, Pepper. 2005. "Institutional Change in Contemporary Capitalism: Coordinated Financial Systems Since 1990." *World Politics* 57(2): 173–99.

Cumming, Douglas. 2010. *Venture Capital: Investment Strategies, Structures and Policies.* Hoboken, NJ: John Wiley & Sons, 306.

Da Rin, Marco, Thomas Hellmann, Manju Puri. 2013. "A Survey of Venture Capital Research." In *Handbook of the Economics of Finance*, edited by George M. Constantinides, Milton Harris, and Rene M. Stulz. Vol. 2, Part A. Amsterdam: Elsevier B.V., 573–648.

Deeg, Richard. 2009. "The Rise of Internal Capitalist Diversity? Changing Patterns of Finance and Corporate Governance in Europe." *Economy and Society* 38(4): 552–79.

Deeg, Richard, Iain Hardie, and Sylvia Maxfield. 2016. "What Is Patient Capital, and Where Does It Exist?" *Socio-Economic Review* 14(4): 615–25.

Deeg, Richard, and Gregory Jackson. 2007. "Towards a More Dynamic Theory of Capitalist Variety." *Socio-Economic Review* 5(1): 149–79.

De Vecchi, Nicolo. 2003. "The Place of Gestalt Psychology in the Making of Hayek's Thought." *History of Political Economy* 35(1): 135–62.

Dietrich, J. Kimball. 2003. "Venture Capital in APEC Economies." *Report to APEC*, May 15.

DiMaggio, Paul J., and Walter W. Powell. 1983. "The Iron Cage Revisited: Institutional Isomorphism and Collective Rationality in Organizational Fields." *American Sociological Review* 48(2): 147–60.

Dobbin, Frank, Beth Garrett Simmons, and Geoffrey Garrett. 2007. "The Global Diffusion of Public Policies: Social Construction, Coercion, Competition, or Learning?" *Annual Review of Sociology* 33: 449–72.

Doh Joon Chien. 1996. "Government Policy on Small and Medium Enterprises." In *Economic Policy Management in Singapore*, edited by Lim Chong Yah. Addison-Wesley: Singapore, 330–58.

Doidge, Craig, G. Andrew Karolyi, and Rene M. Stulz. 2011. "The U.S. Left Behind: The Rise of IPO Activity around the World." NBER Working Paper 16916. March. Cambridge, MA: NBER.

Dolowitz, D., and D. Marsh. 2000. "Learning from Abroad: The Role of Policy Transfer in Contemporary Policymaking." *Governance* 13(1): 5–24.

Dolowitz, David, and J. C. Sharman. 2009. "Policy Diffusion and Policy Transfer." *Policy Studies* 30(3): 269–88.

Dow Jones VentureSource. 2014. *Venture Capital Report*. New York: Dow Jones.

Drezner, Daniel W. 2005. "Globalization, Harmonization, and Competition: The Different Pathways to Policy Convergence." *Journal of European Public Policy* 12(5): 841–59.

Economic Committee. 1986. "The Singapore Economy: New Directions." *Ministry of Trade and Industry*. Singapore: SNP.

——. 1991. "The Strategic Economic Plan: Towards a Developed Nation." *Ministry of Trade and Industry*. Singapore: SNP.

Economic Development Board (EDB). 1982. *EDB Annual Report 1981–82*, 34–37.

——. 1998a. *Committee on Singapore Competitiveness Report: Executive Summary*.

——. 1998b. *Growing a Knowledge-based Economy: EDB Annual Report 1997*.

——. 2000. *Enabling the Knowledge-based Economy: EDB Annual Report 1999–2000*, 58–59.

——. 2002. *Singapore's Enterprise Ecosystem: EDB Annual Report 2001–2*, 48–51.

——. 2012. *Global Investor Programme*.

Economic Review Committee (ERC). 2002. "Positioning Singapore as a Pre-eminent Financial Centre in Asia: Executive Summary." *Sub-Committee on Services Industries Financial Services Working Group*. September. Singapore.

Economic Strategies Committee. 2010. *Untitled Letter to Prime Minister on Progress and Recommendations*. Singapore.

The Economist. 2017. "British Tech Firms Suffer from Impatient Investors." April 6.

Edquist, Charles. 1997. *Systems of Innovation: Technologies, Institutions and Organizations*. London: Pinter.

Elkins, Zachary, and Beth Simmons. 2005. "On Waves, Clusters, and Diffusion: A Conceptual Framework." *Annals of the American Academy of Political and Social Science* 598: 33–51.

Epley, Nicholas, and Thomas Gilovich. 2006. "The Anchoring-and-Adjustment Heuristic." *Psychological Science* 17: 311–18.

Erlich, Yigal. 2002. "The Yozma Program—Success Factors and Policy." Yozma Group. Tel Aviv, Israel.

Ernst & Young. 2012. *Globalizing Venture Capital: Global Venture Capital Insights and Trends Report*.

——. 2016. *Back to Reality: EY Global Venture Capital Trends 2015*.

EU Business. 2016. "EU Moves to Boost Access to Venture Capital." July 14.

European Commission. 1995. *Green Paper on Innovation*.

Eurostat. 2015. "R&D Expenditure in the EU Stable at Slightly Over 2% of GDP in 2014." Eurostat Newsrelease 209/2015. November 30. http://ec.europa.eu/eurostat/documents/2995521/7092226/9-30112015-AP-EN.pdf/29eeaa3d-29c8-496d-9302-77056be6d586.

Evans, Peter B. 1995. *Embedded Autonomy: States and Industrial Transformation.* Princeton: Princeton University Press.

Executive Office of the [U.S.] President. 2016. *Artificial Intelligence, Automation, and the Economy.* December.

Executive Yuan Development Fund. 2013. "The Goals of Promoting Venture Capital."

Fai, Loke Kok, and Xabryna Kek. 2016. "Govt commits S$9b to New 5-year Plan for R&D Initiatives RIE2020." *Channel News Asia.* January 8.

Falkner, Robert, and Aarti Gupta. 2009. "The Limits of Regulatory Convergence: Globalization and GMO Politics in the South." *International Environmental Agreements* 9(2): 113–33.

Fearon, James, and Alexander Wendt. 2002. "Rationalism versus Constructivism: A Skeptical View." In *Handbook of International Relations,* edited by Walter Carlsnaes, Thomas Risse and Beth A. Simmons. London: Sage Publications, 54–72.

Fenn, George, Nellie Liang, and Stephen Prowse. 1995. "The Economics of the Private Equity Market." Federal Reserve Bank Staff Paper 168.

Fields, Karl J. 2012. "Not of a Piece: Developmental States, Industrial Policy, and Evolving Patterns of Capitalism in Japan, Korea and Taiwan." In *East Asian Capitalism: Diversity, Continuity and Change,* edited by Andrew Walter and Xiaoke Zhang. Oxford: Oxford University Press, 46–67.

Finnemore, Martha. 1996. "Norms, Culture, and World Politics: Insights from Sociology's Institutionalism." *International Organization* 50(2): 325–47.

Finnemore, Martha, and Kathryn Sikkink. 1998. "International Norm Dynamics and Political Change." *International Organization* 52(4): 887–917.

Fitzpatrick, Alex. 2015. "Something Ventured: New Start-ups Are Being Primed by a Major Boom in Funding." *Time* 185(3): 11.

Florini, Ann. 1996. "The Evolution of International Norms." *International Studies Quarterly* 40(3): 363–89.

Forsyth, Douglas J., and Daniel Verdier, eds. 2003. *The Origins of National Financial Systems: Alexander Gerschenkron Reconsidered.* Routledge: London.

Fox, James W. 1996. *The Venture Capital Mirage: Assessing USAID Experience with Equity Investment.* USAID Program and Operations Report No. 17.

Friedman, Thomas. 1999. *The Lexus and the Olive Tree.* New York: Farrar, Strauss.

Fuhrman, Peter. 2016. "How Renimbi Funds Took over Chinese Private Equity (Part I)." *Super Return Live.* March 31.

Fuller, Douglas. 2002. "Globalization for Nation Building: Industrial Policy for High-Technology Products in Taiwan." MIT Japan Working Paper 02.02.

——. 2010. *Innovation Policy and the Limits of Laissez-faire: Hong Kong's Policy in Comparative Perspective.* New York: Palgrave MacMillan.

——. 2016. *Paper Tigers, Hidden Dragons: Firms and the Political Economy of China's Technology Development.* Oxford: Oxford University Press.

Gerschenkron, Alexander. 1962. *Economic Backwardness in Historical Perspective: A Book of Essays.* Cambridge, MA: Belknap Press of Harvard University Press.

Ghosh, Shona. 2017. "A £2 Billion European Investment Fund Has Stopped Giving Money to UK Tech Startups Because of Brexit." *Business Insider.* May 19.

Gilardi, Fabrizio. 2010. "Who Learns from What in Policy Diffusion Processes?" *American Journal of Political Science* 54(3): 650–66.

Gilovich, Thomas, Dale Griffin, and Daniel Kahneman, eds. 2002. *Heuristics and Biases*. New York: Cambridge University Press.

Gilson, Ronald J., and Barnard S. Black. 1999. "Does Venture Capital Require an Active Stock Market?" *Journal of Applied Corporate Finance* 11: 36–48.

GIO. 1994. *The Republic of China Yearbook 2001*. Taipei: GIO.

GIS and Renu Daryanani. 1994. *Hong Kong 1994: A Review of 1993*. GIS: Hong Kong, 85–87, 95.

——. 1995. *Hong Kong 1995: A Review of 1994*. GIS: Hong Kong, 27, 39, 70–111.

GIS and David Roberts. 1990. *Hong Kong 1990: A Review of 1989*, 53–80.

——. 1991. *Hong Kong 1991: A Review of 1990*. GIS: Hong Kong, 67.

——. 1992. *Hong Kong 1992: A Review of 1991*.

GIS and Hugh Witt. 1993. *Hong Kong 1992: A Review of 1992*. GIS: Hong Kong, 49, 70, 72.

Goh, Andrew L. 2005. "Towards an Innovation-Driven Economy through Industrial Policy-Making: An Evolutionary Analysis of Singapore." *Public Sector Innovation Journal* 10(3): 34.

Gold, Thomas B. 1986. *State and Society in the Taiwan Miracle*. Armonk, NY: M. E. Sharpe.

Goldstein, Judith, and Robert Keohane, eds. 1993. *Ideas and Foreign Policy: Beliefs, Institutions and Political Change*. Ithaca, NY: Cornell University Press.

Golomb, Vitaly. 2014. "The Government Once Built Silicon Valley." *TechCrunch*. July 4.

Gompers, Paul, and Josh Lerner. 1999. *The Venture Capital Cycle*. Cambridge, MA: MIT Press.

Goodman, John B., and Louis W. Pauly. 1993. "The Obsolescence of Capital Controls in an Age of Global Markets?" *World Politics* 46(1): 50–82.

Gopalakrishnan, Raju, and Kevin Lim. 2011. "Singapore's PAP Retains Power; Opposition Makes Gains." *Reuters*. May 8.

Government Information Office Executive Yuan, ROC (GIO). 1983. *Republic of China: A Reference Book*. Taipei: United Pacific International: 96–120, 159–61, 189–93, 333–61.

——. 1986. *Republic of China: A Reference Book*. Taipei: Hilit, 196, 237, 288.

——. 1992. *The Republic of China Yearbook 1992*. Taipei: GIO.

——. 1999. *The Republic of China Yearbook 1999*. Taipei: GIO: 172.

——. 2000. *The Republic of China Yearbook 2000*. Taipei: GIO: 104–10, 150, 315.

——. 2001. *The Republic of China Yearbook 2001*. Taipei: GIO: 161, 184, 308–9.

Government Information Services (GIS.) 1995. *Hong Kong 1995*. GIS: Hong Kong, 79–80, 85.

Graduate Institute for Policy Studies (GRIPS). 2011. "Report on Taiwan Mission." *GRIPS Development Forum*. April 7.

——. Development Forum. 2010. "A Report on the Singapore Mission." *Japan International Cooperation Agency*. September 13.

Granovetter, Mark. 1992. "Economic Institutions as Social Constructions: A Framework for Analysis." *Acta Sociologica* 35(1): 3–11.

Greene, J. Megan. 2008. *The Origins of the Developmental State in Taiwan*. Cambridge, MA: Harvard University Press.

GuideMeSingapore. 2013. "Types of Business Entities in Singapore." https://www.guidemesingapore.com/business-guides/incorporation-guides/introduction-to-incorporation/types-of-business-entities-in-singapore. Accessed 16 July 2017.

Gulinello, Christopher. 2005. "Engineering a Venture Capital Market and the Effects of Government Control on Private Ordering: Lessons from the Taiwan Experience." *George Washington International Law Review* 37(4): 845–83.

Ha, Anthony. 2009. "International Venture Funding Rose 5 Percent in 2008." *VentureBeat.* February 18.

Haas, Peter. 1992. "Epistemic Communities and International Policy Coordination." *International Organization* 46(1): 1–35.

Haggard, Stephan. 1990. *Pathways from the Periphery: The Politics of Growth in the Newly Industrializing Countries.* Ithaca, NY: Cornell University Press.

Haggard, Stephan, and Sylvia Maxfield. 1996. "The Political Economy of Financial Internationalization in the Developing World." *International Organization* 50(1): 35–68.

Hall, Peter. 1993. "Policy Paradigms, Social Learning, and the State: The Case of Economic Policymaking in Britain." *Comparative Politics* 25(3): 275–96.

Hall, Peter, and David Soskice. 2001. *Varieties of Capitalism: the Institutional Foundations of Comparative Advantage.* Oxford: Oxford University Press.

Hall, Peter, and Rosemary C. R. Taylor. 1996. "Political Science and the Three New Institutionalisms." MPIFG Discussion Paper 96/6. Cologne, Germany.

Hamilton, Gary G. 1999. *Cosmopolitan Capitalists: Hong Kong and the Chinese Diaspora at the End of the Twentieth Century.* Seattle: University of Washington Press.

Han Fook Kwang, Zuraidah Ibrahim, Chua Mui Hoong, Lydia Lim, Ignatius Low, Rachel Lin, and Robin Chan. 2011. *Lee Kuan Yew: Hard Truths to Keep Singapore Going.* Singapore: Straits Times Press.

Hasson, Avi. 2014. Avi Hasson, chief scientist, in conversation with Dr. Tim Hames, director general, BVCA. November 5. London.

Heerjee, Kaizad. 2000. "The Buzzing eCommerce Scene in Singapore: Dr Kaizad Heerjee, Assistant Chief Executive, Online Development, IDA Singapore—Keynote Address, Launch of eBiz.Connect Networking Session." Pan Pacific Hotel, Singapore. June 14, 2000.

Heritage Foundation. 2017. *Country Rankings.* Washington, DC: Heritage Foundation.

Hirschman, Albert. O. 1970. *Exit, Voice and Loyalty.* Cambridge, MA: Harvard University Press.

HKTDC. 2016. "Private Equity Industry in Hong Kong." January 15.

HMRC. 2015. *VCM50010—VCT: Overview of the VCT Scheme.*

Ho, Kong, Koh Ai Tee, and Shandre M. Thangavelu. 2002. "Enhancing Technopreneurship: Issues and Challenges." In *Singapore Economy in the 21st Century: Issues and Strategies*, edited by Koh Ai Tee, Lim Kim Lian, Hui Weng Tat, Bhanoji Rao, and Meng Kng Chng. Singapore: McGraw Hill, 321–44.

Holzinger, Katharina, and Christoph Knill. 2005. "Causes and Conditions of Cross-national Policy Convergence." *Journal of European Public Policy* 12(5): 775–96.

Hong Kong Audit Commission. 2004. "Commerce, Industry and Technology Bureau, Innovation and Technology Commission: Funding of projects under the Applied Research Fund."

Hong Kong Innovation and Technology Commission. 2011. "Funding Schemes: Applied Research Fund, Background of the Applied Research Fund."

Hong Kong Legal Information Institute. 2013. *Hong Kong Ordinances.*

Hong Kong Legislative Council. 1987. "Official Report of Proceedings: Wednesday, 14 January 1987." *Hong Kong Legislative Council,* 708–45.

Hong Kong Legislative Council Panel on Commerce and Industry. 2010. "Creation of a Favorable Ecological Environment to Facilitate the Realization of Research and Development Results." Trade and Industry Bureau. LC Paper No. CB(1)389/10–11(05). November.

——. 2011. "The Applied Research Fund." Trade and Industry Bureau October LC Paper No. CB(1)75/11–12(01).

——. 2012. "Promotion of Innovation and Technology in Hong Kong." Commerce and Economic Development Bureau LC Paper No. CB(1)1790/11–12(03). May 15.

——. 2013. "2013 Policy Address: Policy Initiatives of Commerce, Industry and Tourism Branch and Innovation and Technology Commission, Commerce and Economic Development Bureau." Commerce and Economic Development Bureau LC Paper No. CB(1)436/12–13(03). January 16.

Hong Kong Legislative Council Panel on Trade and Industry. 1999a. "Information Paper for LegCo Panel on Trade and Industry: Existing Funding Schemes for Manufacturing and Services Industries." Trade and Industry Bureau. February 1. http://www.legco.gov.hk/yr98-99/english/panels/ti/papers/ti0102_4.htm.

——. 1999b. "Applied Research Fund." Trade and Industry Bureau. July 5.

——. 2000. "Applied Research Fund." Trade and Industry Bureau. May 9.

Hong Kong Legislative Council Secretariat Research Division. 2011. "Fact Sheet: Industrial Research Institutes and Industrial Parks in Taiwan." Hong Kong Legislative Secretariat FS17/10–11, March 30.

Hong Kong Public Finance Ordinance. 1999. "Resolution: Under Section 29 of the Public Finance Ordinance (Cap. 2): Innovation and Technology Fund." Hong Kong Public Finance Ordinance, Enclosure 2 to FCR (1999–2000) 36.

Hong Kong Trade and Industry Bureau. 1998. "Item for Finance Committee: New Capital Account—Applied Research Fund." Industry of Industry and Trade FCR (97–98): 114.

Hong Kong Venture Capital and Private Equity Association (HKVCA). 2001. *Year 2000–2001 in Review: Chairman Richard Roque.*

——. 2002. *Year 2001–2 in Review: Chairman Roger Marshall.*

——. 2003. *Year 2002–3 in Review: Chairman Monique Lau.*

——. 2004. *Year 2003–4 in Review: Chairman Kevin Yip.*

——. 2005. *Year 2004–5 in Review: Chairman Hanson Cheah.*

——. 2006. *Year 2005–6 in Review: Chairman Vincent Chan.*

——. 2007. *Year 2006–7 in Review: Chairman Jamie Paton.*

——. 2008. *Year 2007–8 in Review: Chairman Johnny Chan.*

——. 2009. *Year 2008–9 in Review: Chairman Kevin Yip.*

——. 2010. "Annual Report 2009–10." *HKVCA.*

——. 2015. "Asian Private Equity and Private Equity Council" *HKVCA.*

Horwitz, Josh. 2015. "Taiwan Government to Invest in Over $80 Million in Four VC Funds, including 500 Startups." *TechinAsia.* January 26.

Hoskins, Tansy. 2016. "Robot Factories Could Threaten Jobs of Millions of Garment Workers." *The Guardian,* July 16.

Huff, Gregg. 1994. *The Economic Growth of Singapore: Trade and Development in the Twentieth Century.* Cambridge: Cambridge University Press.

Hundt, David. 2014. "Economic Crisis in Korea and the Degraded Developmental State." *Australian Journal of International Affairs* (68)5: 499–514.

Info HK. 2002. "Budget Speech by the Financial Secretary." March 6, 2002.

Information Services Department (ISD, English edition). 2000. *Hong Kong 2000.* ISD: Hong Kong: 102–11, 362–68.

——. 2005. *Hong Kong 2005.* ISD: Hong Kong: 44, 102, 120–31.

——. 2009. *Hong Kong 2009.* ISD: Hong Kong: i, 61, 66, 105.

ISD and Bob Howlett. 1996. *Hong Kong 1996: A Review of 1995 and A Pictorial Review of the Past Fifty Years.* H. Myers, Government Printer: Hong Kong: 27, 99–100.

Innovation and Technology Commission (ITC). 2011. "About Us: Strategic Partner."

Islam, Asif. 2015. "Entrepreneurship and the Allocation of Government Spending under Imperfect Markets." World Bank Policy Research Working Paper 7163. Washington, DC: World Bank.

Iversen, Torben, and David Soskice. 2006. "Electoral Institutions and the Politics of Coalitions: Why Some Democracies Redistribute More Than Others." *American Political Science Review* 100(2): 165–81.

Jacowitz, Karen E., and Daniel Kahneman. 1995. "Measures of Anchoring in Estimation Tasks." *Personality and Social Psychology Bulletin* 21: 1161–66.

Jepperson, Ronald L., Alexander Wendt, and Peter J. Katzenstein. 1996. "Norms, Identity, and Culture in National Security," In *The Culture of National Security: Norms and Identity in World Politics,* edited by Peter J. Katzenstein. New York: Columbia University Press, 33–75.

Jervis, Robert. 1985. "From Balance to Concert: A Study of International Security Cooperation." *World Politics* 38(1): 58–79.

Johnson, Chalmers. 1982. *MITI and the Japanese Miracle.* Palo Alto: Stanford University Press.

Kalberg, Stephen. 1980. "Max Weber's Types of Rationality: Cornerstones for the Analysis of Rationalization Processes in History." *American Journal of Sociology* 85(5): 1145–79.

Kaplan, Morton. 1976. "Means/ends Rationality." *Ethics* 87(1): 61–65.

Katzenstein, Peter J. 1978. "Introduction: Domestic and International Forces and Strategies of Foreign Economic Policy." In *Between Power and Plenty: Foreign Economic Policies of Advanced Industrial States.* Madison: University of Wisconsin Press, 3–22.

——. 1985. *Small States in World Markets: Industrial Policy in Europe.* Ithaca, NY: Cornell University Press.

——, ed. 1996. "Introduction." In *Culture and the Security State: Norms and Identity in World Politics.* New York: Colombia University Press, 1–32.

Katzenstein, P., R. Keohane, and S. Krasner. 1998. "International Organization and the Study of World Politics." *International Organization* 52(4): 645–85.

Kay, John. 2012. *The Kay Review of UK Equity Markets and Long-Term Decision Making.* London: UK Department of Business Innovation and Skills.

Kennedy, Alex. 2011. "Singapore Enters New Era and Founding Father Lee Leaves Cabinet after Historic Opposition Gains." *Associated Press.* May 18.

Kenney, Martin. 2011. "How Venture Capital Became a Component of the US National System of Innovation." *Industrial and Corporate Change* 20(6): 1677–1723.

Kenney, Martin, Han Kyonghee, and Shoko Tanaka. 2002. "Scattering Geese: The Venture Capital Industries of East Asia, A Report to the World Bank." *World Bank.* September 29. Washington, DC: World Bank.

Kenyon, Helen. 2012. "Preqin Special Report: Venture Capital." Preqin Ltd.

Khurshed, Arif, Stephen Lin, and Mingzhu Wang. 2011. "Institutional Block-Holdings of UK Firms: Do Corporate Governance Mechanisms Matter?" *European Journal of Finance* 17: 133–52.

Kim, Mason M. S. 2015. *Comparative Welfare Capitalism in East Asia: Productivist Models of Social Policy.* London: Palgrave Macmillan.

King, Gary, Robert O. Keohane, and Sydney Verba. 1994. *Designing Social Inquiry: Scientific Inference in Qualitative Research.* Princeton: Princeton University Press.

King, Mervyn. 2016. *The End of Alchemy: Money, Banking, and the Future of the Global Economy.* New York: W. W. Norton.

King, Rodney. 2006. *The Singapore Miracle: Myth and Reality.* Inglewood, Australia: Insight Press, 27–34.

Kirby, Carrie. 2002. "Q&A: Stan Shih of Acer Computing Success: Taiwanese Exec Discusses PC Industry, Links to Bay Area." *San Francisco Chronicle*, March 25.

Klingler-Vidra, Robyn. 2014a. "Building a Venture Capital Market in Vietnam: Diffusion of a Neoliberal Market Strategy to a Socialist State." *Asian Studies Review* 38(4): 582–600.

——. 2014b. "The Public Venture Policy Menu: Policies Public Authorities Can Take." *Coller Venture Review* 1a: 36–43.

——. 2015. "Diffusion and Adaptation: Why Even the Silicon Valley Model Is Adapted as It Diffuses to East Asia." *Pacific Review* 29(5): 761–84.

——. 2016. "When Venture Capital Is Patient Capital: Seed Funding as a Source of Patient Capital for High-growth Companies." *Socio-Economic Review* 14(4): 691–708.

Klingler-Vidra, Robyn, Martin Kenney, and Dan Breznitz. 2016. "Policies for Financing Entrepreneurship through Venture Capital: Learning from the Successes of Israel and Taiwan." *International Journal of Innovation and Regional Development* 7(3): 203–21.

Klingler-Vidra, Robyn, and Philip Schleifer. 2014. "Convergence More or Less: Why Do Practices Vary as They Diffuse?" *International Studies Review* 16(2): 264–74.

Klingler-Vidra, Robyn, and Robert Hunter Wade. forthcoming. "The World Bank, the Middle Income Trap and 'Policy Distraction' in Vietnam." Working paper.

Knight, Frank. 1921. *Risk, Uncertainty, and Profit.* Boston, MA: Hart, Schaffner and Marx.

Knill, Christoph. 2005. "Introduction: Cross-national Policy Convergence: Concepts, Approaches and Explanatory Factors." *Journal of European Public Policy* 12:5: 764–74.

Koehn, Peter H. 2001. "One Government, Multiple Systems: Hong Kong Public Administration in Transition." *Public Organization Review: A Global Journal* 1: 97–121.

Kogut, Bruce, and J. Muir Macpherson. 2008. "The Decision to Privatize: Economists and the Construction of Ideas and Policies." In *The Global Diffusion of Marks and Democracy,* edited by Beth A. Simmons, Frank Dobbin, and Geoffrey Garret. Cambridge: Cambridge University Press, 104–40.

Koh, Francis C. C., and Winston T. H. Koh. 2002. "Venture Capital and Economic Growth: An Industry Overview and Singapore's Experience." SMU Economics and Statistics Working Paper Series 21–2002. November.

Koh, Winston T. H., and Poh Kam Wong. 2005. "The Venture Capital Industry in Singapore: A Comparative Study with Taiwan and Israel on the Government's Role." NUS Entrepreneurship Centre Working Papers Reference No.: WP2005–09.

Kohli, Atul. 2004. *State-Directed Development: Political Power and Industrialization in the Global Periphery*, Cambridge: Cambridge University Press.

Kortum, Samuel, and Josh Lerner. 2000. "Assessing the Contribution of Venture Capital to Innovation." *RAND Journal of Economics* 31(4): 674–92.

Kowert, Paul, and Jeffrey Legro. 1996. "Norms, Identity, and Their Limits: A Theoretical Reprise." In *The Culture of National Security: Norms and Identity in World Politics*, edited by Peter J. Katzenstein. New York: Columbia University Press, 451–57.

Krupp, Jason. 2012. "Private Equity Deal Signed with Taiwan." *Business Day*, October 17.

Kuczynski, Pedro-Pablo, and John Williamson. 2003. *After the Washington Consensus: Restarting Growth and Reform in Latin America*. Washington, DC: Institute for International Economics, 325.

Kuo, Yu Ching, and Xiao Han. 2017. "Continuity and Change: Looking into the Future of Taiwan's Innovation and Entrepreneurship Policy." Paper presented at the Joint-Research Symposium on Smart Cities, Innovation and Entrepreneurship in Asia: Challenges and Opportunities, April 20.

Kupor, Scott. 2014. "Why the Structural Changes to the VC Industry Matter." Andreessen Horowitz. July 25. http://a16z.com/2014/07/25/why-the-structural-changes-to-the-vc-industry-matter/

Kwong, Kai-Sun, Chau Leung-Chuen, Francis T. Lui, and Larry D Qiu. 2001. *Industrial Development in Singapore, Taiwan, and South Korea*. Singapore: World Scientific, 27–28.

Kwong, Robin. 2011. "Taiwan Lets Mainland Invest in Technology." *The Financial Times*. February 27.

Lall, Sanjaya. 1996. *Learning from the Asian Tigers: Studies in Technology and Industrial Policy*. London: Macmillan Press.

——. 2004. "Reinventing Industrial Strategy: The Role of Government Policy in Building Industrial Competitiveness." United Nations Conference on Trade and Development, G-24 Discussion Paper Series No. 28. April.

Lapavitsas, C. 2009. "Financialised Capitalism: Crisis and Financial Expropriation." *Historical Materialism* 17(1): 114–48.

Latter, Tony. 2007. *Hands On or Hands Off? The Nature and Process of Economic Policy in Hong Kong*. Hong Kong: Hong Kong University Press.

Lazonick, William. 2009. "The New Economy Business Model and The Crisis of U.S. Capitalism." *Capitalism and Society* 4(2): 1–70.

LeBoeuf, Robyn, and Eldar Shafir. 2006. "The Long and Short of It: Physical Anchoring Effects." *Journal of Behavioral Decision Making* 19: 393–406.

Lechevalier, Sébastien. 2011. *La grande transformation du capitalisme japonais (1980–2010)*. Paris: Presses de Sciences Po.

Lee, Chang Kil, and David Strang. 2008. "The International Diffusion of Public Sector Downsizing: Network Emulation and Theory-Driven Learning." In *The Global Diffusion of Markets and Democracy*, edited by Beth A. Simmons, Frank Dobbin, and Geoffrey Garrett, 141–72. Cambridge: Cambridge University Press.

Lee, Kuan Yew. 2000. *From Third World to First: Singapore and the Asian Economic Boom*, New York: HarperCollins, 543–57, 595–71.

Lee, Hsien Loong. 1998. "Financial Sector Review: A Round-Up and Next Steps Financial Sector Review Group (FSRG) Appreciation Dinner" (speech). FSRG, Singapore, November 27.

Lee, Terence. 2013. "Singapore Government to Pump Extra $39 Million into Early Stage Investment Ecosystem." *TechInAsia*, September 25.

Legislative Council Audit Commission. 2004. "Report No. 42 of the Director of Audit—Chapter 2: Funding of Projects Under the Applied Research Fund." *Legislative Council Audit Commission.*

Legro, Jeffrey. 1996. "Culture and Preferences in the International Cooperation Two-Step." *American Political Science Review* 90: 118–37.

Lenschow, Andrea, Duncan Liefferink, and Sietske Veenman. 2005. "When the Birds Sing: A Framework for Analysing Domestic Factors behind Policy Convergence." *Journal of European Public Policy* 12(5): 797–816.

Lerner, Josh. 2002. "When Bureaucrats Meet Entrepreneurs: The Design of Effective 'Public Venture Capital' Programs." *Economic Journal* 112(477): 73–84.

——. 2009. *Boulevard of Broken Dreams: Why Public Efforts to Boost Entrepreneurship and Venture Capital Have Failed—and What to Do About It.* Princeton: Princeton University Press.

Lerner, Josh, Ann Leamon, James Tighe, and Susana Garcia-Robles. 2014. "Adding Value through Venture Capital in Latin America and the Caribbean." Harvard Business School Working Paper 15–024. October 13.

Levi-Faur, David. 2005a. "Agents of Knowledge' and the Convergence on a 'New World Order': A Review Article." *Journal of European Public Policy* 12(5): 954–65.

——. 2005b. "The Global Diffusion of Regulatory Capitalism." *Annals of the American Academy of Political and Social Science* 598: 12–32.

Levi-Faur, David, Jacint Jordana, and Xavier Fernández i Marín. 2011. "The Global Diffusion of Regulatory Agencies: Channels of Transfer and Stages of Diffusion." *Comparative Political Studies* 44(10): 1343–69.

Levy, Jack S. 1994. "Learning and Foreign Policy: Sweeping a Conceptual Minefield." *International Organization* 48(2): 279–312.

Liang, Peng, and Guoshun Wang. 2010. "Venture Capital in Japan." School of Management Central South University, Changsha, P.R. China Working Paper.

Liu, Manhong Mannie. 2015. "Growing the Venture Dragon: China." *Coller Venture Review* 2: 112–22.

Lockett, Hudson, and Jennifer Hughes. 2016. "UK Becomes Second-Largest Offshore Renimbi Clearing Centre." *Financial Times.* April 28.

Low Tax. 2011. "Hong Kong: Offshore Business Sectors: Venture Capital Sector." Global Tax and Business Portal.

Luk, Helen. 1985. "Survey on Small and Medium Enterprises." Applied Research Corporation—National Productivity Board, Singapore: 2.

Lundvall, B-Å. 1992. *National Systems of Innovation: Towards a Theory of Innovation and Interactive Learning.* London: Pinter.

MacMillan, Douglas. 2016. "Uber Raises $3.5 Billion from Saudi Fund." *Wall Street Journal.* June 1.

Mahoney, James, and Kathleen Thelen. 2010. "A Theory of Gradual Institutional Change." In *Explaining Institutional Change: Ambiguity, Agency and Power*, edited by James Mahoney and Kathleen Thelen. Cambridge: Cambridge University Press, 1–37.

March, James G. 1978. "Bounded Rationality, Ambiguity and the Engineering of Choice." *Bell Journal of Economics* 9(2): 587–608.

March, James G., and Johan P. Olsen. 1998. "The Institutional Dynamics of International Political Orders." *International Organization* 52(4): 943–69.

Marshall, Monty G., and Ted Robert Gurr. 2012. *Polity IV Project*. Vienna, VA: Center for Systemic Peace.

Mathonet, Pierre-Yves, and Thomas Meyer. 2007. *J-Curve Exposure: Managing a Portfolio of Venture Capital and Private Equity Funds*. West Sussex: Wiley Finance.

Maxfield, Sylvia. 1998. *Gatekeepers of Growth: The International Political Economy of Central Banking in Developing Countries*. Princeton: Princeton University Press.

Mazzarol, Tim. 2014. "Growing and Sustaining Entrepreneurial Ecosystems: What They Are and the Role of Government Policy." SEAANZ White Paper WP01–2014.

Mazzucato, Mariana. 2013. *The Entrepreneurial State*. London: Anthem Press.

McDermott, Rose. 2008. "Book Review: *Bounded Rationality and Policy Reform: Social Sector Reform in Latin America*, by K. Weyland." *Comparative Political Studies*. December 1.

McGinnis, Patrick. 2015. "Can Jamaica 'Hack' Entrepreneurship For The Caribbean?" *Forbes*. April 30.

Meseguer, Covadonga. 2006. "Learning and Economic Policy Choices." *European Journal of Political Economy* 22: 156–78.

———. 2009. *Learning, Policy Making, and Market Reforms*. Cambridge: Cambridge University Press.

Meseguer, Covadonga, and Fabrizio Gilardi. 2009. "What Is New in the Study of Policy Diffusion?" *Review of International Political Economy* 16(3): 527–43.

Meyer, John W., John Boli, George M. Thomas, and Francisco O. Ramirez. 1997. "World Society and the Nation-State." *American Journal of Sociology* 103(1): 144–81.

Meyer, John W., and Brian Rowan. 1977. "Institutionalized Organizations: Formal Structure as Myth and Ceremony." *American Journal of Sociology* 83: 340–63.

Miller, Terry, and Anthony B. Kim. 2016. *2016 Index of Economic Freedom*. Washington, DC: Heritage Foundation and Dow Jones.

Mims, Christopher. 2014. "Humanity's Last Great Hope: Venture Capitalists." *Wall Street Journal*. October 20.

Ministry of Economic Affairs, ROC (MoEA). 2012. "Taiwan Signs Venture Capital Cooperation Agreement with New Zealand." *Ministry of Economic Affairs, ROC—What's New*. March 14.

———. 2014. "HeadStart Taiwan Project." *National Development Council*. August.

Ministry of Science and Technology (MoST). 2016. *White Paper on Science and Technology*. Taipei: Republic of China MoST. February.

Ministry of Trade and Industry (MTI) (Singapore). 1985. *Subcommittee Report on Entrepreneurship Development*, 20–27.

———. 1998. *Committee on Singapore's Competitiveness Report*.

Mole, David. 1996. "Introduction." *Managing the New Hong Kong Economy*. New York: Oxford University Press, 1–17.

The Money Project. 2016. *All of the World's Stock Exchanges by Size*. February 16.

Monetary Authority of Singapore. 1998. *Annual Report 1997/98*.

Mosley, Layna. 2000. "Room to Move: International Financial Markets and National Welfare States." *International Organization* 54: 737–73.

Mulcahy, Diane, Bill Weeks, and Harold S. Bradley. 2012. "We Have Met the Enemy . . . and He Is Us: Lessons from Twenty Years of the Kauffman Foundation's Investment in Venture Capital Funds and the Triumph of Hope over Experience." Ewing Marion Kauffman Foundation, Kansas City, MO.

National Development Council (Taiwan). 2014. "HeadStart Taiwan: Regaining the Economic Momentum." National Development Council. July.

——. 2016. *Asia Silicon Valley Development Plan: From IT to IoT—Engineering a New Industrial Transformation for Taiwan.* September.

National Research Foundations (NRF). 2008a. "NRF Seeding Six Venture Funds with SGD10 Million Each to Invest in Singapore-based Early-stage Start-ups." Press Release. July 31.

——. 2008b. "Singapore to Develop a National Innovation and Enterprise Framework for the Next Stage of Economic Growth." Press Release. January 10.

——. 2012. *National Research Foundation Corporate Profile.*

——. 2014. *Innovation and Enterprise Milestones.*

——. 2015. *ESVFIII Call for Proposals.*

——. 2016. "NRF Announces Award of Venture Capital Funds to Four Large Local Enterprises Under its Early Stage Venture Fund Scheme." Press Release. May 17.

National University of Singapore Engineering Faculty (NUS). 2012. "History of Innovation."

National Venture Capital Association. 2011. "Venture Impact Edition 6.0: The Economic Importance of Venture Capital-Backed Companies to the U.S. Economy." *NVCA and IHS Global Insight.*

——. 2012. *Policy Issues: NVCA Policy Overview.*

Nelson, Richard R., and Sidney G. Winter. 1982. *An Evolutionary Theory of Economic Change.* Cambridge, MA: Belknap Press of Harvard University Press.

Nelson, Stephen C., and Peter J. Katzenstein. 2014. "Uncertainty, Risk and the Financial Crisis of 2008." *International Organization* 68(2): 361–92.

North, D. C. 1990. *Institutions, Institutional Change, and Economic Performance.* Cambridge: Cambridge University Press.

Office of the Chief Executive of the Hong Kong Special Administrative Region. 2007. "2007–2008 Policy Address."

——. 2004. "2004–2005 Policy Address: Strengthening Advisory and Statutory Bodies."

Organization for Economic Cooperation and Development (OECD). 1996. *Venture Capital and Innovation.* Paris: OCDE/GD(96)168.

——. 1997. *Government Venture Capital for Technology-based Firms.* Paris: OECD OCDE/GD(97)201.

——. 2003. *Venture Capital: Trends and Policy Recommendations.* Paris: OECD.

——. 2007. *Innovation and Growth: Rationale for Innovation Strategy.* Paris: OECD.

——. 2014. *Institutional Investors and Long-term Investment: Project Report.* Paris: OECD.

Pai, Yasue. 2006. "Comparing Individual Retirement Accounts in Asia: Singapore, Thailand, Hong Kong, and PRC." World Bank Social Protection Discussion Paper No. 0609. Washington, DC: World Bank.

Pandey, I. M., and Angela Jang. 1996. "Venture Capital for Financing Technology in Taiwan." *Technovation* 16(9): 499–514.

Patten, Chris. 1998. *East and West: The Last Governor of Hong Kong on Power, Freedom, and the Future.* London: Macmillan.

Paus, Eva. 2014. "Latin America and the Middle Income Trap." ECLAC. Financing for Development Series, No. 250.

Pempel, T. J., and Keiichi Tsunekawa. 2015. "Introduction." In *Two Crises Different Outcomes: East Asia and Global Finance,* edited by T. J. Pempel and Keiichi Tsunekawa. Ithaca, NY: Cornell University Press, 1–16.

People's Daily. 2000. "HK Financial Secretary to Visit Israel." May 22.

PitchBook. 2016. *European Venture Industry Report 2Q 2016.* Seattle.

Polanyi, K. 2001 [1944]. *The Great Transformation.* New York: Rinehart.

Poulsen, Lauge, and N. Skovgaard. 2014. "Bounded Rationality and the Diffusion of Modern Investment Treaties." *International Studies Quarterly* 58(1): 1–14.

Preqin. 2015a. *Preqin and HKVCA Special Report: Private Equity in Hong Kong.* June.

———. 2015b. *2015 Preqin Global Private Equity and Venture Capital Report.*

Przeworski, Adam, and Fernando Limongi. 1993. "Political Regimes and Economic Growth." *Journal of Economic Perspectives* 7(3): 51–69.

Public Law 96–477. 1980. Available at: http://3197d6d14b5f19f2f440-5e13d29c4c 016cf96cbbfd197c579b45.r81.cf1.rackcdn.com/collection/papers/1940/1940_ SIAA_L.pdf. Accessed May 7, 2015.

Putnam, R. 1988. "'Diplomacy and Domestic Politics: The Logic of Two-Level Games." *International Organization* 42(3): 427–60.

Radaelli, Claudio M. 2005. "Diffusion without Convergence: How Political Context Shapes the Adoption of Regulatory Impact Assessment." *Journal of European Public Policy* 12(5): 924–43.

Ragin, C. C., and H. S. Becker. 1992. *What Is a Case? Exploring the Foundations of Social Inquiry.* Cambridge: Cambridge University Press.

Randhawa, Dipinder S., and Tan Shiuh Ming. 2009. *Finance for SMEs in Singapore.* Singapore: Saw Centre for Financial Studies.

Rapo, Raija, and Marita Seulamo-Vargas. 2010. "Silicon Valley Journal: Experiences of Finnish IT Start-ups from Dot-Com Boom to 2010." *Tekes Review* 267/2010. Helsinki: Tekes. 1–178.

Rethel, Lena. 2010. "Financialization and the Malaysian Political Economy." *Globalizations.* 7(4) (December): 489–506.

Risse-Kappen, Thomas. 1996. "Collective Identity in a Democratic Community: The Case of NATO." In *The Culture of National Security: Norms and Identity in World Politics,* edited by Peter J. Katzenstein. New York: Columbia University Press, 357–99.

Rogers, Everett M. 1995. *Diffusion of Innovations.* Glencoe: Free Press.

Roman, David. 2017. "Singapore Creates S$1 billion Innovation Fund to Drive Growth." *Bloomberg.* April 26.

Rose, R. 1991. "What Is Lesson Drawing?" *Journal of Public Policy* 11(1): 3–30.

Ruggie, John Gerard. 1982. "International Regimes, Transactions, and Change: Embedded Liberalism in the Postwar Economic Order." *International Organization* 36(2): 379–415.

Sabaliauskas, Linas. 2015. "Seeding a Venture Wolf: The Baltics." *Coller Venture Review* 2: 124–30.

Saxenian, AnnaLee. 2008. "Venture Capital in the Periphery: The New Argonauts, Global Search and Local Institution Building." Paper presented at Druid 2008 Conference on Entrepreneurship and Innovation—Organizations, Institutions, Systems and Regions.

Saxenian, AnnaLee, and Chuen-Yueh Li. 2000. "Bay-to-Bay Strategic Alliances: The Network Linkages between Taiwan and the U.S. Venture Capital Industries." *UC Berkeley Papers.*

Scharpf, F. W. 1997. "Economic Integration, Democracy and the Welfare State." *Journal of European Public Policy* 4(1): 18–36.

Scott, W. Richard. 2003. "Institutional Carriers: Reviewing Modes of Transporting Ideas over Time and Space and Considering Their Consequences." *Industrial and Corporate Change* 12(2): 879–94.

Senor, Dan, and Saul Singer. 2009. *Start-up Nation: The Story of Israel's Economic Miracle.* New York: Hachette.

Shih, Chintay, and Shin-Horng Chen. 2010. "On Reform of Hong Kong's Public Research Funding System." In *Innovation Policy and the Limits of Laissez-faire: Hong Kong's Policy in Comparative Perspective,* edited by Douglas Fuller. New York: Palgrave MacMillan, 114–44.

Shipan, Charles R., and Craig Volden. 2008. "The Mechanisms of Policy Diffusion." *American Journal of Political Science* 52(4): 840–57.

Simmons, Beth A., Frank Dobbin, and Geoffrey Garrett. 2006. "Introduction: The International Diffusion of Liberalism." *International Organization* 60(4): 781–810.

——, eds. 2008. *The Global Diffusion of Marks and Democracy.* Cambridge: Cambridge University Press.

Simmons, Beth A., and Zachary Elkins. 2004. "The Globalization of Liberalization: Policy Diffusion in the International Political Economy." *American Political Science Review* 98(1): 171–89.

Simon, Herbert A. 1955. "A Behavioral Model of Rational Choice." *Quarterly Journal of Economics* 69(1): 99–118.

——. 1957. *Models of Man, Social and Rational: Mathematical Essays on Rational Human Behavior in a Social Setting.* New York: John Wiley and Sons.

——. 1979. "Rational Decision Making in Business Organizations." Nobel Prize in Economic Science Lecture, Stockholm, December 8, 1978.

Sivan, Yesha, and Robyn Klingler-Vidra. 2016. "Deep Innovation: Solving Humanity's Big Problems Needs More Commitment." *Coller Venture Review* 3: 4–9.

Skocpol, Theda, and Margaret Weir. 1985. "State Structures and the Possibilities of Keynesian Responses to the Depression in Sweden, Britain and the United States." In *Bringing the State Back In,* edited by P. Evans et al. Cambridge: Cambridge University Press, 107–151.

Smelser, Neil J., and Richard Swedberg. 2005. *The Handbook of Economic Sociology: Second Edition.* Princeton: Princeton University Press.

Sobel, Andrew. 2012. *International Political Economy in Context.* London: Sage.

Solingen, Etel. 2012. "Of Dominoes and Firewalls: The Domestic, Regional, and Global Politics of International Diffusion." *International Studies Quarterly* 56: 631–44.

Solingen, Etel, and Tanya A. Börzel. 2014. "Introduction to Presidential Issue: The Politics of International Diffusion—A Symposium." *International Studies Review* 16(2): 173–87.

South China Morning Post. 2017a. "Transparency Key to Success of Hi-tech Park at Lok Ma Chau." January 6.

——. 2017b. "Hong Kong Budget 2017 As It Happened: Paul Chan Announces HK$ 92 Billion Surplus." February 22.

Spencer, Barbara, and James Brander. 1983. "International R&D Rivalry and Industrial Strategy." *Review of Economic Studies* 50(4): 707–22.

Stark, David, and Balasz Vedres. 2012. "Political Holes in the Economy: The Business Network of Partisan Firms in Hungary." *American Sociological Review* 77(5): 700–722.

Steiner, Miriam. 1983. "The Search for Order in a Disorderly World: Worldviews and Prescriptive Decision Paradigms." *International Organization* 37(3): 373–413.

Stillman, Robert D. 2002. "Government Support for Venture Capital." Beijing Forum on SME Financing, Final Report TA 3534-PRC Appendix V. May.

Strang, David, and Sarah A. Soule. 1998. "Diffusion in Organizations and Social Movements: From Hybrid Corn to Poison Pills." *Annual Review of Sociology* 24: 265–90.

Strange, Susan. 1996. *Retreat of the State: The Diffusion of Power in the World Economy.* Cambridge: Cambridge University Press.

Streeck, Wolfgang, and Kathleen Thelen, eds. 2005. *Beyond Continuity: Institutional Change in Advanced Political Economies.* Oxford: Oxford University Press.

——. 2009. "Institutional Change in Advanced Political Economies." In *Debating Varieties of Capitalism*, edited by B. Hancké. Oxford: Oxford University Press, 95–134.

Storz, Cornelia, Bruno Amable, Steven Casper, and Sebastien Lechevalier. 2013. "Bringing Asia into the Comparative Capitalism Perspective." *Socio-Economic Review* 11(2): 217–32.

Storz, Cornelia, and Sebastien Schafer. 2011. *Institutional Diversity and Innovation: Continuing and Emerging Patterns in Japan and China.* London: Routledge.

Suchman, M. 1995. "Managing Legitimacy: Strategic and Institutional Approaches." *Academy of Management Review* 20(3): 571–610.

Sugden, Robert. 1989. "Spontaneous order." *Journal of Economic Perspectives* 3: 85–97.

Suster, Mark. 2014. "The Changing Structure of the VC Industry." Both Sides of the Table. July 22. http://bothsidesofthetable.com/the-changing-structure-of-the-vc-industry-1cb41db9c433.

Swank, Duane. 2008. "Tax Policy in an Era of Internationalization: An Assessment of a Conditional Diffusion Model of the Spread of Neoliberalism." In *The Global Diffusion of Marks and Democracy*, edited by Beth A. Simmons, Frank Dobbin, and Geoffrey Garret. Cambridge: Cambridge University Press, 64–103.

Taiwan Venture Capital Association (TVCA). 2006. *Venture Capital as a Policy Tool.*

——. 2015. *2014 Yearbook* (in Chinese).

Talmor, Eli. 2015. "Coller Institute of Venture History of Venture Table." *Coller Venture Review* 2: 28–83.

Tan, Augustine H. H. 1999. "Official Efforts to Attract FDI: Case of Singapore's EDB." 1999 EWC/KDI Conference on Industrial Globalization in the 21st Century: Impact and Consequences for East Asia and Korea. August.

Tan, Chwee Huat, Joseph Lim, and Wilson Chen. 2004. "Competing International Financial Centers: A Comparative Study between Hong Kong and Singapore." Paper for Saw Centre for Financial Studies and ISEAS Conference in November 2004—Singapore as a Financial Centre: Development and Prospects. NUS.

Tang, Shu-hung. 1996. "Reforming Hong Kong's Fiscal System." In *Managing the New Hong Kong Economy*, edited by David Mole. New York: Oxford University Press, 35–53.

Taylor, Mark Zachary. 2016. *The Politics of Innovation: Why Some Countries Are Better Than Others at Science and Technology.* New York: Oxford University Press.

Tech City UK. 2015. *Future Fifty.*

Tegos, Michael. 2015. "Singapore's National Research Foundation to Invest Another $28M in Start-ups." *Tech In Asia.* September.

Teng, Harold Siow Song. 2011. *Government Policy and Critical Success: Factors of Small Businesses in Singapore.* Newcastle upon Tyne: Cambridge Scholars Publishing, 35–36.

Thelen, Kathleen, and Sven Steinmo. 1992. "Historical Institutionalism in Comparative Perspective." In *Structuring Politics: Historical Institutionalism in Comparative*

Analysis, edited by Sven Steinmo, Kathleen Thelen, and Frank Longstreth. Cambridge: Cambridge University Press, 1–32.

3i. 2017. "Our History." http://www.3i.com/about-us/our-history. Accessed April 5, 2017.

Thurbon, Elizabeth. 2016. *Developmental Mindset: The Revival of Financial Activism in South Korea*. Ithaca, NY: Cornell University Press.

Tom, Mikey. 2017. "Startups Increasingly Turning to Debt Financing Despite Dangers." *PitchBook*. March 29.

Townley, Barbara. 2008. *Reason's Neglect: Rationality and Organizing*. Oxford: Oxford University Press.

Tsai, Kuen-Hung, and Jiann-Chyuan Wang. 2004. "The Innovation Policy and Performance of Innovation in Taiwan's Technology-Intensive Industries." *Problems and Perspectives in Management* 2(1): 62–75.

Tversky, Amos, and Daniel Kahneman. 1973. "Availability: A Heuristic for Judging Frequency and Probability." *Cognitive Psychology* 5: 207–32.

——. 1983. "Extensional Versus Intuitive Reasoning: The Conjunction Fallacy in Probability Judgment." *Psychological Review* 90: 293–315.

United Nations Conference on Trade and Development (UNCTAD). 1997. "Experiences of Country Funds and Venture Capital Funds in Developing Countries." UNCTAD/GDS/GFSB/1. June 16.

Van Der Kamp, Jake. 2017. "Lok Ma Chau Loop Has Nothing to Do with Hi-tech—Its All about Profit." *South China Morning Post*. January 8.

van der Zwan, N. 2014. "Making Sense of Financialization." *Socio-Economic Review* 12: 99–129.

Vartiainen, Juhana. 1999. "The Economics of Successful State Intervention in Industrial Transformation." In *The Developmental State*, edited by Meredith Woo-Cumings. Ithaca, NY: Cornell University Press, 200–234.

Vietnam Breaking News. 2016. "Vietnam Opens Its Doors to Venture Capital." April 22.

Vogel, Steven. 1998. *Freer Markets, More Rules: Regulatory Reform in Advanced Industrial Countries*. Ithaca, NY: Cornell University Press.

Volden, Craig, Michael M. Ting, and Daniel P. Carpenter. 2008. "A Formal Model of Learning and Policy Diffusion." *American Political Science Review* 102(3): 319–32.

Wade, Robert H. 2004 [1990]. *Governing the Market: Theory and the Role of Government in East Asian Industrialization*. Princeton: Princeton University Press.

——. 2016. "The American Paradox: Ideology of Free Markets and Practice of Directional Thrust." *Cambridge Journal of Economics* 41(3): 859–80.

Wadhwa, Vivek. 2013. "Silicon Valley Can't Be Copied." *MIT Technology Review*. July 3.

Wallen, Patrick. 2017. "How Trump Will Impact Venture Capital: The Future of QSBS." *TechCrunch*. March 24.

Walter, Andrew, and Xiaoke Zhang. 2012. *East Asian Capitalism: Diversity, Continuity and Change*. Oxford: Oxford University Press.

Wang, Angela & Company. 2006. "China: New Measures for the Administration of PRC Venture Capital." *Mondaq* May 8.

Wang, Clement K. 2002. "Differences in the Governance Structure of Venture Capital: The Singapore Venture Capital Industry." Centre for Entrepreneurship National University of Singapore. November.

Wang, Lee-rong. 1995. "Taiwan's Venture Capital: Policies and Impacts." *Journal of Industry Studies* 2(1): 83–94.

Waltz, Kenneth. 1979. *Theory of International Politics.* Reading, MA: Addison-Wesley.

Weber, Max. 1968 [1921]. *Economy and Society.* Edited by Guenther Roth and Claus Wittich. New York: Bedminister.

Weins, Jason, and Jordan Bell-Masterson. 2015. "How Entrepreneurs Access Capital and Get Funded." *Entrepreneurship Policy Digest.* June 2.

Weiss, Linda. 2014. *America Inc.? Innovation and Enterprise in the National Security State.* Ithaca, NY: Cornell University Press.

Weyland, Kurt. 2005. "The Diffusion of Innovations: How Cognitive Heuristics Shaped Bolivia's Pension Reform." *Comparative Politics* 38(1): 21–42.

——. 2006. *Bounded Rationality and Policy Diffusion: Social Sector Reform in Latin America.* Princeton: Princeton University Press.

——. 2010. "The Diffusion of Regime Contention in European Democratization, 1830–1940." *Comparative Political Studies* 43(8/9): 1148–76.

——. 2012. "Diffusion Waves in European Democratization: The Impact of Organizational Development." *Comparative Politics* 45(1): 25–45.

Whitley, Richard. 1992. *Business Systems in East Asia.* London: Sage.

——. 1999. *Divergent Capitalisms. The Social Structuring and Change of Business Systems.* Oxford: Oxford University Press.

——. 2007. *Business Systems and Organizational Capabilities: The Institutional Structuring of Competitive Competences.* Oxford: Oxford University Press.

Wiener, Antje. 2014. *A Theory of Contestation.* Berlin: SpringerBriefs in Political Science.

Wilkin, Sam. 2004. "Maintaining Singapore's Miracle." *Country Risk.* August 17.

Williamson, John. 2004. "A Short History of the Washington Consensus." Washington: Institute for International Economics.

Witt, Michael A., and Gordon Redding. 2013. *The Oxford Handbook of Asian Business Systems.* Oxford: Oxford University Press.

Wong Poh-Kam. 2003. "From Using to Creating Technology: The Evolution of Singapore's National Innovation System and the Changing Role of Public Policy." In *Foreign Direct Investment, Technology Development and Competitiveness in East Asia,* edited by S. Lall and S. Urata. Cheltenham, UK: Edward Elgar, 191–238.

——. 2011. "Overview of Government Schemes to Promote Venture Investing in Singapore." Presentation in Australia.

Wong, Teresa Y. C. 1996. "Going Up-market: An Industrial Policy for Hong Kong in the 1990s." In *Managing the New Hong Kong Economy,* edited by David Mole. New York: Oxford University Press, 18–34.

Woo-Cumings, Meredith. 1999. *The Developmental State.* Ithaca, NY: Cornell University Press.

Wood, Julia. 2014. Is Singapore the Next Silicon Valley? *CNBC News.* March 6.

Yeandle, Mark, and Michael Mainelli. 2016. *Global Financial Centers Index 19.* Long Finance. March.

Yeh, Anthony Gar-on, and Jiang Xu. 2006. "Turning of the Dragon Head: Changing Role of Hong Kong in the Regional Development of the Pearl River Delta." In *Developing a Competitive Pearl River Delta in South China Under One Country-Two Systems,* edited by Anthony Gar-on Yeh, Victor Fung-shuen Sit, Guanghan Chen, and Yunyuan Zhou. Hong Kong: Hong Kong University Press, 63–95.

Yeh, Thomas M. F. 2006. "Venture Capital Industry Development in Taiwan." Fourteenth Conference on Pacific Basin Finance, Economics and Accounting. July 14.

Yeo, Y., and M. Painter. 2011. "Diffusion, Transmutation, and Regulatory Regime in Socialist Market Economies: Telecoms Reform in China and Vietnam." *Pacific Review* 24(4): 375–95.

Yeoh, Chin. 2017. *Private Equity in Hong Kong: Market and Regulatory Overview.* Practical Law. London: Thomson Reuters.

Yeung, Henry Wai-chung. 2016. *Strategic Coupling: East Asian Industrial Transformation in the New Global Economy.* Ithaca, NY: Cornell University Press.

Youngson, A. J. 1982. *Hong Kong Economic Growth and Policy.* Hong Kong: Oxford University Press.

Yuen, Homan. 2016. "Seed Investing Is Bifurcating." *TechCrunch.* July 1.

Yung, Chester. 2014. "Thousands March for Democracy in Hong Kong." *Wall Street Journal.* January 1.

Zhang, Maria Yue, and Mark Dodgson. 2014. *High-tech entrepreneurship in Asia: Innovation, Industry and Institutional Dynamics in Mobile Payments.* London: Edward Elgar.

Zhang Zhibin. 2011. *Dynamics of the Singapore Success Story: Insights by Ngiam Tong Dow.* Singapore: CENGAGE Learning, 177–83.

Zhou, Laura. 2017. "Hong Kong-southern China Greater Bay Area 'to Rival New York, Tokyo.'" *South China Morning Post.* March 6.

Zider, Bob. 1998. "How Venture Capital Works." *Harvard Business Review* November-December: 131–139.

Zysman, John. 1983. *Governments, Markets, and Growth: Financial Systems and the Politics of Industrial Change.* Ithaca, NY: Cornell University Press.

Index

Lightning Source UK Ltd.
Milton Keynes UK
UKHW041838010922
408136UK00003B/93/J